SØREN

Søren Kierkegaard

Subjectivity, Irony, and the Crisis of Modernity

JON STEWART

OXFORD
UNIVERSITY PRESS

OXFORD
UNIVERSITY PRESS

Great Clarendon Street, Oxford, OX2 6DP,
United Kingdom

Oxford University Press is a department of the University of Oxford.
It furthers the University's objective of excellence in research, scholarship,
and education by publishing worldwide. Oxford is a registered trade mark of
Oxford University Press in the UK and in certain other countries

First published 2015
First published in paperback 2018

Published in the United States of America by Oxford University Press
198 Madison Avenue, New York, NY 10016, United States of America

British Library Cataloguing in Publication Data
Data available

Library of Congress Cataloging in Publication Data
Data available

ISBN 978–0–19–874770–3 (Hbk.)
ISBN 978–0–19–878522–4 (Pbk.)

For Katalin

Preface

There are many different introductory books on the Danish thinker Søren Kierkegaard and many different ways to present his thought to beginning students. Each of these has its own set of strengths and weaknesses. While the approach used in this book has, I believe, distinct advantages, it is, of course, just *one* approach. My goal here is not to give the reader an exhaustive or even particularly representative overview of Kierkegaard's complex thought or authorship. Instead, the strategy is to develop a single strand of his thought that derives from the Greek philosopher Socrates. As will be seen, this is a very central strand that has profound explanatory power for understanding Kierkegaard's motivation, method, and writing style.

The strategy taken here has some clear pedagogical advantages. By interpreting Kierkegaard as a figure who is trying to imitate specific aspects of Socrates' life and thought, the work approaches Kierkegaard by means of something that is presumably at least somewhat familiar to students and first-time readers (namely, the dialogues of Plato and the figure of Socrates). Moreover, it provides a useful insight into many very odd or counterintuitive elements of Kierkegaard's thought, which are otherwise difficult to explain. The Socratic dimension also helps to provide a degree of continuity throughout Kierkegaard's very heterogeneous writings, since it is present from the beginning to the end of his authorship.

The present work differs significantly from more traditional introductory texts on Kierkegaard. Many of these approach Kierkegaard by introducing his thought in terms of the so-called stages of existence: the aesthetic, the ethical, and the religious. This structure has been the mainstay of Kierkegaard introductions for almost a century and has been used so often that it is today a cliché. The problem with this is that it is overly schematic and does not fully do justice to the richness of Kierkegaard's thought. Moreover, it is not clear to what degree Kierkegaard himself ever conceived of his work as a whole in this way, and the importance of this famous developmental scheme can in a sense be regarded simply as a result of its constant repetition in the secondary literature.

Moreover, traditional introductions also tend to separate Kierkegaard's life from his thought by presenting his biography, at best, in an initial chapter and then going on to treat his thought as something separate and distinct from his life. By contrast, the present work integrates the biographical aspect with the account of Kierkegaard's thought and writings. This allows the reader to appreciate his works more fully by seeing them in the context of his concrete place and time. Often some of the mystery of Kierkegaard's work disappears when one sees how his thought developed as a response to a specific work or idea of one of his contemporaries.

Finally, there has long been a tradition of Kierkegaard apologetics in introductory works. Scholars naturally and rightly feel the need to defend Kierkegaard against misconceptions of his thought, but this often goes further and needlessly places him on a pedestal. The present work, by contrast, tries to take a sober look at Kierkegaard and to see him for who he was: a human being with the shortcomings and weaknesses of other human beings. An attempt is made to give a balanced assessment and to highlight Kierkegaard's unique genius, but at the same time not to ignore the other aspects of his character. The work attempts to underscore the counterintuitive and radical nature of Kierkegaard's thought that is often undermined in apologetic readings.

Make no mistake, Kierkegaard is a profoundly complex author, and no single introduction will be able to cover every aspect of his thought. Any attempt to give an overview will invariably focus on certain aspects in preference to others. Some scholars might object that the approach used here leaves out certain important elements of Kierkegaard's thought or that certain of his main works get short shrift. They will complain that all too much time is spent with Kierkegaard's early work *The Concept of Irony* at the expense of his mature works. But this is all question begging, since it presupposes ahead of time what the central aspects of Kierkegaard's thought are and assumes that *The Concept of Irony* is simply a piece of *juvenilia* that can be readily expedited. So the real test of any introduction to Kierkegaard is how well the chosen approach illuminates the totality of his thought. The present work makes a strong case for the importance of Socrates and in this way opens up to the introductory student of Kierkegaard the basic premises of his thinking. This allows the student a basic orientation in Kierkegaard's thought that will facilitate later independent study. The goal is to provide the readers with some basic categories and tools so that they will be able to read Kierkegaard fruitfully on their own and thus discover for themselves new aspects and dimensions of his thought which could not be treated here in any depth.

I openly acknowledge my reliance on a handful of outstanding scholarly studies on the relation of Kierkegaard to Socrates, such as those of Himmelstrup, Howland, Kloeden, Muench, and Scopetea.[1] The present work adds nothing with regard to new research to this topic but rather makes use of the previous research to introduce Kierkegaard in a new way. Likewise, I make no claim to have broken any new ground with my reading of *The Concept of Irony* and am glad to recognize my debt to the research of scholars such as K. Brian Söderquist.[2] If the present work does provide something new, this lies in the application of this material in an introductory context. The goal is not to present new research, but instead to open the door for new readers to start to understand and appreciate the genius of Søren Kierkegaard.

---

[1] Jens Himmelstrup, *Søren Kierkegaards Opfattelse af Sokrates. En Studie i dansk Filosofis Historie*, Copenhagen: Arnold Busck 1924. Jacob Howland, *Kierkegaard and Socrates: A Study in Philosophy and Faith*, New York: Cambridge University Press 2006. Wolfdietrich von Kloeden, *Kierkegaard und Sokrates. Søren Kierkegaards Sokratesrezeption*, Rheinland-Westfalen-Lippe: Evangelische Fachhochschule 1991 (*Schriftenreihe der Evangelischen Fachhochschule Rheinland-Westafalen-Lippe*, vol. 16). Paul Muench, "The Socratic Method of Kierkegaard's Pseudonym Johannes Climacus: Indirect Communication and the Art of 'Taking Away,'" in *Kierkegaard and the Word(s): Essays on Hermeneutics and Communication*, ed. by Poul Houe and Gordon D. Marino, Copenhagen: C. A. Reitzel 2003, pp. 139–50. Paul Muench, "Kierkegaard's Socratic Pseudonym: A Profile of Johannes Climacus," in *Kierkegaard's Concluding Unscientific Postscript: A Critical Guide*, ed. by Rick Anthony Furtak, Cambridge: Cambridge University Press 2010, pp. 25–44. Sophia Scopetea, *Kierkegaard og græciteten. En kamp med ironi*, Copenhagen: C. A. Reitzel 1995. See also the articles in Jon Stewart and Katalin Nun (eds), *Kierkegaard and the Greek World*, Tome I, *Socrates and Plato*, Aldershot: Ashgate 2010 (*Kierkegaard Research: Sources, Reception, and Resources*, vol. 2). See also the Bibliography.

[2] K. Brian Söderquist, *The Isolated Self: Irony as Truth and Untruth in Søren Kierkegaard's On The Concept of Irony*, Copenhagen: C. A. Reitzel 2007 (*Danish Golden Age Studies*, vol. 1).

Acknowledgments

This book is generally conceived as a basic introduction to the life and work of Søren Kierkegaard. Much of the text was developed in connection with a Massive Open Online Course (MOOC) with the same title that appeared under the aegis of the University of Copenhagen on the Coursera platform from October 7 to December 2, 2013. The course had some 24,000 enrolled online students, and the enormous positive response that it received was the inspiration to develop the idea presented in the course into an introductory text suitable for classroom use. The present book is generally a faithful reproduction of the manuscript of the online course; however, some additions and stylistic modifications have been made.

The approach and general conception were worked out in close cooperation with Dr. Timothy Hall, who was the main administrator for the course. His useful suggestions and critical feedback substantially affected the direction of the manuscript. The text has also been improved by the questions and comments of the many teaching assistants who helped with the realization of the course: Karl Aho, Joseph Ballan, Hjördis Becker-Lindenthal, Matthew Brake, Victoria Davies, Stephen DeRose, Joaquim Hernandez-Dispaux, Jennifer Hincapié Sánchez, Luke Johnson, Wojciech Kaftanski, Katarzyna Krawerenda-Wajda, Irina Kruchinina, Laura Liva, Daniel Marrs, Frances Maughan-Brown, Cody Lewis Oaks, Azucena Palavicini Sánchez, George Patios, Humberto Quaglio, Troy Smith, Emma Sørgaard, Michael Stark, Shalon van Tine, and Tian Wangjinjian. In the context of the online course, I was glad to have the constant help and support of Jesper Tang Nielsen from the Faculty of Theology of the University of Copenhagen.

The manuscript has also profited from the useful suggestions of established Kierkegaard scholars Paul Muench, Peter Šajda, and K. Brian Söderquist, who generously shared with me their knowledge of Kierkegaard's *corpus* and not least of all *The Concept of Irony*. Their work provided the original inspiration for the selection of some of the main themes and texts for the course. While writing the manuscript, I consulted regularly with Niels Jørgen Cappelørn on a number of historical details regarding Kierkegaard's life and times. Katalin

Nun, Loy Stewart, and Finn Gredal Jensen selflessly read through the text at different stages and offered their critical comments. Katalin contributed to helping me to develop a text that was both academically responsible and interesting to beginners. She also helped to organize and edit the illustrations that appear here. Loy gave some good advice about how to streamline the work and make it more focused and stylistically felicitous. Finn was a particularly valuable consultant due to his knowledge of Plato and ancient philosophy. I gratefully acknowledge the cooperation of the Søren Kierkegaard Research Centre and the Royal Library's Photographic Atelier for allowing me to reproduce here some of the pictures in the Centre's archives. To all of the people involved in both the production of the online course and the manuscript, I owe a profound debt of gratitude.

Contents

Figures   xvii

Introduction   1

1. The Life and Work of Kierkegaard as a "Socratic Task"   6
   1.1. Kierkegaard's Family and the School of Civic Virtue   7
   1.2. Introduction to *The Concept of Irony*   10
   1.3. Socratic Irony and Ignorance   12
   1.4. Socrates and *Aporia*   14
   1.5. Socrates and the Sophists   15
   1.6. Socrates' Mission and the Gadfly   16
   1.7. Socrates' Daimon   18
   1.8. Socrates' Maieutics   19
   1.9. The Socrates of Copenhagen   20

2. Hegel's View of Socrates   22
   2.1. Martensen and the University of Copenhagen in
        the 1830s   22
   2.2. Introduction to Hegel   27
   2.3. Hegel's Understanding of Socrates in the History of
        Western Culture   29
   2.4. A Truth for Which to Live and Die   31
   2.5. Hegel's View of the Socratic Method and Irony   33
   2.6. Hegel's Interpretation of Socrates' Maieutics and
        Aporia   35
   2.7. Hegel's Interpretation of Socrates, the Good, and
        the Sophists   37
   2.8. Hegel's Interpretation of the Daimon of Socrates   40
   2.9. Hegel's Analysis of Socrates' Trial   41
   2.10. The Conflict of Tradition and Individual Freedom   44

3. Kierkegaard's View of Socrates   46
   3.1. Kierkegaard's View of Socrates' Daimon   46
   3.2. Martensen's Faust   48
   3.3. Kierkegaard's Analysis of Socrates' Trial   50

3.4. Doubt and *The Conflict between the Old and
the New Soap Cellars*   53
3.5. Kierkegaard's *Johannes Climacus, or De omnibus
dubitandum est*   56
3.6. The Sophists and the Legacy of Socrates   58
3.7. Socrates and Christ   60
3.8. Andreas Frederik Beck and the First Review of
The Concept of Irony   61
3.9. Knowledge as a Double-Edged Sword   64

4. Kierkegaard, Heiberg, and History   67
4.1. Kierkegaard's Introduction to Part Two   68
4.2. German Romanticism   70
4.3. Kierkegaard's "Observations for Orientation"   71
4.4. Johan Ludvig Heiberg's *On the Significance of
Philosophy for the Present Age*   74
4.5. Kierkegaard's "The World Historical Validity of Irony" 76
4.6. Kierkegaard's Criticism of Hegel on Socratic and
Romantic Irony   79
4.7. Kierkegaard's Criticism of Hegel on History
and Socrates   81
4.8. The Modern Struggle for Individuality   85

5. Kierkegaard and Romantic Subjectivism   87
5.1. Introduction to Fichte   89
5.2. Hegel's and Kierkegaard's Analyses of Fichte   90
5.3. The Appropriation of Fichte's Theory by Schlegel
and Tieck   93
5.4. Kierkegaard's Analysis of Schlegel   96
5.5. Kierkegaard and Poul Martin Møller   99
5.6. Kierkegaard's Idea of Controlled Irony   101
5.7. Kierkegaard's Defense and the Reception of the Work 104
5.8. Kierkegaard and Regine Olsen   105
5.9. The Modern Problem of Creating Oneself   108

6. The Conception of Kierkegaard's Socratic Task and the
Beginning of the Authorship: 1843   111
6.1. Kierkegaard's Stay in Berlin   112
6.2. The Debate about Mediation and the Conception
of *Either/Or*   115
6.3. The Aesthete A as a Romantic Ironist: Diapsalmata 117

6.4.	The Immediate Reception of *Either/Or*	121
6.5.	The Next Works in Kierkegaard's Authorship	123
6.6.	The Universal and the Single Individual	125
6.7.	The Paradox of Faith	127
6.8.	The Modern Conflict of Law and Conscience	129

7. Kierkegaard's Socratic Task and the Development of the
Pseudonymous Works: 1844–6   132

7.1.	Kierkegaard's *Philosophical Fragments*	133
7.2.	Kierkegaard's *The Concept of Anxiety*	135
7.3.	Kierkegaard's *Prefaces* and the Polemic with Johan Ludvig Heiberg	138
7.4.	Kierkegaard's *Stages on Life's Way*	142
7.5.	The Conflict with *The Corsair*	144
7.6.	Introduction to Kierkegaard's *Concluding Unscientific Postscript*	149
7.7.	Kierkegaard's "The Issue in the Fragments"	152
7.8.	Kierkegaard's "A First and Last Explanation"	155
7.9.	The Parallel Authorship	158
7.10.	The Journals and Notebooks	161
7.11.	Socrates and Christianity as Subjective Truth	163

8. Kierkegaard's Socratic Task and the Second Half of the
Authorship: 1846–55   166

8.1.	Kierkegaard's Views of Society and His Relation to King Christian VIII	166
8.2.	Socrates in *Upbuilding Discourses in Various Spirits* and *Works of Love*	169
8.3.	Kierkegaard's *The Point of View*	172
8.4.	The Revolutions of 1848 and *The Sickness unto Death*	174
8.5.	Kierkegaard's *Practice in Christianity*	177
8.6.	The Attack on the Church	180
8.7.	The Last Issue of *The Moment*	182
8.8.	Kierkegaard's Illness and Death	185
8.9.	Kierkegaard's Funeral and Burial	185
8.10.	Kierkegaard's Legacy	189
8.11.	Christian Appropriation	191

Bibliography	195
Index	205

Figures

Fig. 0.1. The title page of Kierkegaard's *The Concept of Irony* (1841)   3

Fig. 1.1. Nytorv in Copenhagen (Kierkegaard's house is next to the house on the right-hand corner)   7

Fig. 2.1. Hans Lassen Martensen (1808–84)   24

Fig. 2.2. The courtyard of Regensen College with the Round Tower (*c.* 1840)   25

Fig. 2.3. The Lime Court of the University of Copenhagen with the Church of Our Lady in the background   26

Fig. 2.4. G. W. F. Hegel (1770–1831)   28

Fig. 3.1. The first page of *The Conflict between the Old and the New Soap Cellars* in the *Journal DD* (*c.* 1837–8)   54

Fig. 3.2. Manuscript from *Johannes Climacus, or De omnibus dubitandum est* (*c.* 1842–3)   56

Fig. 4.1. Johan Ludvig Heiberg (1791–1860)   74

Fig. 5.1. Johann Gottlieb Fichte (1762–1814)   89

Fig. 5.2. Friedrich von Schlegel (1772–1829)   97

Fig. 5.3. The Stock Exchange in Copenhagen   106

Fig. 5.4. Regine Olsen (1822–1904)   107

Fig. 6.1. The University of Berlin   113

Fig. 7.1. Title page of *The Corsair*   145

Figs. 7.2 and 7.3. Satirical images of Kierkegaard from *The Corsair*   148

Fig. 7.4. Draft of "A First and Last Explanation"   156

Fig. 7.5. Kierkegaard's parallel authorship   160

Fig. 7.6. The cover of Kierkegaard's *Journal NB6*   162

Fig. 8.1. The interior of the Church of Our Lady   178

Fig. 8.2. Bishop Jakob Peter Mynster (1775–1854)   181

Fig. 8.3. Eggert Christopher Tryde (1781–1860)   186

Introduction

In the twenty-first century we live in a complex and fast-changing world. The experience of each new generation differs radically from that of the previous one. For example, in the generation of my parents nobody had a computer or a smart phone, but today virtually everyone has these things. Ask yourself how many things you use your computer and your smart phone for and how much time you spend with them, and you will get some insight into how different your life is from that of the earlier generation. Our experiences and perceptions of the world differ radically from those of people who grew up only forty or fifty years ago. In the past, radical changes of this sort took place over centuries; now, with the rapid pace of technological development, they occur in only a few years. These constant changes over time make people feel uneasy or insecure. Certain traditional practices or things that people have done all of their lives suddenly become obsolete. This leads to an experience of disorientation and alienation with modern life. Everything stable slips away, and there seems to be nothing fixed to hold on to. This is the situation that we face in the twenty-first century.

The Danish philosopher and religious thinker Søren Kierkegaard saw these changes taking place in the first half of the nineteenth century, and he gave a brilliant analysis of them. While Kierkegaard never heard of the Internet and never owned an iPad or a digital camera, nonetheless he had great insight into modernity. Today we can read his works, and they can help us to understand the world around us and our place in it.

In this book we will examine the thought of Søren Kierkegaard, a unique figure, who has inspired, provoked, fascinated, and irritated people ever since he walked the streets of Copenhagen. Today, scholars argue about whether he was a philosopher, a theologian, an inspirational writer, a literary author, a psychologist, or something else. In the end he was a little bit of all of these things, and his highly creative form of writing makes it difficult to say exactly what genre he was using or what academic field he belonged to.

This feature of his writing is reflected in the complex history of the reception of his thought. His works have had an enormous influence on a number of different fields, for example, philosophy, theology, religious studies, literary theory, aesthetics, and psychology. That a single thinker can appeal to people in so many different fields is interesting in itself, but the truly odd thing about this reception is that he has had an appeal to people who radically disagree with one another and thus represent conflicting positions. He has been seen as an advocate of both progressive and reactionary political views. He has been celebrated as both an existentialist and an essentialist. He has been hailed as both a critic of German Romanticism and a follower of it. One explanation for this odd and unique aspect of his reception is that there is something undetermined or open-ended about Kierkegaard's writings that allows him, in a sense, to speak to everyone, and in his works, rich and diverse as they are, readers always seem to find something that gives them a special insight into their own life or situation.

In this book we will explore how Kierkegaard deals with the problems associated with relativism, the lack of meaning, and the crisis of religious faith that are typical of modern life. In his work *The Concept of Irony* from 1841 Kierkegaard examines different forms of subjectivism and relativism as they are conceived as criticisms of traditional culture (see Fig. 0.1). What do we mean by these terms, "subjectivism" and "relativism"? We say, for example, that a certain law or custom is "merely" relative in the sense that it is only accepted in one culture or society but rejected in others. When we make statements of this sort, they are usually critical and intended to undermine the validity of the law or custom at issue. In other words, if something is *merely* relative, then it does not have absolute validity or authority, and therefore we can choose to follow it or not. This is the way that we are used to talking about things like relativism and subjectivism.

Kierkegaard refers to these different tendencies under the heading of "irony." Why does he use this term? Sometimes when people today say that something is ironic, they mean that it was an unfortunate or a fateful event, for example, in the sense that one might say that when a

Om

Begrebet Ironi

med stadigt Hensyn til Socrates.

Af

S. A. Kierkegaard.

ἀλλὰ δὴ ὧδ᾽ ἔχει· ἄν τέ τις εἰς κολυμβή-
θραν σμικρὰν ἐμπέσῃ ἄν τε εἰς τὸ μέγι-
στον πέλαγος μέσον, ὅμως γε νεῖ οὐδὲν
ἧττον. Πάνυ μὲν οὖν. ᾽Ουκοῦν καὶ ἡμῖν
νευστέον καὶ πειρατέον σώζεσθαι ἐκ τοῦ
λόγου, ἤτοι δελφῖνά τιν᾽ ἐλπίζοντας ἡμᾶς
ἀπολαβεῖν ἂν ἤ τινα ἄλλην ἄπορον σω-
τηρίαν.

De republica L. 5 § 153 D

Kjøbenhavn.

Paa Boghandler P. G. Philipsens Forlag.

Trykt i Bianco Lunos Bogtrykkeri.

1841.

Fig. 0.1. The title page of Kierkegaard's *The Concept of Irony* (1841)

bad thing happens to a bad person, this is ironic. But this is not what Kierkegaard means. Instead, when we are ironic about something, we say the opposite of what we really mean, and the context alerts the listener to this. For example, in Copenhagen when we are having bad weather with violent rain or heavy snow, I might say, "It's wonderful weather that we are having." Since the person addressed knows that the weather at the moment is in fact very poor, they immediately know that I do not mean literally what I am saying but rather that I am being ironic. This is the way irony is commonly used. But irony can also be used in a critical manner. For example, in politics, if I disagree with a specific policy or a proposed law, I might say, "That's a great policy," or "That's a great law," thereby meaning exactly the opposite. It is this critical sense of irony that is the kind of thing that Kierkegaard has in mind when he associates it with subjectivism and relativism. With this kind of irony one can criticize accepted customs and practices and, indeed, absolutely anything at all.

In *The Concept of Irony* Kierkegaard compares irony in the form used by the ancient Greek philosopher Socrates with modern irony, which is represented by the German Romantics in his own day. In both cases an attempt was made to use critical reflection to call into question traditional beliefs and ways of thinking. While Kierkegaard is critical of the Romantics, he has great praise for Socrates. Indeed, he takes Socrates as his model in his attempt to criticize his own Danish culture and its conception of religion in the nineteenth century. By contrast, the Romantics are seen to represent a typical modern kind of problem that was just mentioned: subjectivism, relativism, nihilism, alienation, lack of meaning, and so forth. As the modern movements of existentialism, post-structuralism, and post-modernism reveal, the issues that Kierkegaard addressed are still among the central problems of philosophy today.

The present work is intended as an introduction to the life and thought of Søren Kierkegaard for people who have no prior knowledge. My goal is threefold. First, I wish to explore Kierkegaard's analysis and understanding of the pressing issues of modernity and to try to come to terms with the relevance of his views for our lives today. Second, I will examine how Kierkegaard sought insight into these modern issues, somewhat paradoxically, from the ancient philosopher Socrates. I want to try to understand why Kierkegaard used Socrates as a model for his own work and writing. Third, although this work is not conceived as a biography, I intend to trace Kierkegaard's life and his relations to his contemporaries, using the first two topics, just mentioned as the interpretive keys.

I will focus on *The Concept of Irony* as a crucially important text at the beginning of Kierkegaard's literary career. This is a book that has been somewhat neglected in Kierkegaard studies, and some people believe that Kierkegaard himself dismissed it as an insignificant early work. However, I want to show that this is not the case and that, on the contrary, it is an absolutely essential text for understanding Kierkegaard's thought as a philosopher and religious thinker. Although it was only the second book that he wrote, it nevertheless played a determining role in Kierkegaard's later development and writings. Indeed, it can be said that in *The Concept of Irony* he laid the groundwork for much of what would appear in his famous later books such as *Either/Or* and *Fear and Trembling*. By studying this work, we will be able to gain an understanding of Kierkegaard's life, writings, and relevance for our heterogeneous and fast-moving world today. We will discover that although Kierkegaard died in 1855, he still has some valuable insights for us living today in the twenty-first century.

1

The Life and Work of Kierkegaard as a "Socratic Task"

At the end of his life, Kierkegaard, looking back on his work, wrote that his undertaking was a "Socratic task."[1] Moreover, he said, "The only analogy I have before me is Socrates."[2] What did he mean by this? He seems to have taken Socrates, or at least his own special version of Socrates, as his model in his own life. In his writings he took himself to be doing something like what Socrates was doing with his philosophy. So in order to understand what he meant by this, we first need to see how he understood Socrates and what he took Socrates to stand for. Once we have identified the key elements of Kierkegaard's understanding of the character and philosophy of Socrates, we can see how he tried to make use of these in his own work. The obvious place to start with this is *The Concept of Irony*, which contains Kierkegaard's most detailed explanation of the figure of the Greek philosopher.

In this chapter we will first look at Kierkegaard's early life: his family background and his education at the School of Civic Virtue in Copenhagen. We will then turn to *The Concept of Irony* and try to understand its structure and argumentative strategy. Finally, we will look at a couple of Plato's dialogues, the *Euthyphro* and the *Apology*, in which we will see some of the key elements of Socrates' philosophy portrayed. Specifically, we will explore the following themes: Socrates' irony, his ability to reduce his dialogue partner to what is called *aporia* or being at a loss, his relation to the Sophists, his

---

[1] Kierkegaard, *The Moment and Late Writings*, trans. by Howard V. Hong and Edna H. Hong, Princeton: Princeton University Press 1998, p. 341.
[2] Ibid.

self-understanding as the gadfly of Athens, his daimon or personal spirit, and finally, his art of midwifery or "maieutics." Our goal here is to understand these ideas in the original context of Socrates' thought as portrayed by Plato. Then we will go on to see how Kierkegaard understands them and appropriates them for his own purposes.

1.1. Kierkegaard's Family and the School of Civic Virtue

Søren Kierkegaard was born in Copenhagen on May 5, 1813. He came into the world in a house that stood on a square called Nytorv, or the New Market. The house was demolished in 1908, but we can see it portrayed in pictures from the period (see Fig. 1.1). The building stood next door to the dominant structure of the square, the court-house with the large neo-classical columns.

Fig. 1.1. Nytorv in Copenhagen (Kierkegaard's house is next to the house on the right-hand corner)

Kierkegaard lived during a rich period in Danish cultural life that is often referred to as the Danish Golden Age—a period usually conceived as covering roughly the first half of the nineteenth century. His contemporaries included famous figures such as the author Hans Christian Andersen (1805–75), the physicist Hans Christian Ørsted (1777–1851), and the sculptor Bertel Thorvaldsen (1770–1844). Copenhagen was a relatively small town at that time with some 115,000 inhabitants.[3] This meant that most of the important writers, poets, scientists, and artists knew each other personally and mutually enriched each other's work. For example, Kierkegaard's first book, *From the Papers of One Still Living*, was published in 1838 and was a criticism of a novel by Andersen.

Although this was a rich cultural period in Denmark, with regard to economics, at the time of Kierkegaard's birth Copenhagen was a poor city in an impoverished country. This was due in large part to Denmark's ill-starred attempt to assert its Neutrality in the Napoleonic Wars, which resulted in the British bombardment of Copenhagen in 1807 and the subsequent loss of the Danish fleet. Years of rapid inflation and economic uncertainty followed. In 1813, the year when he was born, the Danish state went bankrupt. From one day to the next the Danish currency became virtually worthless. Only very few people managed to preserve their wealth and property during these difficult times, and Kierkegaard's father, Michael Pedersen Kierkegaard (1756–1838), was one of these few. He bought the house on Nytorv in 1809, a couple of years before Kierkegaard's birth. Michael Pedersen Kierkegaard was born into a very poor family. He came from Jutland to Copenhagen when he was 12 years old to become an apprentice in the wool business of one of his uncles. After about ten years he had his own business, and in time he became rich.

Kierkegaard's mother, Ane Sørensdatter Lund (1768–1834), was his father's second wife. She was the maidservant in the house of Kierkegaard's father, and they married in 1797, some thirteen months after the death of the father's first wife; at the time, Ane was pregnant with their first daughter, who was born five months after their marriage. In the course of the next fifteen years they would have a total of seven children, of which Søren was the youngest. Kierkegaard is surprisingly silent about his mother and her role in his upbringing.

---

[3] See Bruce H. Kirmmse, *Kierkegaard in Golden Age Denmark*, Bloomington and Indianapolis: Indiana University Press 1990, p. 25.

Kierkegaard's father was a profoundly religious man, and Kierkegaard was raised in the tradition of Lutheran Christianity. This stamped the character of the entire family. Søren's elder brother, Peter Christian Kierkegaard (1805–88), went on to study theology and become a leading pastor and bishop in the Danish Church. Kierkegaard's father is said to have had a depressed character resulting from an obsession with his own sinfulness. It is thought that his sons inherited this trait.

When Kierkegaard was a boy his nickname around the house was "the Fork." The reason for this was that one day when he was asked what he wanted to be when he grew up, he replied, "A fork." When asked why, he responded, "Then I could 'spear' anything I wanted on the dinner table." When he was then asked, "But what if we come after you?" he replied, "Then I'll spear you."[4] This story evidences the fact that the young Kierkegaard was a provocative lad, who enjoyed getting the better of people.

As a boy Kierkegaard attended the School of Civic Virtue, where he learned Latin and Greek and developed an interest in the classics. Originally founded in 1787, the school was divided in 1789 into two schools, one in Copenhagen and one in nearby Christianshavn. From 1821 until he was admitted to the university in 1830, Kierkegaard attended the Copenhagen school, which was located in the street Klareboderne, a short walk from his family home. It was a respected educational institution for the sons of wealthy bourgeois families. The school was an intensive one that focused on classical education in Latin, Greek, and Hebrew. During his time at the school Kierkegaard came to love Greek culture and literature. His readings in Greek included Homer's *Iliad* and *Odyssey*, some of Herodotus' *Histories*, and some of the New Testament.[5] Most importantly, he also read some of the dialogues of the Greek philosopher Plato, specifically, the *Euthyphro*, the *Apology*, and the *Crito*. He also studied another important source of the life and teachings of Socrates, namely, Xenophon's *Memorabilia of Socrates*.[6] The school thus

---

[4] *Encounters with Kierkegaard: A Life as Seen by His Contemporaries*, trans. and ed. by Bruce H. Kirmmse, Princeton: Princeton University Press 1996, p. 3.

[5] Ibid., p. 15, and the note on p. 273.

[6] See Tonny Aagaard Olesen, "Kierkegaard's Socrates Sources: Eighteenth- and Nineteenth-Century Danish Scholarship," in *Kierkegaard and the Greek World*, Tome I, *Socrates and Plato*, ed. by Jon Stewart and Katalin Nun, Aldershot: Ashgate 2010 (*Kierkegaard Research: Sources, Reception, and Resources*, vol. 2), pp. 221f.

provided him with a thorough knowledge of the philosopher Socrates, who would fascinate him for the rest of his life.

But looking back at his time at the school, Kierkegaard probably did not have so many fond memories. By all accounts he did not have friends and was often teased for his odd clothes. His thick wool stockings caused him to receive the unenviable nickname Søren Sock. But the young Kierkegaard was not one to sit by passively and allow himself to be antagonized if he could help it. On the contrary, contemporary reports unanimously recount that he himself had a tendency to tease and irritate his fellow pupils with his superior intellect. He enjoyed demonstrating his cleverness by making his classmates look silly. Unfortunately, since he was not the largest boy in the class, his provocations had the negative consequence that he was occasionally beaten by the others for the humiliation that they had suffered at his hands.[7] In any case, these negative experiences did not prevent him from returning to the school later in life to teach Latin.

All of Kierkegaard's brothers and sisters died at a fairly young age, with the sole exception of his elder brother, Peter Christian. The early deaths of his siblings caused a shadow of melancholy to hover over their family home. By 1834, when Kierkegaard was just 21 years old, only he, his brother Peter Christian, and his father remained. All of the others—five brothers and sisters, and his mother—were dead.

1.2. Introduction to *The Concept of Irony*

After graduating from the School of Civic Virtue, Kierkegaard was accepted as a student at the University of Copenhagen. There he wrote *The Concept of Irony* as his master's thesis. The book is divided into two large parts. Part One is entitled "The Position of Socrates Viewed as Irony." Here the young author compares the picture of Socrates that is presented by the three main ancient sources: Plato, Xenophon, and the comic writer Aristophanes. As we know, Plato and Xenophon were both students of Socrates and wrote dialogues in which they presented their beloved teacher as the main speaker.

---

[7] *Encounters with Kierkegaard*, pp. 4–5, p. 7, p. 10.

Aristophanes parodied Socrates in a humorous manner in the comedy *The Clouds*. By comparing and contrasting these ancient sources, Kierkegaard hopes to arrive at the true picture of Socrates. The view that Kierkegaard consistently urges throughout his analysis is that Socrates has no philosophical doctrine or theory, but rather merely refutes what others say without presenting any constructive alternative. In this sense Socrates represents a negative, destructive force. Kierkegaard does not mean that Socrates is negative in the sense that we now refer to someone having a negative disposition, that is, someone who is pessimistic. Rather, Socrates is negative in the sense that he undermines the position of others but refuses to present a positive thesis or doctrine himself. In this first part of the work Kierkegaard wants to establish that this interpretation of Socrates is well grounded in the ancient sources.

This first part of *The Concept of Irony* is followed by an appendix called "Hegel's View of Socrates." This refers to the treatment of Socrates by the German philosopher G. W. F. Hegel in his lectures. Hegel's interpretation of the thought of Socrates and its role in the development of philosophy and culture was profoundly influential at the time. Kierkegaard knew this, and he made a careful study of Hegel's different accounts of Socrates, which he critically built on in his master's thesis. So in order to understand Kierkegaard's picture of Socrates, we must also have some insight into Hegel's interpretation and Kierkegaard's response to it. This will be the subject of the second chapter.

Part Two of Kierkegaard's work is simply entitled "The Concept of Irony." It is here that he treats the modern forms of irony in the Romantics and examines the thought of the German writers Friedrich von Schlegel, Karl Wilhelm Ferdinand Solger, and Ludwig Tieck. While Socratic irony was given a generally positive treatment, the Romantics are criticized for using irony in the service of relativism or nihilism; their goal is simply to undermine bourgeois society, but there is no truth or deeper meaning that they wish to propose to replace it.

The final short section of *The Concept of Irony* is entitled "Irony as a Controlled Element, the Truth of Irony." This section has been quite controversial in the secondary literature. It seems to be Kierkegaard's presentation of his own view of the proper and appropriate use of irony. It was impossible for Kierkegaard to go back to ancient Athens and use irony in the same way that Socrates did, since the historical and cultural background had changed so radically since that time. Romantic irony was likewise no alternative given Kierkegaard's criticism of it in the preceding pages. So instead, he suggests a limited form of irony, which he believes is the most appropriate in his own day. This is what he calls "controlled irony."

1.3. Socratic Irony and Ignorance

The central focus of attention in most of *The Concept of Irony* is without doubt Socrates. But it was not just in *The Concept of Irony* that Kierkegaard examined the teachings of this philosopher. Rather he was fascinated with the figure of Socrates, to whom he returned throughout his life. What was it about the ancient Greek philosopher that interested Kierkegaard? And what is meant by "Socratic irony"?

Socrates lived in ancient Athens in the fifth century BC, and his work was, as noted, recorded in the form of dialogues by his student Plato. In 399 BC Socrates was brought up on charges by his fellow Athenians and sentenced to death. The *Apology* is an account of his trial, and the *Phaedo* is an account of his final hours and death by drinking hemlock. Socrates spent much of his time walking around the city and talking with people. He went to people who claimed to know something about a given topic and asked them about it. Claiming to be ignorant, he begged his discussion partners to enlighten him on whatever topic they claimed to know something about. Thus he would begin a dialogue with them.

What is known as "Socratic irony" usually appears at the beginning of these exchanges when Socrates gets his interlocutor to explain something to him or to give a definition of something. One can see this illustrated in the dialogue the *Euthyphro*. In this work Socrates goes to the courthouse at Athens to attend to the legal proceedings that had been raised against him, and there he meets an acquaintance, Euthyphro. The two greet and ask each other what business they have at court. To Socrates' astonishment, Euthyphro explains that he is bringing charges against his own father. Needless to say, this is something very unusual, especially in ancient Greece, where respect for one's father was a virtually absolute value. Socrates can immediately see the obvious contradiction between the love and respect that one owes one's father and Euthyphro's action. But instead of pointing out this contradiction, he pretends to assume that there must be some-thing that *he* has not understood and that Euthyphro must have some special knowledge of the matter. Socrates exclaims, "Good heavens! Of course, most people have no idea, Euthyphro, what the rights of such a case are. I imagine that it isn't everyone that may take such a course [of action], but only one who is far advanced in wisdom."[8] This sounds like a compliment to the ears of Euthyphro, who fails to see the irony in it. So he responds self-confidently, "Far indeed, Socrates."[9]

Euthyphro goes on to assure Socrates that he is in fact an expert in such things, and Socrates seems to assent to this. One can also see Socratic irony at the end of the dialogue when Euthyphro, growing tired of Socrates refuting every answer that he gives, suddenly runs off. As Euthyphro hastens away, Socrates feigns a great disappoint-ment, claiming he thought that he was going to learn something about piety from him. Socrates seems almost to heckle Euthyphro, saying that, without his instruction, he is condemned to live in the ignorance of his own views for the rest of his life.

By claiming not to know anything himself and by getting Euthy-phro to boast about having expert knowledge, Socrates is free to ask Euthyphro questions, pretending to want to learn from him. Euthy-phro would look silly if, after having claimed to be an expert, he refused to answer him. What Socrates realized was that it was easy to get people talking when one flattered them for their expertise. So in this way the Socratic dialogue is initiated. Socrates' irony is a key factor in this process. Initially, he seems to be ironic, first, about not knowing anything, since clearly the ensuing discussion demonstrates that he in fact knows something about the topic, and, second, about granting that Euthyphro knows something or is an expert.

Kierkegaard was fascinated by this since he saw in his own Danish society of the nineteenth century many people like Euthyphro, who claimed to have knowledge of things about which they were in fact ignorant. He observed Socrates' use of irony to bait these people so as to draw them out. Then once they began to explain what they thought they had understood, they could be refuted. Kierkegaard studied

---

[8] Plato, *Euthyphro*, in *The Last Days of Socrates*, trans. by Hugh Tredennick, Harmondsworth: Penguin 1954, p. 22.

[9] Ibid.

Socrates' method carefully and considered ways in which he could use it to his own advantage in the discussions taking place in his own day.

1.4. Socrates and *Aporia*

In addition to irony, another important element of the Socratic dialogue for Kierkegaard is what is known as *aporia* (ἀπορία). This is a Greek word, which means "being at a loss" or "being unable to answer." Socrates brings Euthyphro and his other interlocutors to a state of *aporia* in the course of the dialogue. Socrates asks for a definition of piety, which Euthyphro gives. But upon Socrates' cross-examination, they both agree that this is not satisfactory, and so Socrates asks for a better definition. The same thing happens with the second definition, the third, and so on, so that in the end no real definition or result is achieved. Losing patience with Socrates and seeing that he is beginning to look more and more foolish, Euthyphro suddenly claims that he has an important appointment and hastens away. Thus the dialogue itself ends in *aporia* since no definition of piety is ever agreed to. For this reason, it is said that this is one of Plato's "aporetic" dialogues, that is, one that ends with no definitive conclusion to the question under examination.

Usually when one writes a philosophical treatise or tract, the goal is to demonstrate a specific thesis, to establish a specific point. One states the thesis at the beginning, and in the body of the work one proceeds to give arguments for it. Against this background, the procedure of Socrates is very unusual since it does not establish anything at all. Rather, the result is purely negative. All that one has learned is that the handful of definitions of piety that have been proposed are incorrect, but one still does not know what piety is. No positive definition has survived the critical examination.

This appealed to Kierkegaard very much, and he enjoyed seeing in Socrates a thinker of negativity in this sense. Socrates' goal was not to establish a positive doctrine, but rather to get others to reconsider their long-held views by pointing out that they rested on uncertain foundations. Five years after *The Concept of Irony*, Kierkegaard returned to this feature of Socrates' philosophizing in his *Journal JJ*, where he writes, "The fact that several of Plato's dialogues end without result has a far deeper reason than I had earlier thought.... [It makes] the reader or listener self-active."[10] Kierkegaard was fascinated by the fact that although Socrates was only doing something negative, he nonetheless brought other people to be reflective and reconsider certain aspects of their beliefs and lives. Through his questioning, Socrates led his interlocutors into the process of philosophical thinking, since they could not simply be passive recipients of a teaching presented by Socrates or someone else. Kierkegaard was then inspired to try to imitate this aspect of Socrates' method in his own writings.

1.5. Socrates and the Sophists

In the fifth century BC there were in Athens a number of travelling scholars of rhetoric who would give lessons to the sons of rich families for a fee. These figures were known as Sophists. They claimed to be able to teach useful skills such as public speaking, logical reasoning, and argumentation along with providing a general education. These were important skills to have in the democracy of Athens, where political issues were constantly debated.

While the Sophists were successful at attracting students and earning a living in this way, they were not always popular with everyone. Like some lawyers today, they had a somewhat shady reputation for being able to twist words and to win cases for implausible or even wrongful positions. They were charismatic personalities and eloquent speakers who could seduce people with language. It was said that they were less interested in the truth than in winning the argument.

Since Socrates was often seen in the streets apparently giving instruction to young men, many of the people of Athens associated him with the Sophists, and thus one of the charges leveled against him was that he made the weaker argument the stronger, since this was what the Sophists were known to do. But Socrates vehemently

---

[10] *Kierkegaard's Journals and Notebooks*, ed. by Niels Jørgen Cappelørn et al., vols 1–11, Princeton: Princeton University Press 2007ff., vol. 2, p. 276, JJ:482. In the *Concluding Unscientific Postscript*, he writes, "the most one person can do for another is to unsettle him" (Kierkegaard, *Concluding Unscientific Postscript*, vols 1–2, trans. by Howard V. Hong and Edna H. Hong, Princeton: Princeton University Press 1992, vol. 1, p. 387).

rejected this association,[11] arguing that unlike the Sophists, he did not claim to know anything and thus did not teach anything. The young men came to listen to his discussions simply because they found it amusing to see him interrogate people in his special way. Since Socrates purported not to teach anything, he never demanded any kind of fee in contrast to the Sophists, who lived on the money that they received for their instruction.

Kierkegaard was attentive to Socrates' polemic with the Sophists, which is portrayed in many of the dialogues of Plato. He saw many people in the Copenhagen of his own day whom he regarded as the modern version of the Sophists. They claimed to know something about Christianity and to teach this, while benefiting materially from their positions in the Church. While they enjoyed a comfortable life with financial security, they taught a version of Christianity that Kierkegaard found to be deeply problematic. Moreover, Kierkegaard also regards some scientists and scholars as Sophists due to the fact that they claim to have discovered the final truth about things and yet not possess the proper amount of humility with regard to such things. He thus resolved to use Socrates' method to undermine these self-satisfied and overly confident people.

1.6. Socrates' Mission and the Gadfly

Socrates' procedure of questioning people irritated a number of his fellow citizens who felt publicly humiliated, especially when he refuted them in front of a crowd of bemused young men. This was one of the reasons why some of his enemies raised charges against him and forced him to defend himself in a court of law. When asked to explain why he goes around Athens and harasses his fellow citizens in this way, Socrates told the story of a friend of his who went to the Oracle at Delphi.[12] In ancient Greek society the oracle was a revered religious institution, where it was believed the god Apollo spoke through the priestesses. Whenever an important decision needed to be made either about some private matter or about some larger matter of state, it was customary to go to the oracle in order to ask

---

[11] Plato, *Apology*, in *The Last Days of Socrates*, p. 48.
[12] Plato, *Apology*, pp. 49ff.

the god if a given plan would prosper. A friend of Socrates asked the god if there was anyone who was wiser than Socrates, and the god replied, through the priestess, that there was no one.

When his friend returned to Athens and reported this, Socrates was perplexed by the answer since he could not think of anything that he had any special knowledge about. Indeed, he saw many people around him whom he considered to be much wiser than he about a number of different things. So he set out to ask these different people about what they knew. As it turned out, as he went around from one person to the next, each of them pretended, like Euthyphro, to be a great expert at something, but in the end, after Socrates' questioning, it became obvious that they knew nothing at all. Socrates was then led to the conclusion that he was wiser in the sense that he at least knew that he did not know, in contrast to the others who erroneously claimed that they did know.[13] This, he thought, must be the meaning of the oracle. Socrates' knowledge was not some *positive* knowledge about some concrete sphere of thought or activity, but rather a *negative* knowledge. Paradoxically, Socrates' knowledge is that he does not know anything at all.

Since this insight had come from the god at the oracle, Socrates came to believe that he had been given a divine mission, and it was his religious duty to go around Athens and to test people's claims to knowledge. This was his explanation to the jurors for why he acted the way he did. Socrates uses the image of a gadfly as an analogy to his action. A gadfly irritates a horse by constantly buzzing around and landing on it. Socrates sees himself as doing the same thing with his fellow Athenians. Plato quotes him as saying, "It seems to me that God has attached me to this city to perform the office of such a fly; and all day long I never cease to settle here, there, and everywhere, rousing, persuading, reproving every one of you."[14] Socrates thus portrayed himself as *the gadfly of Athens* who performed a beneficial, albeit irritating, function of keeping people from falling into complacency and constantly keeping them on their guard with respect to their claims to knowledge. He regarded his work as a religious calling; he did not interrogate people on the streets because he enjoyed doing so or because he personally thought it was a good idea, but rather he

---

[13] Ibid., p. 50.   [14] Ibid., p. 63.

saw himself as following the command of the god. It was his religious duty to do so.

This was an image that Kierkegaard relished, and he came to conceive of his own task as like that of Socrates. He believed that through his writings he could in effect be *the gadfly of Copenhagen*, keeping his fellow countrymen from falling into complacency.[15] He believed that the people in his own day had a mistaken conception of Christianity and needed a gadfly to force them to examine their views critically and revise them. His goal was not to convince people of a positive doctrine by means of discursive arguments intended to persuade skeptically disposed readers. Likewise, his goal was not to become popular or make friends with people with his writings. Rather, his aim was to follow Socrates' example of provoking and irritating them in a way that would cause them to see the errors in their beliefs.

1.7. Socrates' Daimon

One of the charges that was raised against Socrates was that he worshiped foreign gods that were not worshiped in Athens. This charge refers to what Socrates called his "daimon" (δαιμόνιον). This is a Greek word that means literally a god or spirit. In the Platonic dialogues mention is made of Socrates' daimon as a kind of personal spirit or inner voice that advises him. Modern scholars have had difficulties making sense of this: some try to interpret it as the voice of conscience, while others regard it as something like a guardian angel. At his trial Socrates explained the daimon as follows: "I am subject to a divine or supernatural experience. . . . It began in my early childhood—a sort of voice which comes to me; and when it comes it always dissuades me from what I am proposing to do, and never urges me on."[16] So Socrates claims that he has a private inner voice that prevents him from getting into trouble by telling him not to do something that is ill considered or that might lead to negative consequences. But like Socrates himself, the daimon never offers positive suggestions for what he should do.

---

[15] *Kierkegaard's Journals and Notebooks*, vol. 2, p. 275, JJ:477.
[16] Plato *Apology*, pp. 63f.

Socrates believed the daimon was helping him fulfill his divine mission. When the jurors convicted him of the charges and sentenced him to death, he claimed that he was not concerned since throughout the entire proceedings of the trial, his daimon never raised an objection to anything that he was saying or doing—which he took to mean that everything was going according to the divine will.[17] He thus concluded that he had nothing to fear.

This was also an idea that Kierkegaard identified with. In the Christian tradition we are used to talking about concepts such as divine providence or the idea that God is directing the universe with a specific purpose in mind. In his work *The Point of View for My Work as an Author*, in which he reflects on his life and his writing career, Kierkegaard explains his conviction that his life has been driven by an invisible divine "governance" (*Styrelse*). God had a plan for his life, which Kierkegaard unwittingly realized. Although he did not always understand the divine plan himself, Kierkegaard felt that God was in a sense guiding him in his writings in the same way that Socrates' daimon was guiding him. Just like socrates, Kierkegaard saw his own work as a kind of divine mission. Kierkegaard believed that God would lead him in the right direction, just as Socrates believed that his daimon would keep him away from harm.

1.8. Socrates' Maieutics

Another feature of Socrates' thought is what is referred to as "maieutics" or the art of midwifery. This word comes from the Greek adjective μαιευτικός, meaning "of or about midwifery." Socrates explained that his mother was a midwife and that he took this art from her. When he questions people, the goal, he claims, is to get them to come to a truth themselves. He believed that they implicitly had the truth within themselves but without knowing this consciously. But this knowledge can be brought to light with the kind of leading questioning that Socrates engages in.

A famous example of this is when Socrates questions an uneducated slave boy in the dialogue the *Meno*, and merely by questioning,

---

[17] Ibid., p. 74.

without stating anything positive himself, he is able to lead the boy to an understanding of some of the basic principles of geometry. Everyone present is astonished that the boy apparently knew geometry all the time without ever having had any instruction in it. This is consistent with Socrates' repeated claim that he did not teach anything. He claims merely to be the midwife who assists in the birth of ideas, but he himself does not produce them. He simply helps others to produce them and to evaluate them subsequently. The ideas lie hidden in the individuals themselves, without them even being aware of their presence. (This led Socrates to a doctrine of innate ideas, that is, the notion that we are born with certain ideas right from the start, and that we know things before actually having any experience of the world. The task of the questioner is then simply to help us remember what we already know ahead of time but have forgotten.)

Socrates' maieutics is a motif that Kierkegaard also uses for his writing. He did not want to state explicitly what he thought Christianity was but instead wished to help others to arrive at their own conception of it. Kierkegaard wanted to avoid giving the impression that he wanted to teach people, and they just needed to follow his instruction. He believed Christianity was meaningful only to the extent that the believer experienced it himself, and so a vicarious belief based solely on the authority of another person's teaching was insufficient and even misleading. Instead, Kierkegaard insisted that Christianity is all about an inward relation in each individual, and so the goal was to help people to find this in themselves. So just like Socrates, Kierkegaard believed he could facilitate this, but it was ultimately the other person who was doing the work of discovering the truth or the inward relation in him- or herself.

1.9. The Socrates of Copenhagen

One of the few friends that Kierkegaard had throughout his life was a man named Emil Boesen, who was a pastor in the Danish Church. Boesen recalled the importance of Kierkegaard's master's thesis for the philosopher's later development, explaining, "It was ... most probably while [Kierkegaard] was writing *The Concept of Irony* ... that he first gained a clear understanding of what he himself wanted to do and what his abilities were."[18] Boesen suggests that there was something about his work in this context that helped Kierkegaard to decide to become an author and helped him to find out specifically what kind of an author he wanted to be. What was this? Much evidence supports the claim that Socrates was the key for Kierkegaard. All of the points that we have touched on here came to be important for him in one way or another: ignorance, *aporia*, the Sophists, the gadfly, the daimon, maieutics, and, of course, Socrates' irony.

In many of his most important works Kierkegaard returns to the figure of Socrates. He is discussed at some length in the *Philosophical Fragments* as a form of learning that is contrasted with Christianity. Likewise, reference is made to Socrates in the satirical work *Prefaces* from 1844. A long section of *Stages on Life's Way* entitled "In vino veritas" is modeled on Plato's dialogue *The Symposium*. Throughout his edifying discourses Socrates is referred to indirectly as "the simple wise man of old." Socrates appears in scattered passages in the *Concluding Unscientific Postscript* and is likewise discussed in connection with a theory of Christian ethics in *Works of Love*. Kierkegaard also invokes Socrates in *The Sickness unto Death* as an alternative to the modern age. Finally, Socrates is mentioned as a kind of model in the final issue of *The Moment* shortly before Kierkegaard's death. In short, Socrates is a constant presence in his authorship.

Kierkegaard recognized problems in nineteenth-century Denmark that were analogous to the problems that confronted the Greeks in the fifth century BC. Human nature being what it is, he recognized many of his own contemporaries in the characters portrayed in the dialogues of Plato. Kierkegaard hit upon the idea that what was needed in his own time was a new Socrates. By this he meant not someone who would come up with a new philosophy or a new doctrine, but rather someone who would disturb and provoke people and shake them from their complacency. This was the goal that he decided to set for himself. He would become the new Socrates—the Socrates of Copenhagen.

---

[18] *Encounters with Kierkegaard*, p. 29.

2

Hegel's View of Socrates

Kierkegaard's understanding of Socrates was of course based on his reading of the texts of Plato, Xenophon, and Aristophanes, that is, the primary Greek sources. But it was also largely shaped by the interpretation of the German philosopher G. W. F. Hegel, with whom he was in a constant critical dialogue in *The Concept of Irony*. Hegel's philosophy was highly popular at the University of Copenhagen in the late 1830s when Kierkegaard was a student and was writing this work. In this chapter we will explore first the presence of Hegel at the university during Kierkegaard's time and then go through Hegel's analysis of Socrates, treating the same topics that we introduced in the previous chapter: Socratic irony, *aporia*, the daimon, etc. We will see how Kierkegaard is inspired and influenced by the important historical role that Hegel ascribes to the person of Socrates.

2.1. Martensen and the University of Copenhagen in the 1830s

What does it mean to say that we are "autonomous"? For most people today "autonomy" is just a fancy word for "freedom." Literally, autonomy just means that one is able to give a law to oneself; in other words, one can decide for oneself what one wishes to do. To say that someone is not autonomous means that that person is subject to external laws that often contradict what one wants to do. So in this sense we all generally think autonomy is a good thing, just as we think freedom is a good thing. I do not want someone telling me what to do or imposing arbitrary rules and regulations on me that limit my freedom. While today autonomy is conceived as a universally positive thing, this was not always the case. In some societies the main value is not for people to go out and act on their own desires and wishes; instead, the most important thing is for them to conform to a set of rules that has been agreed upon by their family, culture, or society. This includes dressing in a certain way or acting in accordance with accepted norms. Such societies perceive autonomous acts as signs of arrogance and disregard of one's family or tradition.

This is an issue that is also often associated with religion. For example, in religious ceremonies, everyone is expected to participate and perform the ceremony in the same way. It is impossible to be an individualist or a nonconformist in a ceremonial context. Similarly, in religion there is usually a core body of dogma that all the followers are supposed to believe. It is not about creating some new idea or personal truth, but rather following the established set of beliefs that everyone follows. For these reasons a religious congregation or community is often a close-knit group with shared values and ways of thinking.

In Christianity it is thought that human beings are finite and sinful. They are unable to obtain salvation through their own actions and require the assistance of divine grace. In this context it is considered not just arrogant but even irreligious to act as if one could determine the truth for oneself. In this sense autonomy is conceived as a negative thing. This issue, which is still very much alive today, was also important in Kierkegaard's time. It was thematized by a young Danish scholar named Hans Lassen Martensen (see Fig. 2.1).

When Kierkegaard was a student at the University of Copenhagen in the 1830s, the philosophy of Hegel was something of a fad among the students. The excitement surrounding Hegel's thought was created by Martensen, who was just five years older than Kierkegaard. In 1834 Martensen embarked on a two-year trip that took him to Berlin, Heidelberg, Munich, Vienna, and Paris. On his journey Martensen met most all of the leading figures in Prussia and the German states who were discussing Hegel's philosophy at this time.[1] This was a formative event in his life.

When he returned to Copenhagen in 1836, Martensen began an illustrious academic career. On July 12, 1837 he defended his dissertation, which was entitled *On the Autonomy of Human*

---

[1] At the time Germany was, of course, not a unified political entity but rather consisted of a patchwork of autonomous small duchies, principalities, and kingdoms.

Fig. 2.1. Hans Lassen
Martensen (1808–84)

Self-Consciousness.[2] His public oral defense was held at Regensen College, where animated discussions about his lectures often took place among the students (see Fig. 2.2).

In this work he critically treated the systems of the German thinkers Kant, Schleiermacher, and Hegel. Martensen argued that their philosophies all represented systems of autonomy that he believed focused one-sidedly on the power of the individual. He argued that this fails to recognize the profound dependency of human beings on God. With this topic Martensen can in a sense be said to anticipate Kierkegaard's topic of irony. In both cases what is at issue is the role of the individual or the subject vis-à-vis the objective

---

[2] This work is available in English as *The Autonomy of Human Self-Consciousness in Modern Dogmatic Theology*, in *Between Hegel and Kierkegaard: Hans L. Martensen's Philosophy of Religion*, translations by Curtis L. Thompson and David J. Kangas, Atlanta: Scholars' Press 1997, pp. 73–147. For a useful introduction to Martensen, see Robert Leslie Horn, *Positivity and Dialectic: A Study of the Theological Method of Hans Lassen Martensen*, Copenhagen: C. A. Reitzel 2007 (*Danish Golden Age Studies*, vol. 2).

Fig. 2.2. The courtyard of Regensen College with the Round Tower (*c.* 1840)

order of things. Both Martensen and Kierkegaard were in agreement that modern subjectivity or relativism had gone too far. Martensen's key term for this is "modern autonomy," while Kierkegaard's is "irony," but in the end they are talking about the same set of issues.

Martensen began lecturing at the University of Copenhagen in the fall of 1837 (see Fig. 2.3). His courses soon became the talk of the university. Students from all disciplines flocked to hear what he had to say, since he was in a sense giving an account of what he had learned on his trip about the most recent developments in philosophy and theology in the German-speaking states. To the consternation and amazement of the older, more conservative faculty, Martensen became a kind of academic celebrity. To the students he was an exciting young scholar, who could speak to them in a way that they had not experienced before. He presented the basic ideas of Hegel, which all of Prussia and Germany were talking about. One of Martensen's students describes his

Fig. 2.3. The Lime Court of the University of Copenhagen with the Church of Our Lady in the background

encounter with these lectures as his "intellectual awakening."[3] He writes:

> The man, who through his lectures made such a strong impression on me and many others was a young instructor, who...had been appointed to give lectures on more recent history of philosophy...for us first-year students. It was H.L. Martensen...he brought new life into the...new university building....Martensen...for many years filled the largest auditoriums with nothing but zealous auditors. What immediately won me over to him was the fresh enthusiasm which surrounded him in comparison to the other instructors....He spoke precisely about what I thirsted to hear, and did so at times with a

[3] Christian Hostrup, *Erindringer fra min Barndom og Ungdom*, Copenhagen: Gyldendalske Boghandels Forlag 1891, p. 80.

warmth which I found doubly impressive in the cold temple of the sciences.[4]

Among the students in Martensen's lecture hall was the young Søren Kierkegaard. His notes to Martensen's course can be found in his *Notebook 4*.[5] Here Kierkegaard could witness first-hand the sensation that Hegel and German philosophy were making among his fellow students. He was disturbed by Martensen's success and frustrated by the avid interest that his fellow students showed in these lectures.

While Kierkegaard clearly felt alienated from the group of students that idolized Martensen, he knew that if he were going to write his master's thesis on irony, he would have to take Hegel's views on the subject seriously. In a handful of different texts Hegel had treated the topic of irony in both its Socratic and Romantic forms. So Kierkegaard read carefully Hegel's texts with a special eye to this issue.

2.2. Introduction to Hegel

Hegel was born in Stuttgart in 1770 and was one of the leading figures in the philosophical tradition known as German idealism (see Fig. 2.4). He penned a handful of important works on different topics: the *Phenomenology of Spirit* (1807), the *Science of Logic* (1812–16), the *Encyclopedia of the Philosophical Sciences* (1817), and the *Philosophy of Right* (1821). After having lived at important cultural centers such as Tübingen, Berne, Frankfurt am Main, Jena, Nuremberg, and Heidelberg, Hegel's career culminated in a professorship at the Royal Friedrich Wilhelm's University, which is today the Humboldt University in Berlin. He spent the last decade of his life in Berlin, where his philosophy exercised great influence. His lectures there in the 1820s attracted students from all over Europe.

---

[4] Ibid., pp. 81f.
[5] *Kierkegaard's Journals and Notebooks*, ed. by Niels Jørgen Cappelørn et al., Princeton: Princeton University Press 2007, vol. 3, pp. 125–42, Not4:3–12.

Fig. 2.4. G. W. F. Hegel
(1770–1831)

After he died on November 14, 1831 his students formed a society dedicated to publishing a complete edition of his works. They believed that Hegel's lectures constituted an important aspect of his thought that was not well known outside his lecture hall, and so in their edition they decided to include not just the works that Hegel had published in his own lifetime but also four of his most important lecture courses. Since Hegel himself did not leave behind complete notes, the individual editors were assigned the task of collecting and collating student notes and producing continuous texts from them. These were then published as the *Lectures on the Philosophy of Religion*, the *Lectures on Aesthetics*, the *Lectures on the Philosophy of History*, and the *Lectures on the History of Philosophy*. Kierkegaard owned copies of all of these works, and *The Concept of Irony* refers to or quotes directly three of the four.

Hegel's most extended account of Socrates appears in the first volume of the three-volume *Lectures on the History of Philosophy*, which appeared from 1833 to 1836, edited by Karl Ludwig Michelet. We shall look at Hegel's analysis and see how it is relevant for Kierkegaard's understanding of Socrates in *The Concept of Irony*. In his investigation Hegel makes use of the three main sources of Socrates' life and teachings: Plato, Xenophon, and Aristophanes— the same three sources that Kierkegaard uses in his analysis of Socratic irony in *The Concept of Irony*.

2.3. Hegel's Understanding of Socrates in the History of Western Culture

Hegel gave a sweeping story about the development of Western philosophy and culture, but did so in a way that always kept in view the relevance of this story for his own time.[6] This was the period after the French Revolution and the Napoleonic Wars, and students were fascinated to study the forces of history that Hegel described not just because this shed light on some particular period in history, but rather because it helped them to understand the developments in their own age.

In his lectures he portrays Socrates as what he calls a "mental turning point" in the history of philosophy and culture.[7] Prior to Socrates, the so-called pre-Socratic philosophers were concerned with understanding the world of nature. They were in a sense the first natural scientists, who tried to explain the world without appealing to any divine agency. They were thus primarily interested in the object-ive world as they found it outside themselves. By contrast, Socrates was the first to turn the focus inward, to the realm of thought. He believed that understanding how people thought was prior to and more important than understanding the natural world, for in order to "understand" the natural world, we must first know what it means to understand anything at all. Kierkegaard was attentive to this distinc-tion between Socrates' thought and the natural sciences, which he discusses in his journals.[8]

According to Hegel, this marked a revolutionary idea not just in Greek philosophy but also in history generally. The Greeks lived in accordance with time-honored customs and traditions that they took to be divinely sanctioned. This is the broad sphere of what Hegel calls in German "*Sittlichkeit*," which is usually translated as "ethics," or "ethical life." By this, however, he means not just the customary ethics that a given people like the Greeks follow, but also the broad spheres of religion, laws, traditions, and established patterns of social inter-action. For Hegel, the Greeks had previously believed that this

---

[6] For Hegel's account of Socrates, see *Lectures on the History of Philosophy*, vols. 1–3, trans. by E. S. Haldane, London: K. Paul, Trench, Trübner 1892–6; Lincoln and London: University of Nebraska Press 1955, vol. 1, pp. 384–448.

[7] Ibid., vol. 1, p. 384.

[8] See *Kierkegaard's Journals and Notebooks*, vol. 4, pp. 57–73, NB:70–87.

objective sphere of customary ethics was true, as it were, by nature; in other words, when they acted in accordance with tradition and custom, this was not just the arbitrary will of some specific individual, but rather it was true in itself. These traditions and customs were prescribed by the gods and thus *de facto* true. This is the beginning of what is known today as the tradition of *natural law*, that is, the idea that some things are right or wrong by nature.

According to Hegel, the conception of traditional ethical life is exemplified in Sophocles' tragedy *Antigone*. In this work a conflict arises between the young woman Antigone and the King of Thebes, Creon. Antigone's brother Polyneices had been killed in a failed revolt against the state. Creon decrees that the bodies of the rebels should not be buried but rather should be left exposed to the wild animals and the elements. Anyone caught trying to bury one of the rebels would be punished by death. This was a serious matter in Greek society, since the question of funeral rites was considered sacred.

Antigone regards Creon's decree as arbitrary, the corrupt opinion of a tyrant. It is not true in itself but rather just his personal view. The fact that he is the king and thus has the sanction of law behind him does not change this. For Antigone, there is a higher law, the divinely sanctioned practice that dictates that deceased family members be buried with the customary funeral honors. In the lectures Hegel quotes this work, where Antigone refers to this as "the eternal law of the gods."[9] For Antigone, the funeral rites are an objective fact of nature that she must obey, even if her action is illegal by human laws. The laws of nature are absolute, whereas human laws are arbitrary.

Hegel takes this to be exemplary for the Greek view prior to Socrates. The revolution of thought that Socrates brought about was to shift this emphasis from the outward objective sphere that was given by the gods as true forever, to the inward sphere of the individual. As Hegel explains, "Socrates' principle is that man... must attain to truth through himself."[10] For Socrates, one should not blindly accept custom and tradition but rather critically examine them and come to a conclusion about them for oneself.

But note that this does not mean that whatever the subject happens to think is true and has validity. Hegel believes that there is still an

---

[9] Hegel, *Lectures on the History of Philosophy*, vol. 1, p. 386.   [10] Ibid.

objective truth, but that it must be reached and recognized by the individual subject through rational examination. The problem with the Greek view prior to Socrates was that the sphere of accepted custom and tradition was in a sense tyrannical. It was thought to be beyond question, and one's own personal opinion about it did not matter. For Antigone, it is an absolute truth that the surviving family members must give the funeral rites to deceased relatives regardless of what Creon or anyone else may think about it. It is simply true in itself.

But for Socrates and for the modern view, each individual has the right to give his or her assent to the truth. This recognizes the rationality of the individual to know and understand the truth. So the revolution that Socrates began in the Greek world and that led to our modern conception is that the subject is a constitutive element of the truth. To the Greeks this was a new and shocking idea that in the end cost Socrates his life.

2.4. A Truth for Which to Live and Die

The idea of a subjective truth was one that greatly appealed to the young Kierkegaard. In the summer of 1835 he came to northern Zealand, to the north of Copenhagen, where he visited the small towns and villages at his leisure. He records his impressions from this journey in his first journal, called simply *Journal AA*. This was an important period for the young student Kierkegaard, who seemed not to be making particularly rapid progress with his studies. One reason for this was perhaps that he was still somewhat unsure of what he wanted to do with his life. He recounts some of his doubts and uncertainties about which path to take. On August 1, 1835 in the fishing village of Gilleleje, he writes,

> What I really need is to be clear about *what I am to do*, not what I must know. . . . It is a question of understanding my destiny, of seeing what the Deity really wants *me* to do; the thing is to find a truth which is a truth *for me*, to find *the idea for which I am willing to live and die*.[11]

---

[11] *Kierkegaard's Journals and Notebooks*, vol. 1, p. 19, AA:12.

Here the young Kierkegaard states explicitly that he urgently needs to discover a subjective, personal truth, as he says "a truth *for me*." Like Socrates, he rejects the objective truths that are accepted by society. He continues,

> what use would it be in this respect if I were to discover a so-called objective truth, or if I worked my way through the philosophers' systems...? And what use would it be in that respect to be able to work out a theory of the state...which I myself did not inhabit but merely held up for others to see?[12]

Here he rejects *objective* knowledge, which, he believes, lacks something fundamental. Like Socrates, he believes the truth must be found within himself.

It is interesting to note the way in which Kierkegaard also includes Christianity in his account of objective truth. He writes, "What use would it be to be able to propound the meaning of Christianity, to explain many separate facts, if it had no deeper meaning for *me* and *my life*?"[13] Here he recognizes that Christianity can be regarded as something external and outward, as one objective truth among others. The academic fields of theology such as dogmatics or Church history might be thought to fall into this category. For example, what some Church council decided is an objective fact, but this has nothing to do with the individual's relation to that fact. Again, like Socrates, Kierkegaard believes that the deeper truth is not the *objective* one but rather the *subjective* one that lies within.

In these passages from his journal Kierkegaard has up until now been giving an account of his own views, but then he connects this discussion directly with Socrates. For Kierkegaard as for Socrates, knowledge of external things is irrelevant without knowledge of oneself as subject. He writes, "One must first learn to know oneself before knowing anything else.... Only when the person has inwardly understood *himself*, and then sees the way forward on his path, does his life acquire repose and meaning."[14] Kierkegaard claims that one must first begin with skepticism or "irony" in order to work through it. He writes, "true knowing begins with a not-knowing (Socrates)."[15] After an individual's belief in traditional truths has been shaken by means of the Socratic method, he is in a position to identify his own subjective truths. One must thus start from a position of what

---

[12] Ibid.   [13] Ibid.   [14] Ibid., p. 22.   [15] Ibid.

Kierkegaard calls "not-knowing," so that one is freed from the traditional beliefs which one has been raised with and lived with all
one's life.

Many years later in 1846 in the *Concluding Unscientific Postscript*,
Kierkegaard develops this distinction in some detail. At the beginning
of the work he explains that "the objective issue" is "about the truth of
Christianity."[16] This is the objective truth about Christianity such as
can be determined by, for example, the historical record, the sources,
etc. By contrast, there is also the subjective truth, which "is about the
individual's relation to Christianity."[17] The question of one's personal, inward, subjective relation to Christianity is, for Kierkegaard, a
much deeper and more important truth than all of the external,
objective truths that can be established. This fundamental distinction
between subjective and objective, discussed in the *Postscript*, finds its
origins in Kierkegaard's reflections in Gilleleje in 1835, and these
reflections are closely related to Socrates' revolution of thought that
turned away from external custom and tradition and gave validity to
what was inward and subjective.

2.5. Hegel's View of the Socratic Method and Irony

Hegel discusses Socrates' method and identifies two important features.[18] First, Socrates goes out among different kinds of people in the
context of their daily lives. He then strikes up a conversation with
them about their occupations or interests. In this way he manages
to draw them into a discussion. He then tries to get them to move
from their immediate experience with specific individual cases to a
universal truth. It is this movement from particular to universal that,
according to Hegel, constitutes the first element of the Socratic
method. We can see this in the dialogue, the *Euthyphro*, where
Euthyphro gives Socrates a number of examples of piety, and then

---

[16] Kierkegaard, *Concluding Unscientific Postscript*, vols. 1–2, trans. by Howard
V. Hong and Edna H. Hong, Princeton: Princeton University Press 1992, vol. 1, p. 17.
[17] Ibid.
[18] For Hegel's account of the Socratic method, see *Lectures on the History of
Philosophy*, vol. 1, pp. 397–406.

Socrates asks what all of the particular cases have in common.[19] Instead of hearing specific instances of piety, Socrates wants to find out what the essence or nature of piety is in itself. Similarly, in other dialogues he is interested not in examples of beauty but in beauty itself, not in examples of justice but in justice itself, etc.

The second part of the Socratic method is the causing of confusion between the idea or definition proposed and the actual experience of the individual—a conflict between the universal and the particular. Socrates' implicit goal is to show that his interlocutors have unreflectively accepted certain things to be true without examining them carefully. Thus by pointing out the contradictions in their views, Socrates in effect calls on the individual to go back and examine them critically. The key is that *the individual* with his or her own reason must test whatever is claimed to be true.

Hegel also examines Socratic irony, which was so important for Kierkegaard. He explains that Socrates began by getting his interlocutor to say something about the topic based on the generally accepted understanding of things. In order to get the other person to do this, Socrates pretends that he himself is ignorant of the matter in question and requires instruction in it. Once the other person begins to set forth the accepted view, Socrates can go to work on it and demonstrate the contradictions involved in it. In this way Socrates believed that he was helping the other person to come to the realization that he knew nothing.

A key question about Socrates' use of irony is whether or not Socrates really means it when he says that he knows nothing and is thus in need of instruction. In other words, is this ironic, or does Socrates really believe that he knows nothing? One might be suspicious of his claim to know nothing, since in the course of the ensuing discussion he clearly shows much greater intellectual acumen than his interlocutor. He is constantly either giving examples that seem to betray knowledge of specific things or quoting texts, for example, Homer, both of which require knowledge. Or, at a minimum, he seems to have knowledge of forms of argumentation, since he is so effective at pointing out flaws in reasoning. But Hegel says, "It may actually be said that Socrates knew nothing, for he did not reach the

---

[19] Plato, *Euthyphro*, in *The Last Days of Socrates*, trans. by Hugh Tredennick, Harmondsworth: Penguin 1954, p. 26.

systematic construction of a philosophy."[20] Here Hegel refers to *aporia* or the fact that dialogues like the *Euthyphro* do not end up with any positive result. This would seem to prove the claim that Socrates really does not know anything. This would imply that the irony consists not in this claim, which after all is true, but rather in the feigned belief that his interlocutor knows the truth and can teach it to him.

Hegel points out that when we use universal terms such as truth, justice, and beauty, we all have some vague sense of what these signify, and because of this we can communicate with each other by means of language, which makes use of such terms. But each of us has different intuitions about what these terms mean, and so in order to determine their meaning more exactly, we need to analyze them in more detail. This is what Socrates' method tries to do. By means of irony, Socrates attempts to get his interlocutor to make the given concept concrete or, as Hegel says, to develop it so that it ceases to be vague and abstract.[21]

2.6. Hegel's Interpretation of Socrates' Maieutics and *Aporia*

Hegel also mentions "maieutics" or the art of midwifery as an important element of Socrates' method. According to his interpretation, this amounts to the production of the universal from the particulars.[22] The inexperienced or untrained mind lives in a world of immediate perception, the sphere of particular sense impressions. But these particulars necessarily imply a universal, for otherwise one would not know what the particulars are. For example, one sees a number of particular dogs but would not be able to recognize them as dogs if one did not have the universal idea of dog in one's mind. A category is necessary for us to classify things and thus understand them for what they are. So when Socrates is practicing his maieutics or art of midwifery, he is helping his interlocutors to reach or recover the universal which lies implicitly in their own minds.

For Hegel, this is a kind of educational process that takes place in every person as they grow. We begin in the world of perceptions and particular cases, examples, and images, and only later do we learn to

---

[20] Hegel, *Lectures on the History of Philosophy*, vol. 1, p. 399.
[21] Ibid., p. 400.   [22] Ibid., p. 402.

think abstractly and to talk about abstract ideas or universals.[23] For the educated mind already familiar with the realm of thought, the constant stream of examples given in the Platonic dialogues appears tedious and unnecessary. But the point is that they are supposed to play a didactical function and to lead the uneducated or unreflective individual into the realm of thought. Since every human being possesses the faculty of reason, everyone is capable of abstract thought, but by the same token everyone needs the benefit of education or Socratic questioning to be able to become aware of this sphere.

Hegel also discusses the concept of *aporia* or the negative ending in the dialogues.[24] He points out that Socrates tries to lead his interlocutors into confusion by showing the contradictions in their views. Often he gets them to give a preliminary definition of something and then proceeds to show that the thing is just the opposite of what the proposed definition states. After this happens a few times, Socrates' dialogue partner becomes frustrated and gives up, leaving the discussion with no positive result. We thus have an *aporetic* dialogue. Hegel notes that it lies in the nature of philosophy to begin with a conundrum or a puzzle to be solved. So in this way Socrates has prepared the way for philosophy.

But Hegel's implicit critical point is that Socrates has stopped short with the negative and failed to realize the positive or constructive element that lies in negation. Hegel gives the example of the contradiction of being and nothing.[25] We are accustomed to think of these two ideas as absolutely independent of one another: being exists independently on its own and has nothing to do with nothingness. And vice versa, when we think of nothingness, this is a concept that exists on its own, independent of the concept of being. Thus both terms—being and nothing—are thought to be isolated, independent, and irreducible. Indeed, being contradicts nothing and vice versa. Where the one exists, the other does not. But, Hegel argues, when we examine these concepts more closely, we realize that we cannot think of the concept of being without the concept of nothing, and vice versa. The one necessarily implies the other. Thus, instead of being two isolated, atomic concepts, these in fact constitute a single higher, complex concept: *becoming*. Becoming contains both being and nothing. Something *becomes* when it comes into being, and it equally

---

[23] Ibid., p. 403.   [24] Ibid., pp. 404–6.   [25] Ibid., p. 404.

becomes when it perishes and ceases to be. In this way from what initially appeared to be an irresolvable contradiction, there emerges a new, positive concept. The movement looked initially as if it were stuck in contradiction and negation, as if it were aporetic: the contradiction of being and nothing. But ultimately this proved only to be a passing stage, and in the end something positive and constructive resulted. This is a fundamental idea in Hegel's metaphysics. The concept of negation is not simply a non-starter, but instead also forms the foundation for a positive development. So Hegel is critical of Socrates for stopping with the negation instead of recognizing the positive developments that result from contradiction.

But this is precisely what attracted Kierkegaard to Socrates. The Greek philosopher did not try to go on to develop something positive, but intentionally remained in the negative, in contradiction. Kierkegaard criticizes, among others, Martensen's zealous students for their desire "to go further" or specifically "to go further than Socrates." This criticism has its origin in this point in Hegel. Socrates, according to Hegel, prepared the ground for philosophy by means of negation. He cleared away the mistaken beliefs so that philosophy could go to work from the ground up. But Socrates himself never got past the negation. He failed to recognize the positive dimension of the dialectic. Thus what was needed was to go beyond Socrates, and supply the positive element and begin to construct a philosophical position or theory. But, for Kierkegaard, the whole point with Socrates was negation, and all talk of going beyond was an absurdity. So while Hegel and Kierkegaard agree that Socrates represents a position of negation, their normative assessment of this is completely different.

2.7. Hegel's Interpretation of Socrates, the Good, and the Sophists

Socrates tries to define the abstract concept of the Good.[26] According to Hegel, his great contribution in the development of human thought was the realization that the Good must be developed by the individual and cannot simply be blindly accepted as given by one's culture, established tradition, family, etc. By focusing on the subject,

---

[26] For Hegel's account of the Socrates and the Good, see ibid., pp. 406–25.

Socrates seemed to be like the Sophists, who did not recognize any absolute or external truth. Hegel cites the famous saying from the Sophist Protagoras: "Man is the measure of all things."[27] For Hegel, this means that each individual has his or her own truth. This is a statement of relativism. But this is not Socrates' position. According to his view, the Good is something absolute and universal, even though there is a subjective element involved in it. For Socrates, there is still an objective truth, but the key is that it must be reached by the individual by means of rationality and critical reflection. As Hegel puts it, for Socrates, "man has this outside within him."[28] The objective truth is not simply to be found in the external sphere around us, but rather also in the mind of each individual. While the Sophists use critical reflection to justify their own arbitrary, self-serving claims, Socrates believes that this tool can be used to reach an objective truth that will be agreed upon by everyone.

With Socrates there is a move from the outward to the inward, but the notion of truth is always maintained. Hegel calls this the "unity of the subjective and the objective."[29] The individual must seek the truth or the universal of ethics in him- or herself by means of thought and reason. But thought and reason are universals that other rational people can also attain. In this sense ethics is also something outward and public. So Hegel claims that there is a relation between the inward universal and the outward universal. While the two can be in contradiction, they can also align and be in agreement. Insofar as the subjective side is based on rationality, it is more than the individual's arbitrary whims or moods. Hegel explains, "Socrates opposed to the contingent and particular inward, that universal, true inward of thought. Socrates awakened this real conscience, for he not only said that man is the measure of all things, but man as thinking is the measure of all things."[30] The Sophists are relativists, since subjectivity means for them the contingency of the individual, that is, feelings, whims, moods, etc. But, for Socrates, subjectivity and inwardness are about thought, and since thought is about universals it is also something that can connect us with others and with an "objective" truth.

The revolutionary dimension of Socrates' philosophy was that he introduced reflective morality (*Moralität*) in contrast to established morality or ethics (*Sittlichkeit*). Reflective morality involves individuals

---

[27] Ibid., p. 406.   [28] Ibid., p. 387.   [29] Ibid.   [30] Ibid., p. 411.

consciously considering for themselves what was good instead of merely accepting it uncritically from their parents, ancestors, or society. For Hegel, this marked a major historical shift that set off an entirely new movement of thought that continues to this day: "In the universal consciousness, in the spirit of the people to which [Socrates] belongs, we see the natural turn to reflective morality. . . . The spirit of the world here begins to change, a change which was later on carried to its completion."[31] But like most revolutionary movements, this one was frightening to the people at the time. For the Greeks prior to Socrates, ethics was always an established matter in traditions, customs, and the state. The individual's reflection on or assent to this played no role. But then came Socrates who began to ask critical questions about these kinds of things and to assert the importance of the individual. For the Greeks, this was a terrifying thing since it threatened to undermine all of the traditions, customs, and truths that they had always held most dear. Thus Socrates was regarded as not just a nuisance but also a real and serious threat to Greek life.

The truth of ethics was formerly thought to be visible in the outward sphere of the state and society. Now, however, Socrates claims that it is to be sought inwardly in the individual. This is a radical new thought. One could no longer be complacent about morality and simply adopt what tradition and custom dictated. Now each individual had to be critical and reflective, and enter upon his or her own journey to reach the truth of ethics. While this Socratic revolution is destructive since it spells the demise of public morality, it is also a liberation since it frees people from the tyranny of custom. One no longer needs to go along with custom simply because it is custom. Now one can call custom and tradition into question and reject aspects of them that one cannot assent to. This is the modern principle that Socrates initiated in antiquity.

The criticism of public morality can be seen as consistent with Socrates' claim that he does not teach anything. With regard to ethics and morals, nothing can be learned that comes from the outside. This entire sphere of public morality imposes itself from without. Hegel uses the example of impressing a stamp on wax to illustrate the way in which we learn public morality when we are young.[32] But this is not what is essential about ethics. On the contrary, what is essential is the

---

[31] Ibid., p. 407.   [32] Ibid., p. 410.

inward dimension. Here individuals must do the work for themselves. They must find the truth of ethics inwardly. This is what Socrates helps them to find, so to speak, as a midwife, but he does not teach anything or provide anything positive himself.

2.8. Hegel's Interpretation of the Daimon of Socrates

Hegel interprets the daimon of Socrates in terms of the revolutionary role that Socrates played in Greek life.[33] He points out that the daimon is different from Socrates' own will and intelligence.[34] It tells him not to do things that he might otherwise have been inclined to do. Hegel draws the analogy between the daimon, which Socrates consulted in important personal matters, and the Oracle at Delphi, which the Greeks consulted in important issues of different kinds. Hegel explains, however, that the difference is that the oracle is public, that is, it is openly available and objective. By contrast, Socrates' daimonic oracle is inward. It is as if he had within himself his own personal oracle that speaks only to him. This idea offended the religious sensibilities of his fellow Athenians.

For the Greeks, the laws and the customs were sanctioned by the gods. They were not personal or subjective decisions of individuals; rather, the individual played no role here whatsoever. Similarly, when a weighty decision had to be made about a course of action, either in one's private affairs or in a matter of the state or community, it was thought that this was not a matter for any individual to decide, but rather this was something that only the gods could determine. The Greeks did not possess what Hegel calls "subjective freedom," that is, the idea that the individual has the right to decide for him- or herself about important matters. It thus struck the Greeks as highly arrogant and inappropriate when a specific individual claimed to be able to make such decisions for himself, and when he claimed to have his own personal oracle that no one else could see or hear. This is precisely what Socrates seemed to be doing by asserting the authority of his daimon above traditional law and custom.

---

[33] For Hegel's account of the daimon, see ibid., pp. 421–5.
[34] Ibid., p. 422.

According to Hegel, Socrates' daimon represents a position that is midway between the externality of the oracle and the inwardness of the human mind of the individual. It is a transitional form from objective to subjective morality. On the one hand, the daimon is something inward and not something outward like the Oracle at Delphi. It is as if the oracle had been transferred from the objective, external sphere to the inward sphere of the person of Socrates. But, on the other hand, although the daimon is something inward, within him, it is not identical with the will of Socrates itself. The daimon opposes Socrates when he wants to do something that is ill advised. So Socrates' own subjective will leads him in one direction, but the daimon contradicts this and leads him in another. In this sense the daimon, although something inward in Socrates himself, is also something outward and distinct from his will. It is an external authority (like the oracle) that corrects his will and advises him about what to do. In this sense the daimon is not objectively external, like the oracle, nor is it a straightforward affirmation of the subjective will of Socrates; rather, it is somewhere in between.

According to Hegel, the daimon can be seen as a movement from the external to the internal, but the movement is not yet complete. Socrates represents the great revolution of thought that shows the infinite and irreducible value of the subjective. But no revolution begins and ends in a single day. Socrates marked the beginning of it, but the subsequent course of history had to develop it further. Socrates was not yet in a position to present and defend his own private will as the truth, and so he had recourse to the daimon, which pointed to the subjective and the inward side of his personality but stopped short of being identical with his will. Only in the modern world have we reached the point where we celebrate the truth and validity of the will of the individual, but it took the course of more than 2000 years of cultural and historical development after Socrates to reach this point. Socrates began the revolutionary movement, but he did not finish it.

2.9. Hegel's Analysis of Socrates' Trial

In *The Concept of Irony* Kierkegaard examines the account of Socrates' trial in Plato's work *The Apology*. He largely draws on Hegel's analysis of these same events in the *Lectures on the History of Philosophy*,[35] and so it is there that we need to start. In his account of the trial of Socrates, Hegel refers to the historian of philosophy Wilhelm Gottlieb Tennemann, who was also one of Kierkegaard's most important sources for ancient philosophy. For Hegel, Tennemann represented the prevailing view of the day that claimed that Socrates was a morally righteous and upstanding person, and his condemnation was a gross injustice that exemplified how the rabble or factions can exercise power in democracies. For years Socrates had been lionized in this manner by scholars sympathetic to him. Hegel finds this view naïve, since it fails to understand the important revolutionary role of Socrates in Greek society.

The first charge leveled against Socrates is that he did not honor the national gods of Athens, but instead introduced new gods.[36] As has just been discussed, this refers to Socrates' claim to have a daimon. To the Greek mind, Socrates was in a sense claiming to replace the oracle with his own private self-consciousness, and to place his personal opinion and views above that of the gods. The famous saying "Know thyself" meant for Socrates that each individual must look within him- or herself to discover what is true. This implied that one should disregard the traditional public morality that was sanctioned by the gods. Socrates seemed to be denying the validity of this and encouraging the individual to look not outwardly for the truth, but inwardly. According to Hegel's view, these were revolutionary ideas. The notion of a personal daimon in contrast to the oracle or the gods of the state amounted to the introduction of a new god. Hegel concludes that on this score Socrates is indeed guilty as charged.

The second charge is that Socrates corrupted the youth.[37] This charge refers to the claim that Socrates led the son of a certain Anytus to disobey him by telling the son that he was fit for something better than the profession that his father had planned for him. Anytus was a tanner by trade, and this kind of handwork was held in disdain as menial labor among the Greeks. Anytus had planned for his son to follow him in this profession, but the son was reluctant to do so since,

---

[35] For Hegel's account of the trial, see ibid., pp. 425–48.   [36] Ibid., pp. 432–5.
[37] Ibid., pp. 435–8. The story of Anytus and his son appears not in Plato's *Apology* but in Xenophon's parallel account. See Xenophon, *Socrates' Defense*, in *Conversations of Socrates*, trans. by Hugh Tredennick and Robin Waterfield, Harmondsworth: Penguin 1990, pp. 48–9.

with Socrates' encouragement, he felt that being a tanner was beneath him and that he had talents and intellect that made him suited for much more prestigious jobs.

Hegel believes that, based on the testimony, this charge was also well founded. He points out that in Greek society at the time, the bond between parents and their children was something sacred. Obedience to one's parents was among the highest of values. Socrates had undermined this by encouraging Anytus' son in the idea that he, in his role as an individual with specific gifts and talents, was more important than in his role as a son with clearly defined obligations and duties. While in our modern world Socrates' actions do not seem so offensive, since we too value the importance of the individual, in ancient Athens this was a serious breach of ethics and custom. This was a part of the revolution that Socrates stood for: it placed the individual above established custom and tradition.

Hegel also analyzes the final episode of the trial of Socrates. According to Athenian law, after the defendant was found guilty and given a preliminary sentence, he was able to propose an alternative punishment.[38] This procedure allowed the jury to be merciful if they saw a degree of contrition on the part of the defendant. By proposing an alternative penalty, the convicted person acknowledged his guilt and recognized the legitimacy and authority of the court. But Socrates in effect made sport of the situation by apparently ironically proposing that he be given free meals and be supported financially by the state for the public service that he was providing. According to Hegel, by doing this, Socrates refused to acknowledge the validity of the court's decision and thus his own guilt. Here again Hegel finds Socrates' position problematic. No state can allow individuals to put themselves above the law or to judge themselves solely based on their own private views in opposition or contradiction to the established customs, traditions, and laws of society. Given this, it is hardly surprising that the Athenians lost their patience with Socrates and stuck with the original sentence of the death penalty.

When Hegel claims that Socrates was indeed guilty of the charges, his point is not that he has no sympathy or understanding for Socrates in this situation. Rather, what he is saying is that when seen from the historical perspective, given the traditions and values

---

[38] Hegel, *Lectures on the History of Philosophy*, vol. 1, pp. 440–5.

of Greek society at the time, the charges against Socrates were well founded. Hegel explains the conflict as follows:

> The Spirit [of the Athenians] in itself, its constitution, its whole life, rested . . . on a moral ground, on religion, and could not exist without this absolutely secure basis. Thus because Socrates makes the truth rest on the judgment of inward consciousness, he enters upon a struggle with the Athenian people as to what is right and true.[39]

What Socrates was doing was undermining the traditions, public morality, and values of the state. Socrates set off a revolution that led to the recognition of the individual as something absolute and irreducible. In this sense he is the forerunner of some of the values of our modern world. So it is natural that from our perspective today we find him a sympathetic figure. Hegel reminds us, however, that this should not make us lose sight of the radicality of Socrates' message in his own time.

2.10. The Conflict of Tradition and Individual Freedom

Some people might ask why this set of issues that Hegel addresses in connection with his interpretation of Socrates is so important. How are these questions relevant for us today? Hegel and Kierkegaard both recognized in the story of Socrates' conflict with Greek society an important forerunner of the problems of modernity. In other words, Socrates' story is not just about the fate of one man in Athens in the fifth century BC, but rather it is also the story of modern existence.

We have all grown up in a world that is rapidly changing, and these changes have often led to conflicts in traditional customs and practices. One does not have to think too hard to identify controversial issues today about the role of the individual and the demands of the culture. Throughout the world, there are conflicts between cultural traditions and individual autonomy. Some people find it objectionable that young men are obliged to follow in the profession of their fathers, that women are obliged to cover their hair in public, that parents pre-arrange the marriages of their children, or that certain classes of people are forbidden from doing certain kinds of work.

---

[39] Ibid., p. 426.

Today it strikes us as objectionable when people are coerced to follow the crowd when it means acting against their own conscience. It is said that practices of this sort encroach on the freedom of the individual. These tensions go right to the heart of what Hegel understands by the concept of subjective freedom. He believes that there is something unique and irreducible about each and every individual that should be respected. Individuals should be granted the right to use their rationality to consent to the practices and values that they inherit from their culture.

The birth of subjective freedom was a major turning point in world history, but the revolution of freedom continues as we try to negotiate the difficult relation between the rights of the individual and demands of the society and tradition. Here we can see that the issues to which Hegel is attentive in Socrates are in fact of central importance to our world today. Socrates represented the rights of the individual against the voice of established custom. He asked people to question their accepted beliefs and to look within themselves for the truth. The conflict between Socrates and the Athenian state was the forerunner of countless later conflicts that continue to this very day.

Kierkegaard took this idea of subjective freedom from Hegel and developed it in his own way into a theory of the individual in the context of both society and religion. As was the case with Hegel, Kierkegaard's interest in Socrates was not purely or primarily historical. Socrates was a symbol of the constellation of modern issues that concern freedom, alienation, and relativism—the problems of our world of the twenty-first century.

3

Kierkegaard's View of Socrates

In the last chapter we looked at Hegel's analysis of the importance of Socrates for Greek culture and for world history. Kierkegaard studied Hegel's account carefully and, in *The Concept of Irony*, responds to it almost point for point. Our goal in this chapter is to come to terms with Kierkegaard's understanding of Socrates, and to see where he agrees with Hegel and where he disagrees. We will look at Kierkegaard's analysis of Socrates' daimon, his trial and conviction, and his relation to the Sophists and the later schools of philosophy. We will also see that Kierkegaard was quite exercised by the Danish theologian and philosopher Hans Lassen Martensen and his lectures at the University of Copenhagen. We will explore Kierkegaard's response to Martensen's article on Faust, and Kierkegaard's two satirical works that were aimed at Martensen and his students, namely, *The Conflict between the Old and the New Soap Cellars* and *Johannes Climacus, or De omnibus dubitandum est*. Finally, we also want to introduce a lesser-known Danish figure, Andreas Frederik Beck, who wrote an insightful book review of *The Concept of Irony*, which gives us a brief snapshot of the contemporary assessment of the work.

3.1. Kierkegaard's View of Socrates' Daimon

Kierkegaard begins his account of the daimon by poking fun at the attempts of the secondary literature to understand this phenomenon.[1]

---

[1] For Kierkegaard's account of the daimon, see *The Concept of Irony*, trans. by Howard V. Hong and Edna H. Hong, Princeton: Princeton University Press 1989, pp. 157–67.

He then quickly moves on to an analysis of the ancient sources, where he finds an important discrepancy. According to Plato, the daimon was purely negative: it warned Socrates not to do certain things, but it never proposed or demanded positive actions. According to Xenophon's account, however, the daimon was also positive, prompting and enjoining Socrates to do specific things. Kierkegaard was thus obliged to make some kind of judgment about which of the ancient sources to follow on this point, and he wholeheartedly affirms the view of Plato: "What I . . . would like to point out to the reader is significant for the whole conception of Socrates: namely, that this daimon is represented only as warning, not as commanding—that is, as negative and not as positive."[2] He thus believes that Socrates is fundamentally a negative figure and that it is a mistake when one wants to ascribe something positive to him.

This is important to Kierkegaard since he wants to see Socrates' irony as the Greek philosopher's defining characteristic. In its essence irony is negative or destructive: it negates and can thus be used to criticize various elements of the established order. Kierkegaard believes that Xenophon did not properly grasp this important negative mission of Socrates, and for this reason he mistakenly attributed something positive to Socrates' daimon. By contrast, Plato was the more perceptive student who recognized the importance of the negative element in Socrates.

Kierkegaard agrees with Hegel's understanding of the daimon as a part of Socrates' subjectivity that is opposed to the traditional values and customary ethics of Athens. He raises the question: "Was Socrates, as his accusers claimed, in conflict with the state religion by the assumption of this daimon?"[3] He responds, in agreement with Hegel, "Obviously he was. For one thing, it was an entirely polemical relation to the Greek state religion to substitute something completely abstract for the concrete individuality of the gods."[4] He also agrees with Hegel in seeing the daimon as a private alternative to the public oracle that the Greeks revered.[5] While he is

---

[2] Ibid., p. 159. Here and later, I have replaced "daimonion" in the translation of Kierkegaard's text with the more customary version "daimon."

[3] Ibid., p. 160.   [4] Ibid.

[5] Ibid., pp. 160f.: "For another, it was a polemical relation to the state religion to substitute a silence in which a warning voice was audible only on occasion, a voice that . . . never had a thing to do with the substantial interests of political life, never said a word about them, but dealt only with Socrates' and at most his friends' completely

generally quite critical of the contemporary secondary literature on the topic,[6] Kierkegaard quotes extensively from Hegel's account as a support for his own view.[7]

The conclusion of Kierkegaard's analysis makes it clear that his main goal is to demonstrate that the daimon is consistent with Socrates' irony. This is the reason why he is so keen to focus on the negative aspect of the daimon that Hegel does not seem particularly interested in. The daimon represented an aspect of Socrates' subjectivity, and as such it allowed him to distance himself from traditional Greek culture. The daimon was thus part of the Socratic revolution of subjectivity.

3.2. Martensen's Faust

When Kierkegaard was growing up, the work of the famous German writer Johann Wolfgang von Goethe was very popular in Denmark.[8] In particular, Goethe's tragic drama *Faust* was often quoted and much discussed. This is the story of a scholar who sells his soul to the devil in exchange for unlimited knowledge. When Kierkegaard was a student at the University of Copenhagen he became very interested in this legend and in the figure of Faust. In 1836 in his *Journal BB*, he made a bibliography of different interpretations of Goethe's work and of the Faust legend generally.[9] He was

---

private and particular affairs—to substitute this for the Greek life permeated, even in the most insignificant manifestations, by a god-consciousness, to substitute a silence of this divine eloquence echoed in everything." See also Kierkegaard's account of Hegel's interpretation, ibid., pp. 163f.: "Instead of the oracle, Socrates now has his daimon. The daimon in this case now lies in the transition from the oracle's external relation to the individual to the complete inwardness of freedom and, as still being in this transition, is a subject for representation."

[6] In this context he refers to "pharisaical scholars, who strain at a gnat and swallow a camel." Ibid., p. 161.

[7] Ibid., p. 161, p. 162, p. 163, p. 164, p. 165.

[8] For Kierkegaard's use of Goethe and the Goethe fever in Golden Age Denmark, see Katalin Nun and Jon Stewart, "Goethe: A German Classic through the Filter of the Danish Golden Age," in *Kierkegaard and his German Contemporaries*, Tome III, *Literature and Aesthetics*, ed. by Jon Stewart, Aldershot: Ashgate 2007 (*Kierkegaard Research: Sources, Reception, and Resources*, vol. 6), pp. 51–96.

[9] *Kierkegaard's Journals and Notebooks*, ed. by Niels Jørgen Cappelørn et al., vols 1–11, Princeton: Princeton University Press 2007ff., vol. 2, pp. 85–99, BB:12–15.

clearly planning to write something about Faust, and maybe he was even considering it as a possible topic for his master's thesis.

In any case, he became very upset when in June of 1837 Hans Lassen Martensen published an article in the first issue of the academic journal *Perseus* entitled "Observations on the Idea of Faust with Reference to Lenau's *Faust*."[10] When he heard of this, Kierkegaard wrote in his journals: "Oh, how unhappy I am—Martensen has written an essay of Lenau's *Faust!*"[11] Why was Kierkegaard so disturbed by this? Why was he so interested in the figure of Faust in the first place?

The answer to these questions becomes clear when we take a brief look at Martensen's article. Instead of treating Goethe's well-known version of Faust, Martensen chose instead to examine a version written by the Austro-Hungarian poet Niembsch von Strehlenau, who wrote under the pseudonym Nicolaus Lenau. On his journey Martensen had met Lenau personally in Vienna and became interested in his work. Martensen saw in the figure of Faust, as portrayed by Lenau, a representative of the modern world.

As noted in the previous chapter, in his dissertation *On the Autonomy of Human Self-Consciousness in Modern Dogmatic Theology*, Martensen examined the concept of autonomy. He concluded that the idea of humans acting on their own and determining the truth by themselves was a widespread and dangerous modern notion that led away from Christian belief. He sees Faust as exemplifying this principle of autonomy and as a symbol for modern secular knowledge. Faust embodies "the deep feeling of the corruption of the human will, its desire to transgress the divine law, its arrogant striving to seek its center in itself instead of in God."[12] According to the Christian view, humans are by nature sinful and ignorant; they can know nothing without the help of God. It is thus only human pride and arrogance that believe humans can discover the truth on their own. Faust thinks he has no use for Christianity since he can discover the truth by means of secular scientific knowing. Martensen writes, Faust "represents

---

[10] Hans Lassen Martensen, "Betragtninger over Ideen af Faust med Hensyn paa Lenaus *Faust*," *Perseus, Journal for den speculative Idee*, no. 1, 1837, pp. 91–164.

[11] *Søren Kierkegaard's Journals and Papers*, vols 1–6, ed. and trans. by Howard V. Hong and Edna H. Hong, Bloomington and London: Indiana University Press 1967–78, vol. 5, p. 100, no. 5225.

[12] Martensen, "Betragtninger over Ideen af Faust med Hensyn paa Lenaus *Faust*," p. 94.

the human race's striving to ground a realm of *intelligence* without God."[13]

Faust also represents the modern principle of doubt. What cannot be demonstrated by science must be subject to skepticism, and this includes the doctrines of religion. This view rejects traditional beliefs and exposes everything to its merciless doubt. It also leads Faust to despair, and he becomes separated and alienated from society and accepted ethics. Martensen thus portrays Faust as the model for the ills of the modern world.

Kierkegaard's irritated reaction to Martensen's article can be explained by the fact that he too was interested in presenting Faust as a paradigmatic example of modern existence, and Martensen had done so first, thus anticipating Kierkegaard's critical assessment of the modern age. Kierkegaard was interested in Faust for the same reason that he was interested in Socrates: they were both negative figures who called into question traditional beliefs and values. Both Socrates and Faust believed that the critical reasoning of each individual must decide the truth of the matter. Socrates reduces people to *aporia* and ends with a negative conclusion, just as Faust's skepticism leads him to despair.

Kierkegaard is attentive to the fact that both Socrates and Faust represent something at the heart of the modern spirit. He makes this connection explicitly in his *Journal AA* from the year 1837, when Martensen published his article. He writes, "Faust may be seen as parallel to Socrates, for just as the latter expresses the severing of the individual from the state, so Faust, after the abrogation of the Church, depicts the individual severed from its guidance and left to itself."[14] Both Faust and Socrates represent an emphasis on the individual at the cost of a larger institution or aspect of the objective world.

3.3. Kierkegaard's Analysis of Socrates' Trial

Kierkegaard also addresses the condemnation of Socrates.[15] Like Hegel, he is critical of what he calls "the scholarly professional

---

[13] Ibid., p. 97.   [14] *Kierkegaard's Journals and Notebooks*, vol. 1, p. 44, AA:41.
[15] Kierkegaard, *The Concept of Irony*, pp. 167–97.

mourners and the crowd of shallow but lachrymose humanitarians,"[16] who regard Socrates as an honest and righteous man who was unfairly persecuted by the rabble. Also like Hegel, he sees the daimon as something that clearly puts Socrates at odds with traditional religion.

With regard to the question of whether Socrates was an atheist who rejected the gods of the state, Kierkegaard claims that this was based on a misunderstanding. This was a typical charge leveled against ancient Greek philosophers like Anaxagoras, who were interested in exploring the phenomena of nature. The Greek gods were conceived as closely related to the natural forces, for example, Zeus with lightning, and Poseidon with the sea and earthquakes. When the early Greek philosophers took it upon themselves to study nature, they distinguished themselves from the religious tradition that saw the gods as causal agents in nature. Since these philosophers did not make any appeal to the gods in their explanations of the natural world, they were often accused of not believing in the gods at all. Kierkegaard concludes that the charge of atheism against Socrates arose from a mistaken belief that he was also working in this tradition of natural philosophy when in fact he was solely concerned with human knowledge and ethics.

The misunderstanding of his agenda was exacerbated by his well-known claim to ignorance. When Socrates claimed to know nothing, this was mistakenly taken to mean that he knew nothing about the gods worshipped by the state. But this was of course not the point of Socrates' self-proclaimed ignorance. He clearly knew a great deal about the particulars in the world around him, but he claimed not to know the universals and was constantly trying to get people to formulate clear definitions of them: What is piety? What is justice? What is beauty?[17]

Kierkegaard claims that an important element in the condemnation of Socrates was what was regarded as his attempt to alienate individuals from the state. He associates this with the famous maxim, "know yourself." According to Kierkegaard, Socrates' understanding of this command was that each individual should seek the truth in him- or herself. But this meant turning away from the world of objective truth, which included traditional ethics and religion. Kierkegaard explains, "The phrase 'know yourself' means: separate

---

[16] Ibid., p. 167.   [17] Ibid., p. 169.

yourself from the other."[18] The individual is thus alienated from mainstream society, since after the Socratic interrogation it is impossible to continue to maintain traditional values and customs as before. By calling everything into question, Socrates destroys the individual's belief in the things that hold society together. This is, according to Kierkegaard, rightly regarded as a dangerous matter: "it is obvious that Socrates was in conflict with the view of the state—indeed, that from the viewpoint of the state his offensive had to be considered most dangerous, as an attempt to suck its blood and reduce it to a shadow."[19]

Kierkegaard thus agrees with Hegel that the Athenian state was justified in condemning Socrates, since his revolutionary actions were undermining its foundations.[20] But it should be noted, he was not revolutionary in the sense that he was forming a specific political party with a positive platform. Rather, his mission was purely negative: he separated individuals from the state and isolated them from one another by undermining their accepted beliefs in tradition.

Kierkegaard also gives an assessment of the last part of Socrates' trial, where the Greek philosopher proposes his alternative punishment. Kierkegaard draws attention to the fact that in the *Apology* Socrates dwells on the specific number of people who voted for his acquittal and his condemnation. By doing this, Socrates represents the jury as a group of individuals and not as a collective whole or as an impersonal instrument of the Athenian state.[21] Each of them individually made a decision and cast his vote. Socrates thus recognizes the importance of the subjectivity or individuality of each person, but he refuses to recognize the authority of the abstract state or any other collective unit.

Here Kierkegaard is in agreement with Hegel's account, which sees Socrates' condemnation as being the result of his refusal to accept the legitimacy of the court.[22] Kierkegaard explains, "The objective power of the state, its claims upon the activity of the individual, the laws, the courts—everything loses its absolute validity for him."[23] Kierkegaard sees Socrates as occupying a position of complete negativity toward the state.[24] Socrates accepts the truth and validity of each single individual but refuses to accept it in any collective group: the state, the jury, a political party, etc. Athenian society was built upon principles of

[18] Ibid., p. 177.   [19] Ibid., p. 178.   [20] Ibid., pp. 181f.
[21] Ibid., p. 194.   [22] Ibid., p. 193.   [23] Ibid., p. 196.   [24] Ibid.

community and democracy, and thus to call this into question was very alarming for most people. So according to this interpretation, the great menace to Greek society came not from some outside source, but rather from Socrates and his merciless use of irony.

3.4. Doubt and *The Conflict between the Old and the New Soap Cellars*

We have seen that Kierkegaard was irritated by Martensen's success with the students at the University of Copenhagen and that Martensen, like Kierkegaard, was interested in the figure of Faust. One important aspect of Martensen's thought was his characterization of modern philosophy as beginning with the principle of doubt. While medieval philosophy was uncritical and based its views on faith, modern philosophy that began with Descartes realized that it was necessary to begin from the ground up by doubting everything. Descartes saw that many things generally accepted as true in fact prove to be mistaken upon closer scrutiny. This means that much of what we take for granted is thus based upon shaky foundations. In his *Meditations on First Philosophy*, Descartes begins by making an attempt to doubt absolutely everything that he has ever known or been taught so that he can attempt to determine from the start what can firmly be established as true.

Martensen seizes on this image of Descartes applying a systematic method of doubt as a model for modern philosophical thought. He takes a Latin phrase from Descartes' text to capture this: "*De omnibus dubitandum est*" or "One must doubt everything." Martensen used this phrase repeatedly, and it became a kind of shorthand slogan among his students. It seemed initially to be used just as a characterization of the period of modern philosophy in contrast to earlier periods, which were less critical. But through force of repetition it came to take on a prescriptive meaning, which in effect amounted to a call to arms for modern thinkers to apply Descartes' skeptical method. Clearly, Martensen's injunction to doubt everything is closely related to the Socratic method of questioning everything. Descartes does not wish to stop until everything has been called into question, just as Socrates does not wish to stop until he has gained a satisfactory answer to his questions.

Kierkegaard wrote two satirical works about Martensen and his students that he never published. Both take Descartes' universal doubt as a central motif. The first of these works is a comedy entitled *The Conflict between the Old and the New Soap Cellars*, which Kierkegaard wrote in his *Journal DD* probably in the first months of 1838 when he was still a student (see Fig. 3.1). The inspiration for

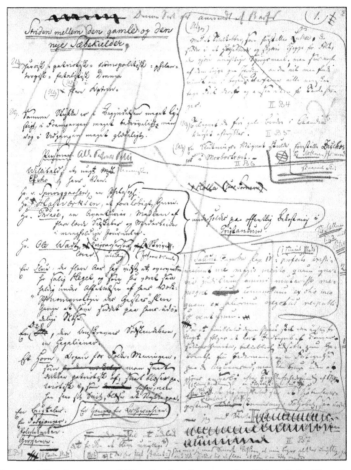

Fig. 3.1. The first page of *The Conflict between the Old and the New Soap Cellars* in the *Journal DD* (c. 1837–8)

this piece came from a square in Copenhagen called Gråbrødre Torv, where during Kierkegaard's time there were rival shops that sold soap. There a new soap vendor moved into the basement of a building next to where an established soap vendor was still operating. To avoid losing business due to the confusion caused by there being two shops, the old soap cellar put up a sign to indicate that his shop was the old, traditional soap cellar.[25] This was the beginning of an amusing rivalry that caught Kierkegaard's attention.

It will be recalled that at his trial Socrates proposed as his penalty that he be maintained at public expense and be provided with free meals at the Prytaneum. This was a public building in Athens, a kind of town hall, where people who had done great deeds for the state, for example, victorious Olympian athletes, would receive free meals at public expense. In his satire Kierkegaard makes use of this idea, but instead of placing Socrates in the Prytaneum, he places Martensen and his students there. Kierkegaard creates a handful of amusing characters, who engage in absurd philosophical conversations. They are constantly using slogans such as "*De omnibus dubitandum est*" that everyone knew from Martensen's lectures and written works. By placing these comic philosophers in the Prytaneum, Kierkegaard seems sarcastically to imply that they, like Socrates, are providing some important public service with their philosophizing and with their attempt to doubt everything. But instead of doing anything meaningful, they simply engage in confused and absurd philosophical conversation, all the while taking themselves very seriously. Kierkegaard thus lampoons Martensen and his students for their sense of self-importance.

It is worth noting that during the period when the piece was written, Martensen lived on the same square in a house just opposite the soap cellars. In September of 1837, that is, when Kierkegaard was a student and when he conceived of the idea of writing the comedy about the soap cellars, he moved into an apartment that stood at the corner of Løvstræde and Niels Hemmingsens Gade (at Løvstræde 7). The apartment was right next to the square with an unimpeded view of Martensen's house.

---

[25] *Kierkegaard's Journals and Notebooks*, vol. 1, pp. 550f., Explanatory Notes.

3.5. Kierkegaard's *Johannes Climacus,*
or De omnibus dubitandum est

The other satirical work that Kierkegaard wrote but never published makes use of Martensen's slogan in its very title, *Johannes Climacus, or De omnibus dubitandum est* (see Fig. 3.2). Johannes Climacus is a name that Kierkegaard later used as a pseudonym when he published *Philosophical Fragments* and the *Concluding Unscientific Postscript.* But the satirical text *De omnibus* was apparently written at some point in 1843 before these two well-known pseudonymous books.

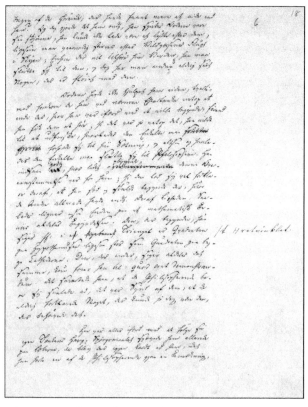

Fig. 3.2. Manuscript from *Johannes Climacus, or De omnibus dubitandum est* (*c.* 1842–3)

De omnibus tells the story of a young student named Johannes Climacus, who attends lectures at the University of Copenhagen and becomes interested in the philosophical discussions about the need to begin by doubting everything. Clearly Kierkegaard intends Climacus to represent one of Martensen's students who is caught up in the flurry of interest surrounding Martensen's lectures. Much of the text is filled with somewhat tedious philosophical deliberations in which Johannes tries to determine exactly what is meant by the demand that one doubt everything in philosophy. There are three different variants of this that he explores in turn: "(1) Philosophy begins with doubt; (2) in order to philosophize, one must have doubted; (3) modern philosophy begins with doubt."[26] Each leads to absurdities.

Although Kierkegaard never finished this work and it breaks off in the middle, the plot was apparently intended to end by showing how Johannes was reduced to despair in his attempt to follow the imperative of doubting everything. In a note Kierkegaard explains the plan for the work that he never realized:

> Johannes does what we are told to do—he actually doubts everything—he suffers through all the pain of doing that. . . . When he has gone as far in that direction as he can go and wants to come back, he cannot do so. . . . Now he despairs, his life is wasted, his youth is spent in these deliberations. Life has not acquired any meaning for him, and all this is the fault of philosophy.[27]

Martensen has irresponsibly enjoined the students to doubt everything, but this would also involve doubting things such as one's religion, one's relations to family, community, etc. To question these things is to isolate oneself. While doubting everything was intended as a kind of academic exercise, the young students take it seriously as a way of life and thereby undermine their own beliefs. But once one has reached this point, it is impossible to go back. Once one has begun the process of critical reflection, one can no longer live in uncritical intimacy with one's former beliefs. This is the view that is suspicious of new knowledge, fearful of what it might bring. As was the case with Socrates, it separates the individual from family and

---

[26] Kierkegaard, *Johannes Climacus, or De omnibus dubitandum est*, trans. by Howard V. Hong and Edna H. Hong, Princeton: Princeton University Press 1985, p. 132.

[27] Ibid., Supplement, pp. 234–5.

community. The conclusion of Kierkegaard's story is that Johannes ends in despair, destroyed by philosophical doubt.

3.6. The Sophists and the Legacy of Socrates

Kierkegaard agrees with Hegel's characterization of Socrates as "a turning point" in history.[28] He proposes his own evaluation of this by analyzing first the relation of Socrates to the movement of the Sophists which preceded him and then his relation to the different schools of philosophy that came after him. By seeing Socrates between these two poles, we can come to a better understanding of his role as a turning point in the development of Greek thought and culture.

The cause of the downfall of Greek life was what Kierkegaard, following Hegel, characterizes as "the arbitrariness of finite subjectivity."[29] This is associated with the Sophists, who are known for their relativism and their denial of any absolute or enduring truth. He explains, "The *Sophists* represent knowledge separating itself in its motley multiplicity from substantial morality by means of the awakening reflection. On the whole, they represented the separated culture for which a need was felt by everyone for whom the fascination of immediacy had faded away."[30] Like Socrates, the Sophists also questioned and criticized the traditional Greek culture, which Kierkegaard refers to as "substantial morality."

The Sophists claimed to teach a practical knowledge that would be beneficial to young men in politics and business. Specifically, they taught the art of speaking and argumentation, by means of which they could make an effective case for whatever they perceived to be to their advantage at the moment. But this argumentation was always in the interest of the one doing the arguing and not in the interest of any higher truth. The Sophists were positive in that they made claims about the world, but negative in that they also questioned or ignored traditional beliefs and higher truths whenever it suited their interests.

---

[28] Kierkegaard, *The Concept of Irony*, p. 200.   [29] Ibid., p. 201.
[30] Ibid., pp. 201f.

In the absence of absolute truth, there is only arbitrary or contingent truth, dictated by the self-interest of the individual. The Sophists elevated these arbitrary and contingent truths into ends in themselves. Without any absolute truths, they and their followers were free to revel in the contingent ones for as long as it served their purposes. Kierkegaard explains this as follows, "In its first form, this education [offered by the Sophists] shakes the foundations of everything, but in its second form it enables every pupil...to make everything firm and fast again. The Sophist, therefore, demonstrates that everything is true."[31] The Sophists can thus give reasons and arguments for anything at all. It is in this sense that we still use the word "sophist" today in a pejorative sense to refer to someone who uses eloquence or specious reasoning to defend questionable opinions or behavior.

Kierkegaard perceived Martensen to be acting sophistically. One of the things that bothered him was that Martensen pretended to assume a posture of radical, disabused skepticism with his well-known claim "*De omnibus dubitandum est*," but this was only an empty slogan. Martensen's point was, like that of Descartes, to emerge from the skepticism and begin to establish something positive: a doctrine, an argument, or a foundational truth claim. This was exactly the way that Kierkegaard describes the Sophists, as we just saw: they shake "the foundations of everything" but then "make everything firm again." For Kierkegaard, the profundity and genius of Socrates are to be found in the fact that he remained in skepticism and negativity, and refused to be drawn into the construction of a positive truth claim. Kierkegaard thus contrasts Socrates with the Sophists by claiming that Socrates was purely negative, whereas the Sophists made positive claims. For example, Protagoras claimed to know what virtue is and to be able to teach it. Socrates claimed not to know what it is and claimed that it could not be taught.[32]

Kierkegaard then argues that Socrates' "irony has a world-historical validity."[33] It is valid for Socrates to use irony in the given historical situation. His irony was aimed at two targets: first, unreflective proponents of traditional Athenian life, and second, self-assured Sophists who were making unfounded positive claims.[34] He saw the former as mired in traditions that were no longer relevant or

---

[31] Ibid., p. 205.   [32] Ibid., p. 208.
[33] Ibid., p. 211.   [34] Ibid., p. 214.

useful and the latter as promoting a shallow self-serving relativism. He thus used irony as a tool to correct what he perceived as misguided behavior by his contemporaries. These were two important aspects of Greek life at the time, and Socrates, with his irony, plays a key historical role in this context. He is not employing irony just to be flippant or to irritate or impress someone; rather, his use of irony was dictated by the times.

Kierkegaard then addresses the other side of the idea of Socrates as a turning point, namely, his legacy. Socrates gave rise to a number of competing schools of philosophy in antiquity. Kierkegaard raises the question of how so many very different views could all claim to have their origin in his thought. If Socrates had had a number of different doctrines, then one might be tempted to think that his legacy is due to the fact that these different doctrines were attractive to different philosophical schools. However, Kierkegaard argues, on the contrary, that Socrates' heterogeneous legacy provides further evidence for the claim that he represents pure negativity. If he had had a positive doctrine with a handful of constructive theses, then these would have been attractive to some people but repellent to others. But the positive nature of his views would invariably have had a limiting effect on the number of his followers. Kierkegaard argues that precisely because socrates had no positive doctrine, people were free to see in his thought anything they wished.[35] He could thus be readily co-opted into whatever views a given philosophical school wished to promote. So while Socrates gave rise to a number of philosophical schools with different positive doctrines, he himself represents what Kierkegaard, following Hegel, calls "infinite negativity."[36]

3.7. Socrates and Christ

In Kierkegaard's time it was common practice to compare Socrates and his fate with Christ. Both were ethically righteous individuals, and both were prosecuted in legal proceedings and executed. There was a body of literature on this comparison, which Kierkegaard was familiar with. One of the most important of these works was the book

---

[35] Ibid., p. 215.   [36] Ibid., p. 216, p. 218.

of the German theologian Ferdinand Christian Baur, entitled *On Christianity in Platonism: Socrates and Christ* from 1837,[37] which Kierkegaard refers to several times in *The Concept of Irony*.[38]

The New Testament portrays Christ as struggling with the scribes and teachers of the law known as the Pharisees who insisted on strict observance of religious ceremonies and practices. In comparative studies like Baur's a parallel was often drawn with Christ's conflict with the Pharisees and Socrates' conflict with the Sophists. Kierkegaard makes this connection himself when he says, "the Sophists are reminiscent of the Pharisees."[39]

This gives us useful insight into the importance of Socrates for Kierkegaard generally. Initially, it was not clear why he would be so interested in Socrates, a pagan philosopher, if his primary goal had something to do with understanding Christianity. Here the connection is clear: Socrates is like Christ, and the Sophists are like the Pharisees. So although Socrates is a pagan philosopher, he displays some important points of commonality with the message of Christ that Kierkegaard believes have been forgotten. Thus, by making use of Socrates' ideas or methods, Kierkegaard believes that he can bring some insight into what he takes to be the confused understanding of Christianity in his own day.

3.8. Andreas Frederik Beck and the First Review
of *The Concept of Irony*

Andreas Frederik Beck was a student at the University of Copenhagen at the same time as Kierkegaard. He was influenced by the German theologian David Friedrich Strauss, who had been a student of Hegel in Berlin. Strauss was known for his monumental study entitled *The Life of Jesus Critically Examined*.[40] This work raised a controversy in

---

[37] Ferdinand Christian Baur, *Das Christliche des Platonismus oder Sokrates und Christus. Eine religionsphilosophische Untersuchung*, Tübingen: Ludw. Friedr. Fues 1837.

[38] Kierkegaard, *The Concept of Irony*, pp. 13–15, p. 31, p. 52, p. 99, p. 220.

[39] Ibid., p. 213.

[40] David Friedrich Strauss, *Das Leben Jesu*, vols 1–2, Tübingen: C. F. Osiander 1835–6. (In English as *The Life of Jesus Critically Examined*, trans. by George Eliot, ed. by Peter C. Hodgson, Ramsey, New Jersey: Sigler Press 1994.)

the German-speaking world by examining the gospel texts in great
detail and concluding that the stories related about Jesus were by and
large myths. The book cost Strauss his position at the University of
Tübingen. In 1839, after it was thought that the controversy had died
down, Strauss was appointed to a post at the University of Zurich in
Switzerland, but when the appointment was made public, it evoked
such large protests that the university could not go through with it
and had to revoke the position.

Beck was interested in bringing Strauss' approach to Denmark. At
the time of Kierkegaard's master's thesis in 1841 he was working on a
book entitled *The Concept of Myth or the Form of Religious Spirit*,
which would be published the following year.[41] He knew Kierkegaard
personally and was keenly interested in *The Concept of Irony*. During
the public defense of a thesis it was possible for people from the
audience to stand up and ask questions about the work, and Beck was
one of these questioners for Kierkegaard's dissertation. The following
year Beck wrote a review of *The Concept of Irony*, which appeared in
the periodical *The Fatherland*.[42]

Today we recognize *The Concept of Irony* as an important work for
understanding our modern world, but at the time it was met with
skepticism. All five of the members of Kierkegaard's thesis committee
complained that it suffered from some serious flaws, especially with
regard to style. The tone of their official statements about it makes it
sound as if they only reluctantly passed the work as a master's thesis
and would very much have liked to have seen some major revisions.
When Beck reviewed the work, however, he saw something more in
it. What was that and what allowed Beck to see it, while the others
were blind to it?

Beck saw that Strauss was trying to understand the life of Jesus by
comparing the different gospel accounts. Where these accounts
differed from one another questions could be raised about their
historical veracity. Beck saw Kierkegaard using the same kind of
methodology in his attempt to reconstruct historically the figure of
Socrates. Instead of Matthew, Mark, Luke, and John, his gospels, so to

---

[41] Frederik Andreas Beck, *Begrebet Mythus eller den religiøse Aands Form*,
Copenhagen: P. G. Philipsen 1842.

[42] Frederik Andreas Beck, "[Review of] *Om Begrebet Ironi, med stadigt Hensyn til
Socrates* af Søren Kierkegaard," *Fædrelandet*, nos. 890 and 897, May 29, and June 5,
1842, cols. 7133–40, 7189–91.

speak, were Plato, Xenophon, and Aristophanes, who each gave a different picture of Socrates. Like Strauss, Kierkegaard had to sift through his sources in order to get to the *real* Socrates.

As a follower of Strauss, Beck could see the importance of Kierkegaard's treatment of history. He appreciated Kierkegaard's methodology of treating the concept not abstractly but in its concrete historical development. Like Kierkegaard, he knew that concepts develop and change over the course of time. Because of this he realized that our modern understanding of things was the result of a long and still ongoing period of development. While the ancient world uncritically accepted the stories of the gospels as true, the modern mind feels compelled to analyze them in a scholarly manner to determine whether or not they are true. In other words, the modern mind wants to determine the truth for itself. This is ultimately very much in line with Kierkegaard's emphasis on inwardness and subjectivity.

Kierkegaard responded to Beck's review in the postscript to his article "Public Confession."[43] Although Beck's account is generally quite positive, Kierkegaard is highly sensitive to the few slightly critical points, and he reacts with satire and irony to them. He objects to the fact that Beck's book on mythology, which had been published in the interim, associates *The Concept of Irony* with Strauss and the left Hegelians. This was a group of thinkers who understood Hegel to be critical of traditional religious belief and used his philosophical methodology to try to undermine Christianity. In addition to Strauss, influential writers such as Ludwig Feuerbach and Bruno Bauer also belonged to this group. Kierkegaard always tried to avoid group affiliations and presumably disagreed with the left Hegelians' rather secular understanding of Christianity. He wanted *The Concept of Irony* to be recognized as an original work that was independent of and outside any particular school of thought. In addition, Kierkegaard reacted negatively to Beck's complaint that certain allusions in the work were difficult to understand. He sarcastically responds that if Beck failed to understand something, then this is a shortcoming on Beck's part and should not be counted as a criticism of the book. Despite the fact

---

[43] Kierkegaard, "Public Confession," in *The Corsair Affair and Articles Related to the Writings*, trans. by Howard V. Hong and Edna H. Hong, Princeton: Princeton University Press 1982, pp. 3–12, see pp. 9–12.

that Beck's review was both perceptive and positive, Kierkegaard was unable to appreciate the elements of praise that it had for his work.

3.9. Knowledge as a Double-Edged Sword

How is Kierkegaard's understanding of Socrates relevant for life today? We have been talking about knowledge, doubt, and traditional values, and in the end these issues come down to a fundamental question about the nature and status of knowledge and its role in human life. This is one of the oldest questions in all of human history. Indeed, we can see it in one of the most ancient stories that is known to us: the story of the Fall in Genesis in the Old Testament. We are told of the first human beings, Adam and Eve, who live in a wonderful garden, which provides them with everything they require to satisfy their needs. They are in harmony with nature and the world around them. But they do not have one thing: knowledge. They live in a kind of ignorant bliss. God tells them that they can enjoy everything they like in the garden, but they may not eat from the tree of knowledge.[44] As we know, according to the story, Adam and Eve, seduced by the snake, defy this prohibition, eat from the tree, and thus gain knowledge. Suddenly, everything changes, and they see the world with different eyes. For the first time they realize that they are naked and feel shame. They are no longer in harmony with the world. Instead of being at home in the garden, they are alienated from it. After discovering their transgression, God exiles them from the garden and casts them out into the wider world, "east of Eden."[45] What this story tells us is that knowledge is a dangerous thing. God knew this all along, and for this reason he told Adam and Eve not to eat from the tree. God was aware that knowledge ends in shame, fear, and alienation. Once human beings have taken this step, they can never go back. The moral to this story is that human beings are not meant to have knowledge. They are happier without it.

The Genesis story is constantly re-enacted in the process of the growth and maturation of each individual. When we are children we live in immediate harmony with our family, culture, and society. But

---

[44] Genesis 2:16–17.   [45] Genesis 3:24.

then as we grow up, we reach a point where we naturally begin to question certain things that we took for granted when we were young. We come to realize that our parents and leaders are fallible and our culture has its problems. This knowledge alienates us from the world around us. Figures like Socrates, Faust, and Johannes Climacus sought knowledge by turning their backs on the established truths of their respective cultures. But this search estranged them from the world. Knowledge is a dangerous thing, and the defenders of traditional values and institutions fear it.

Another perspective on this issue comes from the Enlightenment. According to this view, human beings, as Aristotle says, by nature desire to know. Knowledge is what separates us from the animals, and our very humanity lies in our ability to think rationally and to examine our beliefs critically. As Socrates said, "life without [rational] examination is not worth living."[46] Knowledge enables human beings to reshape their environment and has made possible the great technological and social advances of history. Throughout all of history humans have improved things by means of their ability to acquire new knowledge. For example, there have been great advances in many different fields of science that have concretely improved the lives of people; these include the elimination of diseases such as smallpox and polio, the advances in dentistry and anesthesiology, and one could go on with examples. The advocate of this view claims that it would be completely absurd to deny these advances and that the entire weight of human history supports the famous adage that knowledge is power. According to this perspective, anyone who wishes to try to suppress knowledge is blinded by a backward superstition.

Today most of us would probably agree with the Enlightenment view. We read books about Søren Kierkegaard in order to acquire new *knowledge* that we did not have before. We value knowledge and believe that it is important to have it. The constantly expanding volume of information freely available on the Internet evidences a strong demand for it and a culture that prioritizes its dissemination. It seems uncontroversial that everyone should have the opportunity to learn and acquire new knowledge.

---

[46] Plato, *Apology*, in *The Last Days of Socrates*, trans. by Hugh Tredennick, Harmondsworth: Penguin 1954, p. 72.

While this seems to be very straightforward, our modern world renders this picture problematic. Knowledge is a double-edged sword, and the same Western culture that prides itself on things like skyscrapers and vaccines has also produced concentration camps and biological weapons. Today we have major environmental problems such as global warming and the destruction of the ozone layer that are caused by the by-products of human technology. While it is true that knowledge and technology have helped us to improve our environment, they are proving equally effective in destroying it.

Even the question of the open access to knowledge is not unproblematic. I can share with the readers of this book some knowledge of the thought of Søren Kierkegaard, and this seems not to be a problem. But one can go onto the Internet and find people sharing knowledge about, for example, how to build a bomb. This kind of *knowledge* makes us all very uneasy. Should this be freely accessible to everyone?

Once human beings start on the road to reason, science, and technology, there is no way back. It is a one-way street. The genie is out of the bottle and cannot be put back. As Kierkegaard says of his character Johannes Climacus, once he begins to doubt, and once he starts this process and becomes alienated from this world around him, he cannot return to his previous state of innocence. With considerations of this kind we can begin to see the point behind the story of the Fall in Genesis. The world east of Eden is a dangerous and uncomfortable one. Likewise, the stories of Socrates, Faust, and Johannes Climacus are not just tales from a distant past: they are the story of our perilous world in the twenty-first century.

4

Kierkegaard, Heiberg, and History

Today we occasionally hear talk about the lapse of traditional values and the lack of meaning in modern life. Why is this such a widespread problem today? In the past it was thought that the earth was the center of the universe and had been created expressly to accommodate the human race. Humanity and the individuals who comprised it were God's primary concern. People in those days, of course, were well aware of disease, suffering, and death. But in the face of these it was a great comfort to think that the earth was an absolutely unique and special place that God was personally interested in. God cared about the fate and struggles of individuals.

Historical and scientific developments have altered this view for many. Geologists today tell us that one day the molten rock at the core of the earth will cool off. The earth will stop rotating on its axis and will lose its magnetic field. When this happens its protecting atmosphere will be blown off into space by the solar wind, at which point the earth will be uninhabitable since it will be directly exposed to the dangerous rays of the sun. Astronomers tell us that one day the sun will begin to run out of the fuel that powers it, and it will enter the final stages of its life. When this happens the sun will rapidly expand, becoming a red giant; it will then engulf and incinerate the earth. Our beloved planet will be gone forever, and it will be as if we never existed.

In contrast to the earlier view, this picture offers precious little comfort. If human history is only a fleeting and insignificant episode in a vast and indifferent universe, what is the meaning of my life? In the cosmic play of planets, stars, and galaxies, what importance could my hopes and dreams, struggles and achievements possibly have? The universe seems cruelly indifferent to the things that matter most to me personally. As Macbeth says, the sound and the fury of all of human life amounts to nothing. In the big picture human existence is but a brief flicker of a candle.

This new view can lead to nihilism, the belief that life has no purpose or meaning. When we look at things from this point of view, it is easy to be critical of the events and customs that make up our daily lives. People who take themselves or the actions in their lives very seriously suddenly seem to have lost perspective. They appear to pursue petty goals in their petty lives, all the while pretending that they are achieving something grand and monumental. They fail to see that in the end all of their efforts will amount to nothing. This is the perspective of the modern nihilist.

Kierkegaard was concerned with the problem of the meaninglessness of life, which he regarded as an important modern phenomenon that must be taken seriously. The second part of *The Concept of Irony* treats different forms of what he refers to as "modern irony." The positions that he looks at in this context are very similar to what we now refer to as modern nihilism. So we now turn to this analysis to see what insights it might hold for the modern problem of the absence of meaning in our twenty-first-century world.

4.1. Kierkegaard's Introduction to Part Two

In the Introduction to Part Two of *The Concept of Irony* Kierkegaard reiterates that the goal of the work is to examine the development of irony in its historical forms. As he noted in the Introduction to the book,[1] two elements are required for this analysis: first, the idea or concept of irony, and second, its actual manifestation in the world.[2] On the one hand, we need the concept so that we can recognize specific instances of it. Without the concept of irony in our minds, it would be impossible for us to determine concrete instances of irony in the world. On the other hand, we also need the empirical

---

[1] Kierkegaard, *The Concept of Irony*, trans. by Howard V. Hong and Edna H. Hong, Princeton: Princeton University Press 1989, pp. 9–12.
[2] Ibid., pp. 241f.

phenomenon of irony, since without it, our concept or idea of irony would simply float in the air and have no contact with the real world. So Kierkegaard claims that we must continue to operate with the concept of irony but be sure that we focus on specific instances of it in actuality. The two aspects are intertwined: the concept is defined by the phenomenon, and the phenomenon by the concept.

The first phenomenon of irony that Kierkegaard explored in the first part of the work was, of course, that of Socrates. The Greek philosopher used irony and introduced the notion of subjectivity into the world. According to Kierkegaard, who is following Hegel on this point, this marked a major step in the development of human thinking. After Socrates the idea of subjectivity did not simply disappear. On the contrary, it caught on and in the course of time became more and more important. People began to realize the significance and value of subjectivity in contrast to custom and tradition.

Kierkegaard now says that a new form of irony is present in the modern world, but it is not identical with Socratic irony. Since the time of Socrates subjectivity has had several centuries to develop. The modern world acknowledges the role of subjectivity, thus differing from the ancient Greeks, who, with the exception of Socrates, rejected it. So modern irony arises in a different context and with an entirely different point of departure. In each case irony is an assertion of subjectivity, but since in the modern world subjectivity is already established, it must assert itself in an even more radical manner. Kierkegaard writes, "For a new mode of irony to be able to appear now, it must result from the assertion of subjectivity in a still higher form. It must be subjectivity raised to the second power, a subjectivity's subjectivity, which corresponds to reflection's reflection."[3]

Kierkegaard associates modern irony with the movement of German Romanticism, as represented by figures such as Friedrich von Schlegel, Karl Wilhelm Ferdinand Solger, and Ludwig Tieck. Each of these three figures attempted to employ irony in his specific field. Kierkegaard also notes that Hegel had an important criticism of the Romantics, and he wishes to take this into account in his own analysis. It is to these forms of modern irony that we now turn.

---

[3] Ibid., p. 242.

4.2. German Romanticism

German Romanticism is an intellectual movement that is difficult to define in a few words since it was so diverse and contained so many different elements. Romanticism is usually thought to have arisen in France, England, and the German states in the second half of the eighteenth century as a reaction to the Enlightenment. While the Enlightenment focused on the faculty of reason to criticize the Church and absolute monarchy, Romanticism focused on feeling and emotion. The Enlightenment was regarded as a politically progressive force that swept away superstition and outdated practices and institutions. But the leading figures of Romanticism found something abstract and sterile in it.

The faculty of reason is something that is shared by everyone. Progress in science and mathematics depends on objective evidence and proofs. Scientists are able, at least in theory, to evaluate truth or falsity based on purely rational criteria without regard to their individual preferences and prejudices. We are all able to understand mathematics in the same way since we all possess the faculty of reason. In a sense my own personal opinion about these things does not matter since they are true independent of me. But I can recognize their truth when I employ my reason. According to the Romantics, this means that in order to understand something I must in effect abstract from myself. In my rational faculty there is nothing special or unique about me as a specific person. On the contrary, I share this faculty with everyone else. The Romantics argue that it is only in feeling and emotion that my true self emerges. Only I have the specific set of feelings that I possess at any given point in time. This is what defines my subjectivity and should be cultivated. The Enlightenment's adulation of reason, it was thought, ignores the individual understood in this way.

The Romantics therefore tried to counter the Enlightenment by celebrating individuality. This meant criticizing the Enlightenment's emphasis on science and reason. It also meant rejecting different kinds of conformism in society. Therefore, the Romantics mounted an aggressive attack on bourgeois life and values. Friedrich von Schlegel, for example, wrote a book titled *Lucinde*, which shocked middle-class society of its day with allusions to free sexual acts outside of marriage. The Romantics dreamed of a world in which each individual could break free of society and convention and express his or her true self. In their criticism of the Enlightenment and mainstream society, the Romantics often made use of irony.

Romanticism was also an important trend in Denmark during Kierkegaard's time. The Danish philosopher Henrik Steffens journeyed through Prussia and the German states from 1798 to 1802 and stayed for an extended period in Jena, the hotbed for the German Romantic movement at the time. He met personally August Wilhelm von Schlegel, Friedrich von Schlegel, Ludwig Tieck, Novalis, Goethe, Schiller, and Fichte. After returning to Copenhagen in 1802 he began a series of lectures at Ehler's College, in which he introduced the work of the German Romantics to Denmark. These lectures were attended by some of the leading lights of the Golden Age. From this moment on, Romanticism played an important role in Danish literature, art, philosophy, and religious thinking.

4.3. Kierkegaard's "Observations for Orientation"

The Romantics focused squarely on the value and integrity of the individual. Irony is something that isolates individuals and undermines the social whole. Why is this the case? Kierkegaard points out that the use of irony as a strategic tool requires considered reflection. The ironist looks at the way most people use language and cunningly interjects irony into the conversation. Kierkegaard claims that there is "a certain superiority"[4] in this in that the ironist takes himself to be cleverer than the ordinary person, and his use of language (with irony) is more subtle and sophisticated than ordinary daily speech. The ironist takes joy in using irony and then waiting to see who picks up on it. He takes particular joy when other people fail to notice it and take him to be stating his views straightforwardly. He feels superior to them. The modern ironist is critical of bourgeois life and enjoys criticizing it. He looks down on other people whom he regards as unreflectively caught up in the petty affairs it involves. Unlike them, he believes that he alone sees the hollowness of bourgeois existence and has the courage to expose its shortcomings. This disposition separates the ironist from most everyone else. He regards himself

---

[4] Kierkegaard, *The Concept of Irony*, p. 248.

not as a part of the mainstream, which would mean undermining his individuality, but rather as a loner, an outsider. This is in his eyes the only authentic life.

The goal with modern irony is in a sense the same as with Socratic irony: to expose people who are complacent or overly confident. The ironist pretends to go along with such people, but he subtly undermines their claims and arrogant dispositions indirectly with irony. In this way the ironist, who might be in a less respected position socially, can nonetheless prove himself superior to people who are generally regarded as the pillars of bourgeois society. The ironist thus takes special pleasure in fooling those people who are honored or hold prestigious positions.

Most people are bound by certain customs and conventions of society which dictate their actions. The ironist, by contrast, rejects all such established customs and conventions. He regards himself as being free from them, since he has seen through their facade of legitimacy. He knows that social conventions do not apply outside the society that requires them and regards such requirements as arbitrary. In Kierkegaard's words, "actuality loses its validity" for the ironist.[5] Since he has seen through such customary practices, he is free to ignore them and act as he pleases. Kierkegaard describes this with Hegel's term "subjective freedom," writing, "the salient feature of irony is the subjective freedom that at all times has in its power the possibility of beginning and is not handicapped by earlier situations."[6] Almost all of our behavior follows the pattern of previous behavior, which is governed by customs and traditions. Since the ironist does not believe in these, he is free to start anew or *ex nihilo* each time. He is subjectively free in the sense that he acts based on his own decisions and inclinations and not in accordance with some criterion that comes from without, that is, external custom or tradition.

Kierkegaard describes many different forms of irony, but the key one is what he calls "irony in the eminent sense."[7] One can be ironic about a few things in one's culture that one disapproves of. In this way one aims irony at a specific target, for example, a corrupt institution or a hypocritical individual. But irony in the eminent sense is aimed not just at a few things but rather at an entire culture or way of life.

---

[5] Ibid., p. 253.   [6] Ibid.   [7] Ibid., p. 254.

In Kierkegaard's view the German Romantics wanted not just to criticize specific elements of bourgeois life and keep the rest, but instead to undermine society as a whole. He states that this form of irony "is directed not against this or that particular existing entity but against the entire given actuality at a certain time and under certain conditions."[8] He borrows a phrase from Hegel and refers to this form of irony as "infinite, absolute negativity."[9] Irony is by its very nature something that is critical or *negates* something. This form of irony is *infinite* since it is not satisfied to criticize or negate just specific finite things, but rather wants to criticize everything. It is *absolute* in the sense that it regards everything it criticizes as merely finite conventions. They are arbitrary and unsupported by anything more than custom. The modern ironist, like the Sophists, regards all truths as relative. By contrast, the ironist's own position is absolute; indeed, it is the sole absolute that says that there are no absolutes and all truth is relative.[10]

Kierkegaard notes an unexpected common ground between religious belief and modern irony. At first glance, one might think that these two views are just the opposite of one another since religion represents a part of the traditions and conventions of society that the ironist is constantly trying to undermine. But Kierkegaard enjoins us to look more closely. He recalls the words of Ecclesiastes, "all is vanity."[11] This view says that all aspects of human life are vain and transient in comparison to what is really important, namely, God. Irony comes to the same conclusion about the mundane world of human society. It agrees that all is vanity, but not because it believes that God is the absolute. Instead, its absolute is that there are no absolutes. Religious belief and modern irony both regard most human activity from an absolute perspective that causes them to reject it. They agree that all is vanity, but religious belief concludes the world is vain because it falls short of the divine absolute, while the modern ironist concludes it is vain because there are no absolutes. But what is interesting is that the disposition of both the pious religious believer and the ironist separates them from mainstream society and the daily life of the world, which neither can take seriously. Although the nihilism of the modern ironist seems directly opposed to the faith of the religious believer, this strangely seems to be a case where

---

[8] Ibid.   [9] Ibid., p. 254, p. 259, p. 261.
[10] Ibid., p. 261.   [11] Ibid., p. 257. Ecclesiastes 1:2.

opposites converge. Like the religious believer, the ironist believes his truth sets him free, specifically from the tyranny of custom, tradition, and hypocrisy in the world.

4.4. Johan Ludvig Heiberg's *On the Significance of Philosophy for the Present Age*

An important figure for the young Kierkegaard during his days as a student at the University of Copenhagen was a man named Johan Ludvig Heiberg (see Fig. 4.1). Heiberg came from an intellectual family and was a leading poet, dramatist, and literary critic in Denmark in the 1830s and 1840s.[12] As a child he lived for a time in the so-called Hill House, which belonged to the literary scholar Knud Lyne Rahbek, who was a close friend of his father Peter Andreas Heiberg who had been exiled from the Danish Kingdom. Rahbek's home was known as one of the great literary salons of Golden Age

Fig. 4.1. Johan Ludvig Heiberg (1791–1860)

[12] See Henning Fenger, *The Heibergs*, trans. by Frederick J. Marker, New York: Twayne Publishers, Inc. 1971.

Copenhagen and thus afforded Heiberg the opportunity to meet many writers and cultural figures of the period.

When he was older Heiberg went to Paris, where he studied French vaudeville, which he brought to the stage of the Royal Theater in Copenhagen. He was the editor of the leading journal for aesthetics and criticism of the age, *Kjøbenhavns flyvende Post* or *Copenhagen's Flying Post*. It was in this journal that Kierkegaard published his first articles. Heiberg's wife, Johanne Luise Heiberg, was the leading actress of the day, and Kierkegaard's "The Crisis, and the Crisis in the Life of an Actress" is dedicated to an analysis of her work. Heiberg's mother, Thomasine Buntzen, known as Madame Gyllembourg, was a popular novelist, and Kierkegaard's work *A Literary Review* examines her novel *Two Ages*.[13]

Heiberg's many interests also included philosophy, which he used, among other things, to try to ground his theory of aesthetics. His philosophical orientation came from his experience with Hegel's philosophy. Heiberg learned about Hegel when he was working as a lecturer at the University of Kiel and became so interested in his work that he went to Berlin in 1824 and attended his lectures. This was an exciting period at the University of Berlin when Hegel's power was at its height, and he was surrounded by a large number of adoring students. Heiberg experienced his first-hand encounter with Hegel as one of the great revelations of his life.

Heiberg returned to Copenhagen and began a campaign to introduce Hegel's philosophy to his fellow countrymen.[14] As a part of this effort he wanted to give a series of private lectures on the subject. To announce this he published a short work in March of 1833 entitled *On the Significance of Philosophy for the Present Age*. This work presented some of the basics of Hegel's philosophy and issued an invitation for interested students to sign up for the lectures.

Heiberg begins the treatise by claiming that his age is in a state of crisis. According to his Hegelian theory, there are different periods of history, each with its own values, traditions, and world-view. Each

---

[13] For a useful overview of the Heiberg family's contributions to the Danish Golden Age, see Henning Fenger, *The Heibergs*.

[14] For an overview of Heiberg's attempts to introduce Hegel's philosophy in Denmark, see Jon Stewart, *A History of Hegelianism in Golden Age Denmark*, Tome I, *The Heiberg Period: 1824–1836*, Copenhagen: C. A. Reitzel 2007 (*Danish Golden Age Studies*, vol. 3).

period offers the people at the time a stable picture of reality that they can use to make sense of the world and their lives. From time to time, however, history develops, and new ways of thinking and scientific discoveries appear, with the result that the stable points of orientation begin to falter. Then a period of crisis begins, which eventually results in the collapse of the reigning world-view. In this crisis people feel uncertain and anxious, since their old understanding of the world rests on increasingly shaky foundations.

Heiberg identifies his own time as among these transitional periods. In the wake of the tumults caused by the Enlightenment at the end of the eighteenth century, people had lost their belief in traditional institutions and practices. The Enlightenment criticized monarchial power and rejected traditional religious belief as superstition. According to Heiberg, the result was subjectivism, relativism, and nihilism. People did not know what to believe in any longer. He says that a similar crisis took place during the Roman Empire, when institutions from past ages continued to exist after they had ceased to be relevant or useful. He writes, they were "like a ghost from past ages, which had lost all meaning in the present."[15] In this condition people "felt abandoned by all gods . . . since the entire world of gods was dead."[16] His discussion of the Roman world is clearly intended as an analogy to his own age, in which he believes the traditional views on religion, art, and philosophy have become largely irrelevant. His culture must urgently find a solution before it collapses into a complete relativism and nihilism. This is, for Heiberg, the great challenge of his age.

4.5. Kierkegaard's "The World Historical Validity of Irony"

Kierkegaard's chapter "The World Historical Validity of Irony" takes up Heiberg's understanding of the development of history through periods of stability and crisis. He follows Heiberg by claiming that the world-views of each period are transient and mutable. He writes,

---

[15] Johan Ludvig Heiberg, *On the Significance of Philosophy for the Present Age*, in *Heiberg's On the Significance of Philosophy for the Present Age and Other Texts*, ed. and trans. by Jon Stewart, Copenhagen: C. A. Reitzel 2005 (*Texts from Golden Age Denmark*, vol. 1), p. 90.

[16] Ibid., p. 91.

"The given actuality at a certain time is the actuality valid for the generation and the individuals in that generation."[17] But when the old views cease to be plausible, "this actuality must be displaced by another actuality, and this must occur through and by individuals and the generation."[18] Like Heiberg, he concludes that the changes in the world-views take place by individuals ceasing to believe in the key elements that sustain the common culture.

He tries to understand the use of irony historically at times when a given world-view is in crisis. Instead of talking about the world-view of a specific people or period, Kierkegaard uses the words "existence" and "actuality" to capture this. He explains the situation of a person using irony in a time when a culture's traditions and values are starting to crumble. In such a situation "the whole of existence has become alien to the ironic subject and the ironic subject in turn alien to existence," and as a result, "actuality has lost its validity for the ironic subject."[19] The use of irony results from a sense of alienation from mainstream traditions and values. The ironist is able to perceive that many of the traditions and values are no longer firmly grounded. When this concerns numerous aspects of one's culture, then suddenly, one feels alienated from everything or from the "actuality" of one's time.

Kierkegaard points out that there are two aspects of this development: "the new must forge ahead," and "the old must be displaced."[20] There are people in any given age of crisis who perceive the crisis very clearly. Kierkegaard follows Heiberg on this point, since Heiberg separates the intellectuals of the age from the common masses, claiming that the great minds of the period are the ones leading the vanguard of humanity out of the crisis and into the new age. They have some intuition about the new period that will emerge from the crisis. This is what Kierkegaard describes as the "prophetic individual."[21] Heiberg calls these people the "educated" or "cultivated" people, and in his own age he identifies two figures as the leaders of humanity urging everyone on to embrace a new world-view: Goethe and Hegel.

For Kierkegaard, the ironist is the one who perceives the present crisis clearly. But the ironist has no clear picture of what the future will hold. He has only vague intuitions. Thus, his goal is less to

---

[17] Kierkegaard, *The Concept of Irony*, p. 260.   [18] Ibid., p. 260.
[19] Ibid., p. 259.   [20] Ibid., p. 260.   [21] Ibid.

build the future than to expose the contradictions of the present. He points to the future without knowing exactly what it will entail.[22] Kierkegaard follows what is described at the beginning of *On the Significance of Philosophy for the Present Age* when Heiberg talks about the common culture striving "powerfully forward in manifold directions" without anyone really knowing where they will lead.[23]

Kierkegaard refers to the ironist as "a sacrifice that the world process demands."[24] By this he means that in any age of crisis there will be people who use irony to try to tear away at the decaying structure of the present. The prophets of the new age are without honor in their own time, since they encounter resistance from less perceptive members of their culture who are still invested in tradition. Forward-looking people will invariably be resented and disdained by those of their contemporaries who try to hold on firmly to the old structure. As a result, such prophetic ironists are often subject to persecution.

Kierkegaard describes the ironist as "negatively free"[25] in the sense of being free from the usual demands of custom and tradition. Indeed, the ironist regards the rest of society as unreflective slaves to customary patterns of behavior. He feels liberated by his belief that he is no longer subject to the constraints of society and that the wide world of possibility lies open. He can dress, speak, and act in any way that he wishes, without regard to the social norms. This encourages his intuition that something new is in the process of replacing the old ways.

The key for Kierkegaard is that the ironist must feel this sense of freedom vis-à-vis the established order of things. He writes, "Face-to-face with the given actuality, the subjectivity feels its power, its validity and meaning."[26] This is what Hegel referred to as "subjective freedom." One must realize the absolute and irreducible value of the individual. This realization gradually results from a process of historical development. Our understanding of human beings as individuals has changed radically over time as the principle of subjective freedom has come to be realized. This leads Kierkegaard

---

[22] Ibid., p. 261.
[23] *Heiberg's On the Significance of Philosophy for the Present Age and Other Texts*, p. 87.
[24] Kierkegaard, *The Concept of Irony*, p. 261.   [25] Ibid., p. 262.
[26] Ibid., p. 263.

to conclude: "Insofar as this irony is world-historically justified, the subjectivity's emancipation is carried out in the service of the idea."[27] So for Kierkegaard, the point of irony is not simply to make fun of people or to engage in irony for its own sake. Instead, the justification for irony from a historical perspective is that it is used to focus on and develop the principle of subjective freedom. It is "in the service of" this idea. This was the mission of Socrates. Indeed, Hegel's interpretation was that Socrates was the first to begin to develop subjective freedom.

4.6. Kierkegaard's Criticism of Hegel on Socratic and Romantic Irony

Hegel contrasts Socratic irony and the irony of the German Romantics, and here we see a key idea behind Kierkegaard's work. Hegel points out that although the Romantics claimed Socrates as an inspiration, their use of irony differed significantly from his. Hegel associates Romantic irony with the writer Friedrich von Schlegel, the philologist Friedrich Ast, and the philosopher Johann Gottlieb Fichte—all three of whom are discussed by Kierkegaard in his work.[28] According to Hegel, these authors wish to use irony as a purely negative tool to tear down any idea, custom, belief, institution, or tradition that is not to their liking. In other words, irony can be used in the service of relativism or nihilism to criticize anything and everything. The Romantics have extended the Socratic practice to a universal principle.[29] But, for Hegel, Socrates' goal was not to destroy for the sheer joy of destroying, but rather in order to reach the truth.

For Hegel, it is a mistake to understand Socrates as the originator of this kind of irony.[30] It is true that Socrates placed the focus on the individual and subjectivity, but this was very different from the understanding of subjectivity in the Romantics. Hegel views the

---

[27] Ibid.
[28] Hegel, *Lectures on the History of Philosophy*, vols 1–3, trans. by E. S. Haldane, London: K. Paul, Trench, Trübner 1892–6; Lincoln and London: University of Nebraska Press 1955, vol. 1, p. 400.
[29] Ibid.   [30] Ibid., p. 401.

Romantics as relativists whose attacks on tradition are motivated by little more than the gratification of their ego. He imagines an advocate of this position who says,

> It is I who through my educated thoughts can annul all determinations of right, morality, good, etc., because I am clearly master of them, and I know that if anything seems good to me I can easily subvert it, because things are only true to me in so far as they please me now.[31]

The Romantic can thus change his view at will when it no longer continues to suit him.

While it is true that for Socrates the individual must reach the truth for him- or herself, this does not mean that the truth is arbitrary or relative to each individual. It does not justify a self-satisfied enjoyment of one's own private truth at the expense of a publicly accepted one. Socrates does not arrogantly believe that his views are superior to those of other people. Unlike the Romantics, Socrates does not openly mock accepted custom and tradition. Hegel thus concludes that Socrates' irony is "a manner of speech, a pleasant rallying,"[32] or, in the translation of Kierkegaard's quotation of it in *The Concept of Irony*, "a manner of conversation, sociable pleasantry."[33] This stands in contrast to the Romantics' "satirical laughter or pretense," which treats everything as though it "were nothing but a joke."[34]

Kierkegaard points out that Hegel is generally a quite consistent critic of irony, particularly as it is employed by the German Romantics; indeed, Hegel is uncharacteristically polemical in his treatment of Friedrich von Schlegel. Kierkegaard seems to have a mixed assessment of this. On the one hand, he agrees with Hegel's criticism of the Romantics as relativists and takes Hegel to have performed an important service by criticizing them. He writes, "it is one of Hegel's great merits that he halted or at least wanted to halt the prodigal sons of speculation on their way to perdition."[35] But, on the other hand, he thinks Hegel's animosity toward the Romantics leads him to unfairly overlook the merits of irony in general. Kierkegaard thinks that since Hegel has no patience whatsoever for Romantic irony, he is unable to distinguish this from other forms of irony. In short, Hegel lumps

---

[31] Ibid., pp. 400f.   [32] Ibid., p. 402.
[33] Kierkegaard, *The Concept of Irony*, p. 267.
[34] Hegel, *Lectures on the History of Philosophy*, vol. 1, p. 402.
[35] Kierkegaard, *The Concept of Irony*, p. 265.

together all forms of irony into one negative idea, which he proceeds to criticize. Kierkegaard thinks that Hegel's description of Socratic irony as merely "a manner of conversation, sociable pleasantry"[36] misses the point. This fails to recognize the deeper underlying meaning of Socrates' use of irony.

In other words, for Hegel, the goal of Socrates' irony was simply to start up a discussion that would lead to a determination of the concept or the universal. However, as noted earlier, Hegel is critical of Socrates for never managing to determine the universal successfully or to construct something positive. But, for Kierkegaard, it was precisely the point of Socrates to be negative through and through. His goal was not to construct something but rather to negate.

It is important to appreciate how counterintuitive Kierkegaard's position is here. Usually if there is a problem, our immediate instinct is to try to solve it. If there is a question of a concept, then the goal is to try to define it. We are uncomfortable to remain in a situation with unresolved problems or uncertain situations. We naturally want to resolve them. But Kierkegaard's position is just the opposite of this. For Kierkegaard, resolving something or constructing something is not necessarily beneficial to the individual; rather, it can be a terrible disservice. If one cures doubt or assuages the pain of nihilism by supplying an answer, one robs the individual of his own subjective responsibility to search for the truth. This is even worse if what is constructed and presented as truth is not even true, which is what Kierkegaard regarded the Sophists to be doing in Socrates' time, and what he regarded the priests and academics to be doing in his own time. Kierkegaard's Socrates is negative, that is, in a sense a nihilist, but that is alright: this frees the subject to search for truth subjectively. The key difference between Kierkegaard's Socrates and Kierkegaard's Romantics is that Socrates does not stop the search or cynically make up the truth like the Romantics.

4.7. Kierkegaard's Criticism of Hegel on History and Socrates

The Concept of Irony attempts to trace the use of irony historically in order to understand how and when irony arose and how it

---

[36] Ibid., p. 267.

developed over time. Today this kind of study would fall under the heading "history of ideas." Kierkegaard's work is something of a hybrid. On the one hand, it is not a purely historical work, since he is not interested in history *per se*; he is not tracing kings, wars, and things of that sort. On the other hand, it is not a purely conceptual work either; he is not interested just in the concept of irony on its own, divorced from its historical context. His work rather involves both elements, and this is what he discusses in his Introduction.

First, there is the element of the historical phenomenon, the actual use of irony by the concrete person Socrates that involves understanding Socrates in the context of the ancient Greek world and the Athenian city-state. So there is an empirical element based on the extant sources of Socrates' life and thought: Plato, Xenophon, and Aristophanes. But, second, there is also an abstract, conceptual element, which involves thought. History is not simply a catalogue of raw data. The sources must be interpreted, situations and events must be reconstructed, and connections must be inferred. Certain events must be judged to be central and important, while others are disregarded and cast aside as irrelevant. This is the work of the historian. In order to do this work, one must invariably make use of certain ideas, concepts, or organizational schemes to facilitate one's interpretation of the events. Kierkegaard points out that both of these elements are required to approach subject matter of this kind. It would be absurd to bury oneself in the empirical phenomena alone and leave it at that, since this would not be illuminating in any way. The empirical data need interpretation before they can be meaningful. Likewise, it would be absurd to focus exclusively on the conceptual side without even giving a look to the empirical phenomena, since this would end in complete abstraction, and the analysis would, so to speak, float in the air far away from actual existence and reality. One needs both *particularity*—the raw empirical data of history—and *universality*—the idea or concepts.

Kierkegaard associates the empirical side with history and the conceptual side with philosophy. He recognizes the importance of both for his study:

> Both of them ought to have their rights so that, on the one hand, the phenomenon has its rights and is not to be intimidated and discouraged by philosophy's superiority, and philosophy, on the other hand, is not to

let itself be infatuated by the charms of the particular, is not to be distracted by the superabundance of the particular.[37]

Both sides have their validity, and both are necessary for the kind of study that Kierkegaard is presenting. This is worth noting, since Kierkegaard is often characterized as someone who is anti-conceptual or someone who celebrates existence and actuality while rejecting all forms of abstraction and theory. Here it is clear that he values abstract concepts but believes they must be grounded in experience or concrete phenomena.[38] Thus the book is called not "the empirical phenomenon of irony," but rather "the *concept* of irony."

In his overview of Hegel's understanding of Socrates, Kierkegaard criticizes Hegel for placing too much emphasis on the concept and not enough on the empirical phenomenon. He reproaches Hegel for not being philologically exacting in the sense that he does not make a close study of all of the relevant sources but instead is too quick to focus on the general concept in abstraction from the historical evidence. Hegel is purportedly not worried that perhaps not all of the details from the sources fit into the big picture that he is trying to convey. Kierkegaard caricatures Hegel as the "commander-in-chief of world history" who just takes a "royal glimpse" at things before moving along.[39] Kierkegaard believes that this leads to a distortion of the interpretation of Socrates, since Hegel fails to recognize the inconsistencies in the accounts of Socrates given by the ancient sources: Plato, Xenophon, and Aristophanes. Since Hegel observes Socrates, so to speak, from a bird's-eye view, he fails to see some important details about the person of Socrates, which cannot be reduced to a part of some grand historical narrative.

Kierkegaard's second criticism has to do with Hegel's understanding of Socrates as the founder of morality. Hegel is telling a long story about the development of philosophy and Western culture. He sees Socrates as playing an important role in this development, since the Greek philosopher was the first person to realize the importance of

---

[37] Ibid., pp. 10f.

[38] See *Kierkegaard's Journals and Notebooks*, ed. by Niels Jørgen Cappelørn et al., vols 1–11, Princeton: Princeton University Press 2007ff., vol. 7, p. 70, NB15:103: "It is not as if 'actuality' were devoid of concepts—not at all, no, the concept that is found by conceptually dissolving it into possibility is also present in actuality, but of course there is something more: that it is actuality."

[39] Kierkegaard, *The Concept of Irony*, p. 222.

subjective freedom. This meant that morality was not just about what was already fixed and given outwardly by one's culture, but rather it was something that was inward and concerned one's own thoughts, considerations, and conscience. This was a positive principle that entered into history at this time. According to Hegel, this represented an important step in the development of human culture, and this form of morality is one of the characteristic features of the modern world.

Kierkegaard is critical of this since he thinks it is a mistake to ascribe some positive principle to Socrates. It is wrong to think that Socrates founded some school of philosophy or some social movement. Instead, Kierkegaard wants to insist that Socrates' service historically was entirely negative. He critically dismantled the pretension of the Sophists and the mainstream Athenian citizen. On the one hand, he showed the hollowness of the relativism of the Sophists, and on the other hand, he pointed out that the ideas that his fellow Athenians prided themselves on were baseless and could not stand the test of rational examination. But in both cases, Socrates' contribution is a negative one. He does not at the end present some positive view of his own either to the Sophists or to his fellow citizens. He simply leaves the matter without resolution. At the end there is negation or *aporia*, but no solution. Kierkegaard says that we must hold fast to this picture of Socrates and resist the urge of historians or philosophers to incorporate him in some positive way into a larger narrative about the development of history or philosophy. Hegel has mistakenly given Socrates a positive role of anticipating later developments, but the truth of the matter is that Socrates was not forward-looking, but rather backward-looking. He was responding critically to individuals and institutions that already existed. But this is where it stopped. He was making a negative statement about Greek culture and thought at the time, but he never managed to find the truth or to present something positive for later ages to build upon.

Socrates claims to be seeking the concept of the Good. He is constantly asking for a definition of it and is given answers that reflect Athenian values and views. One by one he undermines all of them. While Kierkegaard agrees with Hegel on this, his critical point is that the focus should be on the eternal search for the Good and not arriving at it.[40] Kierkegaard thus focuses on Socrates' irony as a

---

[40] Ibid., p. 235.

defining feature, since this irony is purely negative. It tears down in the sense that it is critical of specific theses, doctrines, definitions, etc., but it does not build up and is devoid of any positive element. It thus facilitates the never-ending search for truth by not allowing one to stop or remain complacently with any positive conclusion.

4.8. The Modern Struggle for Individuality

Kierkegaard's account of the Romantics and modern irony sounds like an interesting chapter in the history of ideas, but is this really meaningful in any way to our world today? This account raises the important question of who we are as individuals. The problem in the modern world is that as soon as we try to articulate who we are, we immediately run into the problem that there are many other people who share exactly the same characteristics. When I say, for example, that I am a person who enjoys reading about philosophy or a person who is interested in the thought of Søren Kierkegaard, then I have not really said anything that could define who I am as an individual since there are many other people in the world who share exactly these same properties. It then becomes a more urgent question to determine what it is that makes me uniquely who I am.

We often identify ourselves by our clothes, our styles, and our possessions. But take a moment and consider this. I am wearing this shirt, these pants, and these shoes. But none of these things is uniquely mine or expresses something special about me. All of these items are mass produced, and if I were to go outside on the street, it probably would not take me too long to find people wearing the same items. Before mass production, articles like this were made by craftsmen. Each one of these articles was unique, and individuals who possessed them had literally something that was one of a kind. The mass-production techniques of the Industrial Revolution have led to mass-produced clothing for most of us, and the few people who can still afford custom clothing often pay substantial sums for the privilege of expressing their individuality with it. Since the Industrial Revolution virtually everything is made in mass quantities by machines. The world today is made, as it were, by cookie-cutter machines that produce everything around us into preset forms. The danger is that each of us has become just one more product of this machine. Think of Andy Warhol's pictures of soup cans lined up one on top of another. This is an image of modernity. The fear of many of us is to become like one of these soup cans.

Many people try to revolt against this uniformity and assert their individuality by means of hairstyles, tattoos, piercings, and so forth. But what begins as individual expression often degenerates into the latest fad, with the result that so many people are doing the same thing that nothing unique or individual is being expressed. This is our problem in the twenty-first century. The Romantics in Kierkegaard's time saw it coming more than two centuries ago. They struggled to assert the value of the individual against the forces of conformity, but they could not have imagined the challenges that we face today. Most of us believe that there is something special and unique that makes us who we are. But what is it, and how can we express it? When we fail to answer these kinds of questions, we feel disoriented in the world. We feel lost, since we can take no consolation in the community or social groups because they undermine our individuality and make us into faceless members of a larger whole. This is a modern problem where each individual is left to him- or herself. The conflicts between individuality and culture that exercised Socrates and Kierkegaard are still very much with us today. It is intimidating to think of oneself as merely one of seven billion human beings on the planet and in the face of this to try to assert oneself as a special and unique individual.

5

Kierkegaard and Romantic Subjectivism

Modernity presents important challenges to us as we try to understand ourselves and our role in the world. We live today in mass societies, in anonymous cities, where individuals can easily feel lost, dwarfed by the multitude of people. Further, we live in a world where traditional values and beliefs have been shaken at their foundations. Many of the things that used to serve as important points of orientation for people to use to define themselves are no longer viable options.

When I look at myself in the mirror and ask, Who am I?, I want to have a clear and straightforward answer. This is an important question to me personally, as it is to all of us. Somewhere deep down I want to believe that I am a unique and special individual. I want to believe that there is some kind of soul or spirit or mind that makes me the person I am and that distinguishes me from everyone else. I am comforted by this kind of thought since if it is true, then regardless of how many other billions of people there are in the world, there is only one of me, and that is something special and important.

Why does it mean so much to us to believe in such things? This is an important feature of the modern world. In the past, individuality was not such an important thing; indeed, it was suppressed or actively discouraged. People were brought up to believe that the most important thing was not themselves as individuals but rather their relations to larger groups. For example, in traditional cultures it was very important that one belonged to a specific family, and this was what constituted the key element of one's self-identity. Extended families lived together and functioned as a larger social unit. The Romans had great cults celebrating the ancestors of important families. To belong to a specific family dictated every aspect of one's life: one's marriage opportunities, one's profession, one's political orientation, and so forth. In modern society today all of this is gone. Extended families no longer live together, and at best one has the relatively small nuclear family consisting of a father, a mother, and their immediate children. But today, with the frequent rate of divorce and remarriage as well as the rise of different forms of cohabitation, the nuclear family itself is becoming ever more fragmented. In modernity the family is thus quickly reduced to a series of separate individuals and no longer serves the same function as it used to. For however important our families are to us today, it is undeniable that they no longer play the same role for us as they did for people in earlier times. The same thing can be said with other forms of association that were formerly used to define one's identity, for example, affiliation with a specific tribe, a specific guild, a specific religion, etc.

When all of these larger units break down, we are left with scattered individuals. As society changes, people feel uncertain about the loosening of the traditional bonds to these older institutions, and more pressure is put on the individual to define him- or herself in a different way. If one's self-definition does not come from one's affiliation with a family or other larger group, then it must come from oneself. This is the reason for our modern anxiety and uncertainty: the entire weight is placed on our shoulders as individuals. We alone must define ourselves, but how should we do this?

One of the great ideals of the modern world is the notion of the self-made man or woman, that is, the idea that individuals can create a good life for themselves in a capitalist economy based solely on their abilities, their hard work, and their determination. They are not dependent on their families, their guild, or anything else for their advancement. No matter what their background, their race, their religion, they can attain success by virtue of their own merit. According to this modern ideal, people can do it on their own. They can in a sense create themselves.

This is a key issue in Kierkegaard's criticism of Romantic irony that we wish to explore in this chapter. Who are we as individuals? Can we really invent ourselves? Or are we in some important ways grounded by other things in our lives that we have no control over? The idea of a self-made man is supposed to be a positive ideal that encourages people to work hard, but it can also be a frightening prospect. If I can in a sense create myself and have success based on my own abilities, then I can also fail abysmally based on my own lack of ability. I am alone in the modern world. This is a frightening prospect that constitutes an important challenge for people today.

5.1. Introduction to Fichte

Johann Gottlieb Fichte (see Fig. 5.1) was one of the most important German philosophers in the period between Kant and Hegel. He was profoundly influenced by the philosophy of Kant and saw himself as in some ways continuing in the spirit of it, while at the same time correcting what he took to be its shortcomings. In 1807 Fichte, fleeing from the French advances in the Napoleonic Wars, came to Copenhagen, where he met a number of leading Danish scholars.

Fichte was perhaps best known for his theory of subjectivity. He tried to start from the ground up and find out what could be established philosophically with absolute certainty. According to Fichte, what we know immediately is our own thoughts and sensations. This is the subject or the "I," which, as he says, *posits itself* since there is nothing prior to it. The subject is the most basic thing that can be known, and all other knowledge derives from it. By beginning with the subject, he follows Descartes' famous foundational starting point: "I think, therefore I am." We first have knowledge about the self before we have knowledge about the world. While we can doubt the truth of the knowledge about the world, our self-knowledge is immediate and indubitable.

Fig. 5.1. Johann Gottlieb Fichte (1762–1814)

The first proposition in Fichte's work the *Science of Knowledge* is that the subject is identical to itself and does not recognize anything outside itself as having ultimate truth or validity. Fichte tries to capture this with the formulation "I am I" or "I is equal to I," which is often expressed in a shorthand version with an equals sign: "I = I." This formula alludes to the law of identity, one of the fundamental laws of logic that states that everything is identical to itself, or A is A. Fichte takes his proposition "I = I" as foundational, since this law on which it is based is immediately clear to everyone and cannot be called into question. Fichte's "I am I" also refers to the fact that there is a unity of self-consciousness with its representations of the external, objective sphere in general. "I am I" includes not only the subject, but also the world as the subject experiences it. The world is determined by the representations of the subject. I recognize that there are things in the world that are separate from me (I ≠ not-I), but then I also realize that, more importantly, they are an extension of myself in the sense that they are representations produced by my cognitive faculties.

This focus on the subject and the denial of any substantial sphere of objectivity was very attractive to the German Romantics. Fichte seemed to provide them with a metaphysical view that supported their elevation of the individual over the world. Fichte's theory put the focus squarely on the individual and seemed to imply that the objective sphere—that included tradition and bourgeois culture—was something that was dependent on the subject and had no independent grounding on its own.

5.2. Hegel's and Kierkegaard's Analyses of Fichte

Hegel ends his *Lectures on the History of Philosophy* by treating the most important philosophical movements of his own day. In this context he examines the philosophy of Fichte at some length. After presenting Fichte's theory, Hegel issues a couple of criticisms of it. Most importantly, he argues that the "I" that Fichte develops represents merely the individual aspect of self-consciousness.[1] What is missing is the universal or social aspect. The self that Fichte sketches can only stand apart from and opposed to other selves since there is

[1] Hegel, *Lectures on the History of Philosophy*, vols 1–3, trans. by E. S. Haldane, London: K. Paul, Trench, Trübner 1892–6; Lincoln and London: University of Nebraska Press 1955, vol. 3, p. 499.

nothing to unite them. Here Hegel shows himself to be on the side of the advocates of reason and the Enlightenment, since he claims that the individual is essentially defined by the universal capacity of reason and not by the individuality of feeling or sense perception. Since we all share the faculty of reason we can understand things in the same way. Further, we can relate to and understand each other. Fichte's subject lacks this shared rationality and is thus isolated from others. Moreover, Fichte's subject is cut off from the objective sphere in general, which is referred to as the "not-I." Without rationality the individual is unable to recognize and consent to the universal elements in the social sphere as a whole, for example, rational laws, customs, and traditions. Hegel says, "The Fichtean philosophy recognizes the finite spirit alone, and not the infinite; it does not recognize spirit as universal thought."[2] Fichte's philosophy only understands one half of the relation, the subjective half, but it fails to see that the subject through thought and reason has a connection to other people and the world of objectivity and actuality.

The Romantics define humanity in terms of feeling and the senses which they understand to be unique for each individual. Hegel, however, points out that these are faculties that we share with animals. Feeling and the senses do not identify the truly human element in all of us. Instead, it is the faculty of reason that makes possible shared ideas, culture, and civilization. Moreover, it is what unites us with one another, since we need the recognition of other rational human beings to be who we are.

Hegel concludes by identifying Fichte as an important forerunner of the different theories of subjectivism and relativism that are found in German Romanticism. Specifically, he links Fichte's theory of the self-positing ego with Friedrich von Schlegel's theory of irony.[3] Schlegel's ironist does not believe in the truth of anything objective. Instead, Hegel says, "The subject here knows itself to be within itself the Absolute, and all else to it is vain."[4] But Hegel argues that no one can remain in this relativism for long and that at some point one requires a fixed truth or point of orientation. He notes that Schlegel himself ultimately abandoned the viewpoint of irony and converted to Catholicism. For Hegel, this is a demonstration that Schlegel himself in time came to realize the implausibility of this position.

---

[2] Ibid.   [3] Ibid., pp. 507f.   [4] Ibid., p. 507.

Like Hegel, Kierkegaard traces Fichte's theory of the subject back to Kant's epistemology.[5] For Kant, the faculties of the human mind shape the world that we perceive. Space and time are not objective facts about the world, but they are a part of the human perceptual apparatus. The picture that Kant presents is that we receive some sense data from the outside. This data alone is inchoate, but then our mental and perceptual faculties immediately go to work and turn this information into the concrete, determinate objects that we are used to seeing. Kant calls these "representations," since they are not the objects themselves, but rather the result of a cognitive process that organizes the data received by the senses.

There thus arises in Kant a split between our representation of a thing and the thing as it is in itself, apart from any subject that perceives it. Kant argued that this "thing in itself," which Kierkegaard refers to by the German term *"Ding an sich,"* cannot be known since we cannot abstract from our human cognitive faculties to conceive it. These faculties are the way in which we know the world, but they are also in a sense limiting since we can never escape them and know how things are in themselves. This caused a great controversy in the reception of Kant's philosophy, since it gave rise to the skeptical problem that we can never know if our representations of objects in the world are true because we can never compare them to the things in themselves.

Fichte responded to these objections by arguing that the notion of the thing in itself was superfluous. He tried to resolve this problem by reconceiving this Kantian model. Fichte claimed that it was absurd to separate content and form in the way that Kant's view did. In other words, the content of the representations comes from the unknown external object, but the form is supplied by the subject's cognitive faculties. Fichte claims instead that content and form are necessarily connected, and so there is no need to posit something external to the subject. The subject can in a sense produce its own representations. It is upon this basis that he extends his notion of "I is equal to I" to mean that the subject is identical with the external world in the sense that the world is a product of the human cognitive processes. There is a unity of the subject and the object.

---

[5] For Kierkegaard's account of Fichte, see *The Concept of Irony*, trans. by Howard V. Hong and Edna H. Hong, Princeton: Princeton University Press 1989, pp. 272–86.

Kierkegaard's objection to this is much the same as that of Hegel: when the world simply becomes an extension of the human subject and its faculties of cognition, then everything is reduced to subjectivity and nothing objective remains. Kierkegaard writes, "When Fichte infinitized the I in this way, he advanced an idealism beside which any actuality turned pale."[6] Fichte's position represented a radical negation of the world of actuality. What was true and important was the subject, but the world around us had no independent existence.

At a certain level Fichte's position is attractive to Kierkegaard since it represents negativity, that is, a negation of the world. He takes this to be an important improvement over Kant, who did not have this negative element in his philosophy because of the doctrine of the thing in itself, which although unknown, seemed to posit a standard for the objective truth of the world around us. But Fichte, by contrast, negates this world and shows that it is insubstantial. As we have seen, this was what Socrates did in ancient Athens, and Kierkegaard praised him for this negativity. Kierkegaard believes that this negative experience is important for everyone, and he hints at a Christian meaning to this when he paraphrases from scripture, saying that this process of negation is necessary "since everyone who wants to save his soul must lose it."[7] This seems to imply that in order to be a Christian, one must reject or "negate" the world and withdraw into oneself.

5.3. The Appropriation of Fichte's Theory by Schlegel and Tieck

Again following Hegel, Kierkegaard points out that Fichte's theory of the self-positing ego formed the foundation of the theory of irony in later thinkers such as Friedrich von Schlegel and Ludwig Tieck. But, according to Kierkegaard, these thinkers distorted Fichte's theory by trying to apply it in a different context. Kierkegaard makes two related objections: "In the first place, the empirical and finite I was confused with the eternal I; in the second place, metaphysical

---

[6] Ibid., p. 273.
[7] Ibid., p. 274. See Matthew 10:39, Mark 8:35, Luke 9:24, and John 12:25.

actuality was confused with historical actuality."[8] Fichte's primary goal was to create a theory of knowledge that corrected the short-comings of Kant's philosophy. His self-positing "I" thus exists as an abstract concept rather than the lived experience of an individual. By contrast, Schlegel and Tieck took this theoretical entity and recon-ceived it as an actual living and breathing person. In other words, they tried to employ this abstract ego as a model for concrete behavior in the real world.

Specifically, Schlegel and Tieck saw in Fichte's theory a powerful tool with which to criticize the world of bourgeois customs, values, and beliefs. Fichte's ego did not recognize the validity of anything outside itself, and these later Romantic thinkers seized upon this as a way to undermine what they regarded as the old-fashioned and reactionary views in the society of their day.

But again Kierkegaard points out that this differs from Socratic irony, which, as we have seen, was world-historically justified. By contrast, he says that the Romantics' use of irony "was not in the service of world spirit."[9] Socrates examined and undermined specific beliefs that historically were no longer viable. But the Romantics use irony to criticize everything. Their criticism was indiscriminate. Their goal was to tear down society while at the same time glorifying the individual, who is able to create himself. It is true that in any society there are always things that are worthy of criticism—corruption, nepotism, hypocrisy, etc.—but it does not follow that all of society is corrupt, nepotistic, and hypocritical. Thus, the Romantics make the error of universalizing their criticism to everything and end up criticizing things that are quite reasonable and sound. All distinctions get washed away in the Romantics' totalizing criticism.[10] This kind of indiscriminate criticism was never something that Socrates engaged in; on the contrary, at his trial he emphasizes that it is important to follow the laws and traditions of Athens, such as consulting the oracle. The Romantics do not criticize specific antiquated values and institutions in search of a deeper truth, but rather they do so only in order to celebrate and glorify the subjective ego itself.[11] Here Kierkegaard grants the correctness of Hegel's criticism of the

---

[8] Kierkegaard, *The Concept of Irony*, p. 275.   [9] Ibid.
[10] Ibid., p. 276.   [11] Ibid., p. 283.

Romantics: "We also perceive here that this irony was totally unjustified and that Hegel's hostile behavior toward it is entirely in order."[12]

One characteristic of the Romantic ironist is that he can, so to speak, invent himself anew at any given moment. If the truth of his personal history (like everything else) is wholly subjective, then he is free to change it whenever he wishes. There is nothing about his life or past that is substantial or binding. When we tell the story of our lives, we naturally attempt to put things in a positive light or to give things a particular spin in accordance with our interests in the present. Past events that may have seemed insignificant at the time take on a great importance when viewed in the context of the present. Likewise, other events of the past, which were quite important at the time, are forgotten if they seem to have no connection to the present. In this sense our past is not a static fact of the matter but rather to a large degree fluid. The Romantics take this to new heights by constantly telling new stories about their past based on whatever whim or mood happens to strike them. Since, they believe, there is no objective external reality, they are free to interpret things in the world and their past in any way that they please.

Kierkegaard thus points out that the Romantics were not interested in history *per se*, that is, in concrete sources and evidence for what actually happened. Instead, they were fascinated by legends, myths, and fairy tales.[13] Again, Kierkegaard acknowledges the correctness both of Hegel's understanding of the actuality of history and his criticism of Schlegel.[14] For Hegel, there is an objective meaning or *logos* in the development of human history that remains true regardless of differing interpretations. This is true not just of human history, but also of the life of an individual.

Kierkegaard refers to the Romantics' slogan of "living poetically" to capture the view of the ironist.[15] This might be taken to mean that a person has good taste for art and makes this a part of his lifestyle. But this is not the main thing that is meant here. Likewise, we need to be careful since this does not mean what we usually refer to as poetry. Instead, to be poetic in this sense means to write fiction or in this case to live as if one's life were a fiction. So living poetically refers to someone who is constantly able to make up his life anew at any

---

[12] Ibid., p. 275.   [13] Ibid., pp. 277f.
[14] Ibid., p. 278.   [15] Ibid., p. 280.

given moment, to create his life as if he were telling a fictional story. It means making up one's own life with artistic sensitivity in contrast to slavishly following the rules and conventions of society. The element of fiction is key here since it shows that the Romantic ironist is in no way bound to anything in actuality. There is no factual element of his existence that he recognizes as having any validity. Everything is a fiction that he can interpret and reinterpret as he pleases. Kierkegaard is critical of this view since he believes that there are certain irrevocable facts of existence, for example, that we are beings created by God. This is not something that we can choose to reinterpret at random. We are created beings and in this sense are dependent on God. This consequently presents a certain goal in life that Christians try to achieve. The Romantic ironist, however, recognizes no such objective facts or existence and no such goal beyond the finite ones that he himself posits.

5.4. Kierkegaard's Analysis of Schlegel

Kierkegaard goes on to examine in some detail Friedrich von Schlegel's (see Fig. 5.2) appropriation of Fichte's conception of the subject.[16] Kierkegaard follows Hegel in analyzing Schlegel's novel *Lucinde* as representative of Romantic views.[17] The novel traces the love of the young man Julius and his Lucinde. Schlegel's goal was to celebrate the free, passionate Romantic love of his fictional couple. True love can only be found in the unrestrained spontaneous ecstasy that is not governed by other concerns such as prudence, respectability, familial connections, or financial concerns. When the book appeared it was the source of some controversy since it was regarded as immoral and offensive to bourgeois values. Its allusions to the sexual relations of Julius with a variety of different women were considered scandalous by the standards of the day.

Julius is portrayed as someone who does not respect the rules of society. He speaks openly about seducing different women. But these

---

[16] Ibid., pp. 286–301.
[17] Friedrich Schlegel, *Lucinde. Ein Roman*, Berlin: Heinrich Fröhlich 1799. This work is available in English as *Friedrich Schlegel's Lucinde and the Fragments*, trans. by Peter Firchow, Minneapolis: University of Minnesota Press 1971.

Fig. 5.2. Friedrich von
Schlegel (1772–1829)

affairs leave him depressed and disillusioned. Only when he finds his
true love Lucinde is he redeemed. The novel is thus about showing
how Julius finds what might be called a "new immediacy," by discovering the true spontaneous spark of love in a mature relationship
with a woman whom he respects. Julius thus finds his place in the
world again after having lost it. He is saved despite his earlier sins.

Schlegel suggests that it is the rise of bourgeois society that stifles
true love. According to this view, there was an earlier period in
human history when men and women spontaneously came together
based on natural inclination. They were not motivated by things such
as increasing their fortune, securing heirs, or allying themselves with
rich or powerful families. Instead, their love for the other person was
their sole concern. Kierkegaard takes this picture to be somewhat
naïve and suggests the Romantic approach to history tended to
subordinate historic facts to contemporary ideology. Schlegel and
the Romantics pretend to want to reconstruct a past idyllic age, but
in fact this is a fiction that they have created.[18] There never was a time
when human motives were so pure, and it is difficult to imagine a
time when they will ever be so. Kierkegaard also points out that there
is a contradiction in Schlegel's approach. On the one hand, *Lucinde* is
supposed to celebrate a naïve, pristine conception of spontaneous,

[18] Kierkegaard, *The Concept of Irony*, pp. 288f.

immediate love. But, on the other hand, its criticisms of bourgeois morality are based on an elaborate and sophisticated social critique and thus are neither spontaneous nor immediate.[19]

However, the main criticism that Kierkegaard wants to level against Schlegel is that *Lucinde* is not just an attack on a specific idea or value, but rather an attempt to undermine *all* ethics.[20] The view presented is that all ethics and values inherited from traditional culture are ultimately arbitrary, and so the Romantic ironist is at his liberty to reject them and create his own. Moreover, the bourgeois ethics associated with love and marriage are even repressive and detrimental, and so the ironist sees himself as leading a campaign of liberation against this. But this absolute negativity is indiscriminate. Since it criticizes ethics in general, its critique is aimed not just at those elements of bourgeois ethics that are worthy of criticism, but also at those elements that are sound and true. In this sense Schlegel's criticism is unjustified.

We saw that Kierkegaard uses the phrase "living poetically" to describe the ironist, and in this section on Schlegel he explains in more depth what this entails. He writes, "If we ask what poetry is, we may say in general that it is victory over the world; it is through a negation of the imperfect actuality that poetry opens up a higher actuality."[21] To live poetically is to reject traditional customs and values and to posit one's own. In this way one "negates" the world of actuality, that is, the world of established custom. In addition, one creates a "higher actuality" for oneself, that is, one's own set of values.

According to Kierkegaard, Schlegel's attempt to undermine bourgeois ethics in the name of something higher is ultimately unsuccessful, since the ethics that the book *Lucinde* seems to advocate is one of sensual pleasure. While there may admittedly be problems with some aspects of bourgeois ethics, mere striving for the immediate pleasure of the senses can hardly be considered a higher ethical state. The ideological plea that motivates the work is one of freedom and the emancipation from the repression of society, but in exchange one gets instead a base slavery to the natural drives and the need to satisfy the senses. It is difficult to see this as a sublime form of freedom.[22]

---

[19] Ibid., p. 289.   [20] Ibid., p. 290.
[21] Ibid., p. 297.   [22] Ibid., p. 301.

It should be noted that while Kierkegaard was working on this material he was engaged to Regine Olsen, and one wonders to what degree his reading of Schlegel's views of love and bourgeois marriage played a role in his ultimately dissolving the engagement. In any case, this analysis was highly influential for Kierkegaard since he would come to treat the question of the pros and cons of marriage in a number of his later works. For example, in *Either/Or*, the book that he wrote immediately after *The Concept of Irony*, he uses elements from the character of the young Julius as a model for the unnamed author of the first part of the work, the aesthete, who defends the view of Romantic love, and for his picture of the seducer in "The Diary of a Seducer." He also creates the figure of Judge William as the author of the second part of the work. The judge, a married civil servant, defends the virtues of love within the institution of marriage in bourgeois society, and here Kierkegaard can be seen to incorporate elements of the view of the mature Julius. The book *Either/Or* is a dialogue between these two world-views, but the dialogue actually began in this second part of *The Concept of Irony*.

5.5. Kierkegaard and Poul Martin Møller

An important figure in the Danish Golden Age was Poul Martin Møller, who is often thought to have been one of Kierkegaard's great mentors. Møller was, among other things, a scholar of classical studies, who helped to inspire Kierkegaard's love of the ancient Greeks. It is quite possible that he encouraged Kierkegaard to write about the notion of irony in Socrates for his master's thesis. Møller lived in a building just on the other side of the Court House from Kierkegaard's family apartment.

Møller had been professor of philosophy in Norway from 1826 to 1830, before assuming a position at the University of Copenhagen, where he taught from 1831 until his death in 1838. Møller was Kierkegaard's professor, and there is some evidence that the two cultivated a friendship. Evidence of Møller's influence can be seen from the fact that in 1844 Kierkegaard dedicated *The Concept of Anxiety* to him. In that dedication Kierkegaard refers to Møller as, among other things, "the confidant of

Socrates."[23] Kierkegaard also wrote a very flattering passage about Møller in the *Concluding Unscientific Postscript*, in which he discusses Møller's critical relation to Hegelianism.[24]

Møller died in 1838, a couple of months before Kierkegaard's father. These deaths caused a great inner stirring in Kierkegaard. It is thought that Møller's death changed his attitude toward his own life. In the first years at the university Kierkegaard was more interested in the theater, literature, and expensive clothes than in studying theology. Since he came from a rich family, he was under no pressure to complete a degree to secure for himself a livelihood or profession. It was only after the death of Møller and Kierkegaard's father that he began to work seriously, and after a couple of years he finished his studies with *The Concept of Irony* in 1841.

At the time of his death Møller was himself in the process of developing ideas about irony. In his posthumously published works there is a draft of what seems to have been planned as a larger work on this subject. The draft bears the exact title of Kierkegaard's thesis, literally, "On the Concept of Irony." It discusses many of the aspects of irony that Kierkegaard treats in his work. Like Kierkegaard, he examines the theories of Hegel and Fichte and criticizes the Romantics' use of irony to attack modern bourgeois culture. He concludes that the irony of the Romantics "necessarily ends in an absence of all content, in a moral nihilism."[25] The similarities between his and Kierkegaard's work suggest Kierkegaard's master's thesis may have been conceived with Møller as a kind of advisor and then, after his death, completed so as to work out some of the insights that Møller was only beginning to develop.

In his *Journal DD* Kierkegaard recounts a conversation that he had with Møller on June 30, 1837, less than a year before Møller died.[26] The discussion concerned Socrates, and some of the key topics were

---

[23] Kierkegaard, *The Concept of Anxiety*, trans. by Reidar Thomte in collaboration with Albert B. Anderson, Princeton: Princeton University Press 1980, p. 5.

[24] Kierkegaard, *Concluding Unscientific Postscript*, vols 1–2, trans. by Howard V. Hong and Edna H. Hong, Princeton: Princeton University Press 1992, vol. 1, p. 34n.

[25] Poul Martin Møller, "Om Begrebet Ironie," in *Efterladte Skrifter*, ed. by Christian Winther, F. C. Olsen, Christen Thaarup, and L. V. Petersen, vols 1–6, Copenhagen: C. A. Reitzel 1848–50, vol. 3, pp. 152–8; p. 154.

[26] *Kierkegaard's Journals and Notebooks*, ed. by Niels Jørgen Cappelørn et al., vols 1–11, Princeton: Princeton University Press 2007ff., vol. 1, pp. 216–17, DD:18.

irony and humor. Moreover, the comparison was made between Socrates and Jesus. All of these are elements that reappeared in *The Concept of Irony* some four years later.

After Møller's wife died in 1834 at only 29 years of age, he became deeply interested in the question of immortality. In 1837 he published a long article on the recent discussions about immortality that were taking place in the German literature at the time.[27] In it he pointed out what he took to be a major feature in recent intellectual life: nihilism. He saw in German Romanticism and some trends in German philosophy a rejection of traditional Christian values and beliefs with nothing new to replace them. This ended up, according to Møller, as a denial of any meaning or enduring value. Møller was critical of this tendency and insisted that one needed to keep the Christian world-view intact. What Møller terms "nihilism" in the article is closely related to what Kierkegaard refers to as "irony." So there can be no doubt that Møller's critical confrontation with nihilism played a formative role for Kierkegaard in the development of *The Concept of Irony*.

5.6. Kierkegaard's Idea of Controlled Irony

The Concept of Irony concludes with a short chapter entitled "Irony as a Controlled Element, the Truth of Irony."[28] After the detailed analyses in the body of the work, this brief conclusion strikes the reader as almost perfunctory. In it Kierkegaard presents his own alternative to both Socratic irony and Romantic irony. Scholars argue about the meaning of this chapter since there are certain elements of it that can be read themselves as ironic. Thus, while Kierkegaard seems to be presenting the conclusions to the work, some interpreters think that at the same time he is pointing in a different direction.

Kierkegaard begins this chapter with an analysis of irony in the context of art, and he mentions a few authors who, in his opinion,

---

[27] Poul Martin Møller, "Tanker over Muligheden af Beviser for Menneskets Udødelighed, med Hensyn til den nyeste derhen hørende Literatur" ["Thoughts on the Possibility of Proofs of Human Immortality, with Reference to the Most Recent Literature Belonging Thereto"], *Maanedsskrift for Litteratur*, vol. 17, 1837, pp. 1–72, pp. 422–53.

[28] Kierkegaard, *The Concept of Irony*, pp. 324–9.

have made use of it correctly: Shakespeare, Goethe, and Johan Ludvig Heiberg. He claims that these poets are great because they have what he calls "a totality-view of the world."[29] By this he seems to mean that they have an overarching, consistent world-view that allows them to organize their art. In their poems they are able to organize and balance a large number of different elements. Kierkegaard praises them since they are able to use irony effectively as an individual aspect in their works. They are able to find the right time and place to insert individual instances of irony and to employ it to good effect. They are the masters of irony in the sense that they dictate exactly when it is to be used and construct situations where it is most appropriate. This stands in contrast to Romantic irony, which, as we have seen, is totalizing. The Romantics are not able to control irony as one technique among others, but instead they are in effect controlled or dominated by it as the single overriding element. Thus, Kierkegaard recommends what he calls "controlled irony," that is, the use of irony in specific, appropriate cases.

Kierkegaard then moves from the use of irony in art to the use of irony in life. Here he refers to his previous formulation of "living poetically."[30] He appears to suggest a kind of controlled irony that involves generally acknowledging the conventions and customs of one's society but not doing so uncritically. Irony is thus employed against those aspects of society that are deemed flawed but not against society as a whole. He writes,

> In our age there has been much talk about the importance of doubt for science and scholarship, but what doubt is to science, irony is to personal life. Just as scientists maintain that there is no true science without doubt, so it may be maintained with equal justice that no genuinely human life is possible without irony.[31]

This is presumably in part a reference to Martensen's claim that philosophy must begin with doubt with the slogan "*De omnibus dubitandum est.*" Kierkegaard seems to be saying that to be truly human we must all at some point pass through a phase of critical reflection, where we subject our inherited beliefs and practices to critical examination and reject those that are erroneous. He thus implicitly agrees with Socrates' claim that the unexamined life is not

---

[29] Kierkegaard, *The Concept of Irony*, p. 325.
[30] Ibid., p. 326.   [31] Ibid.

worth living, or, put differently, the unexamined life fails to develop fully the faculties that are unique to human beings. He concludes that irony is "the absolute beginning of personal life."[32] By using irony in a controlled manner, the individual can maintain a reflective critical distance on his culture and the established order of things without trying to destroy it and alienating himself from it in the way the Romantics do.

In one of the most important passages in all of Kierkegaard's writings, he connects this view of controlled irony with Christianity. He critically recalls the important scientific advances of the time and notes,

> knowledge not only about the secrets of the human race but even about the secrets of God is offered for sale at such a bargain price today that it all looks very dubious. In our joy over the achievement in our age, we have forgotten that an achievement is worthless if it is not made one's own.[33]

Here he implicitly recalls Socrates and the importance of subjective knowing. Kierkegaard's contemporaries claimed to have impressive knowledge about a number of different things. But this knowledge cannot be accepted at face value. Rather it must be examined by each individual and appropriated by each and every one of us on our own. What Kierkegaard here calls "the secrets of God" cannot be learned as a form of objective knowledge, but instead must be appropriated inwardly by each individual. This argument recurs in many of Kierkegaard's later works. Irony comes in when one wishes to criticize what Kierkegaard takes to be the mistaken view that we can know "the secrets of God" objectively. He believes that this view, widely held in his own day, is worthy of ironic criticism. Thus, irony has an important role to play in the modern world.

In a profoundly provocative passage Kierkegaard plays on the words of Jesus, who says in John chapter 14, verse 6, "I am the way, and the truth and the life." Kierkegaard modifies this and writes, "Irony as the negative is the way; it is not the truth but the way."[34] Here he emphasizes the negative aspect of irony, the aspect that he has argued for throughout the work in reference to Socrates. The implication seems to be that irony is an essential element for coming to Christianity. Irony is necessary to undermine the mistaken

---

[32] Ibid.   [33] Ibid., p. 327.   [34] Ibid.

conceptions of Christianity, which conceive of it as a positive, objective doctrine. Only when free of these misconceptions can one have
the proper relation to Christianity by means of inward appropriation.
Thus, irony as a negative force is not the truth itself but rather
prepares the individual to find the truth on one's own.

5.7. Kierkegaard's Defense and the Reception of the Work

Kierkegaard finished *The Concept of Irony* at the beginning of summer 1841, and he submitted it to the Faculty of Philosophy on June 3.
The dean of the Faculty was the Professor of Philosophy Frederik
Christian Sibbern, who had the task of putting together the committee to evaluate the work. He sent the manuscript to the classical
philologists Johan Nikolai Madvig, Frederik Christian Petersen,
Peter Oluf Brøndsted, the physicist and then rector of the University
of Copenhagen Hans Christian Ørsted, and finally, the young theologian, whom we have already discussed, Hans Lassen Martensen.
The committee was in agreement that the work was certainly
sufficient for the academic degree, but they had serious reservations
about its language and even suggested that it be reworked to eliminate
what they regarded as its stylistic excesses. They further complained
that it did not have the proper scholarly tone for an academic work
and that Kierkegaard's frequent witticisms were inappropriate in an
academic context. Ørsted writes in his report: "Despite the fact that
I certainly see in [*The Concept of Irony*] the expression of significant
intellectual strengths, I nevertheless cannot deny that it makes a
generally unpleasant impression on me, particularly because of two
things, both of which I detest: verbosity and affectation."[35]
On September 29, 1841 Kierkegaard publicly defended his thesis.
In accordance with tradition, the oral defense took place not in
Danish but in Latin. The official opponents or questioners at the
defense were Sibbern and Brøndsted. It was, as already noted, also
possible for people from the audience to ask questions, and in all
seven such unofficial opponents took the opportunity to do so. In the
official report about the event, Sibbern and Brøndsted praised

---

[35] *Encounters with Kierkegaard: A Life as Seen by His Contemporaries*, trans. and
ed. by Bruce H. Kirmmse, Princeton: Princeton University Press 1996, p. 32.

Kierkegaard for his ability to respond convincingly to the questions that were posed.[36]

After his defense Kierkegaard sent a copy of *The Concept of Irony* with a friendly letter to his former teacher of Latin and Greek from the School of Civic Virtue, Ernst Bojesen.[37] In 1840 Bojesen had received a new position at the Sorø Academy, and so he was no longer in Copenhagen. After receiving the book, Bojesen wrote a letter to his fellow philologist Johan Nikolai Madvig, whom he presumably knew was on Kierkegaard's examining committee, and asked him to thank Kierkegaard for him. The letter becomes the occasion for Bojesen to reflect on both the content of *The Concept of Irony* and Kierkegaard's character. He recalls a time, presumably the period while Kierkegaard was a student and was working on his thesis, "when like a modern Socrates, he ran around with everyone in the streets and alleys in order to chat with them or spread his good ideas."[38] It is clear from the account that Bojesen gives that this was a well-known aspect of Kierkegaard's personality and activity. The young Kierkegaard seemed to identify with Socrates and in some ways tried to imitate him.

Kierkegaard must have been relieved to have completed his degree. But, more importantly, *The Concept of Irony* had helped him to develop his own thinking about a number of key issues. As he now contemplated his future, it was inevitable that some of the themes that were important in the context of his master's thesis would be incorporated into both his coming works and his view of life.

5.8. Kierkegaard and Regine Olsen

While Kierkegaard was writing *The Concept of Irony* he had his famous courtship of the young Regine Olsen. He met the 15-year-old Regine in the fall of 1837 when visiting friends in Frederiksberg, at the time a suburb of Copenhagen.[39] Regine lived with her family

---

[36] *Søren Kierkegaards Skrifter*, vols 1–28, K1–K28, ed. by Niels Jørgen Cappelørn et al., Copenhagen: Gad Publishers 1997–2013, vol. K1, p. 144.

[37] *Kierkegaard: Letters and Documents*, trans. by Henrik Rosenmeier, Princeton: Princeton University Press 1978, Letter 48, p. 89.

[38] This letter is printed in the commentaries of *Søren Kierkegaards Skrifter*, vol. K28, pp. 355f, see p. 356.

[39] *Kierkegaard's Journals and Notebooks*, vol. 1, p. 47, AA:53 and AA:54.

Fig. 5.3. The Stock Exchange in Copenhagen

at Børsgade 66, in a house that was right behind the old Stock Exchange (see Fig. 5.3).

Apparently, Kierkegaard and Regine knew each other somewhat for about three years, and it was in August and September of 1840, when Kierkegaard was finishing his thesis, that their courtship reached its most important phase. On September 8, he saw Regine on the street and accompanied her to her home. There was no one else there, and he asked her to play the piano for him as she often did. After a short time, he closed the music book and said to Regine that this was not why he had come. He then in his own idiosyncratic way proposed marriage to her, which apparently took her by surprise. She immediately stood up and rushed him out the door without any response. Kierkegaard then went to her father, a high-ranking civil servant, and asked for her hand in marriage. Regine's father was also surprised, but said that he would go along with it if his daughter agreed. So two days later on September 10 Regine Olsen (see Fig. 5.4) gave her consent, and the two were engaged. This began an engagement that lasted almost a year.

Fig. 5.4. Regine Olsen
(1822–1904)

Shortly after the engagement was agreed to, the two met in the arched passageway behind the royal palace, next to the riding ring.[40] Regine reports that Kierkegaard seemed to have suddenly become distant and cold. She gradually came to understand that this was a part of the melancholy that ran in his family. But it did not deter her from wanting to be Kierkegaard's wife.

At some point, however, Kierkegaard began to have misgivings about the prospect of married life. By August of 1841, he decided that he could not go through with it. His reasons for this have been the source of endless speculation, and many different reasons have been cited that would explain his change of heart. On August 11, 1841 he broke off the engagement by returning the engagement ring to Regine. He wrote to her a farewell letter that, somewhat oddly, he later reprinted verbatim in his pseudonymous work *Stages on Life's Way*.[41]

---

[40] *Encounters with Kierkegaard*, p. 44.
[41] Kierkegaard, *Stages on Life's Way*, trans. by Howard V. Hong and Edna H. Hong, Princeton: Princeton University Press 1988, pp. 329–30: "In order not to keep on rehearsing what must nevertheless happen, what, when it has happened, will certainly provide the strength that is needed—let it then have happened. Above all, forget the one who writes this; forgive a man who, even if he was capable of

Regine was distraught and implored him not to break up with her. Her father invited him to their home and begged him to reconsider his decision, explaining how Regine was upset beyond consolation. Kierkegaard consented to try to console her, but he remained unmoved on the main issue of marrying her. Kierkegaard spoke with her, kissed her for the last time, and left, with Regine finally accepting the situation.

Copenhagen was not a large city at the time, and word of the broken engagement spread quickly. The issue was soon regarded as a public scandal. The Olsen family was outraged and felt publicly humiliated. Kierkegaard subsequently tried to cultivate a public image of being a scoundrel in order to take the blame himself and allow Regine to avoid feeling any wounded pride. The atmosphere in Copenhagen became unpleasant for him, and so he decided to take a trip to Berlin, the capital of Prussia. He departed on a boat on October 25, 1841.

5.9. The Modern Problem of Creating Oneself

Although its relevance is perhaps not immediately obvious, Kierkegaard's critical account of Schlegel and Romantic irony is highly important for us in modern times. The concept of "living poetically" refers to the way in which the Romantic ironist can free himself from the actuality of established society and create himself at will. He presents a public image of himself that demonstrates his ability to live according to his own premises, free from the constraints of bourgeois society. While the formulation "living poetically" might sound like something foreign and not immediately comprehensible, what is described here is not so different from something that is very common to our modern experience. All of us try in one way or another to present a public picture of ourselves that embodies the positive features and character traits that we value: we wish to be seen, for example, as interesting, intelligent, attractive, talented, and so forth.

something, was nevertheless incapable of making a girl happy." The original letter has not survived, but in his journals Kierkegaard writes, "But there had to be a break—I send her back her ring in a letter, which word for word is printed in the imaginary psychological construction" (*Stages on Life's Way*, Supplement, p. 661).

We tell stories about ourselves that highlight these features. Think of online social networking sites. On Facebook we are projecting a certain picture of ourselves to our friends and acquaintances. We are in a sense continually updating a kind of living autobiography.

But there is often a discrepancy between the image we present on Facebook and the totality of one's life, experiences, and personality. We all have certain character flaws that we try to hide or certain experiences that we are embarrassed about or ashamed of. These are not the kinds of things that we are keen to put on our Facebook page, but yet they still belong to who we are as individuals. So there arises a split between the public image that one wishes to cultivate and the true self, which presumably overlaps with the public image but also contains more, and much of which is less flattering.

Here we can see the outlines of Kierkegaard's criticism of the Romantics' view of living poetically. There are people who take the image projected by their Facebook page so seriously that it becomes real. They try to ignore the other parts of their personalities that do not fit with it. This is the problem of authenticity. The authentic person is true to him- or herself in the sense that they know perfectly well that they are projecting a fiction with their Facebook profile, and they are aware of and in touch with the less flattering aspects of their personalities. They are honest with themselves and recognize their flaws, regarding them as areas for improvement. But alas, not everyone is so honest. There are also people who are inauthentic in the sense that they believe a lie that they have told about themselves since it makes them look better in the public eye. They act as though their public image were the truth of their existence and fail to recognize any personal failings or shortcomings. While the Romantic can try to live poetically, and while the modern person can try to live like his public image, this is always in part a fiction that departs from who they really are. These examples illustrate that we intuitively believe that we have some kind of self that cannot be changed randomly simply by reinterpreting our lives or updating our Facebook page. There seem to be inescapable facts, good and bad, about our lives that we cannot authentically ignore.

This then returns us to the questions with which we started: What is that true self? What makes me who I am? Let us suppose I am as honest and authentic as possible, openly recognizing my shortcomings, my failures, my negative character traits, etc. Can I ever succeed completely? Can I ever gain absolute transparency about who I am? We all know people who are too hard on themselves, exaggerating the negative things about their persons and characters. Their self-image is just the opposite of the one we just discussed: rather than overemphasizing the positive, they overemphasize the negative. In the end, neither approach reflects the true self accurately. So given the possibility of self-deception, is it ever possible for us to come to an accurate view of ourselves? We have all experienced instances where other people had a clearer insight into our character or situation than we ourselves did. Other people can see certain things about us clearly from the outside where we might have a blind spot. But other people also have their own agenda and their own forms of self-deception, and so why should we privilege their views over our own?

Here we can see how complex this issue is. We instinctively believe that we are somehow unique and special. We want to believe that we can freely create ourselves in accordance with our interests and abilities. We want to say that there is something absolute and irreducible about our persons and characters, but as soon as we try to define what this is, problems arise. So with his criticism of Schlegel and Romantic irony, Kierkegaard confronts the modern reader with the question that is or should be important to all of us: Who am I?

6

The Conception of Kierkegaard's Socratic Task and the Beginning of the Authorship: 1843

The modern world makes many demands on us. Things are constantly changing, and we are obliged to adapt and learn new things in order to be able to live in this changing world. In a certain sense the modern world is coercive because it does not matter what I may happen to think of these changes since I am in one way or another inevitably obliged to go along with them if I am going to continue to be a participating member of society. But what should I do if certain social or political changes come along that I have serious problems or disagreements with? Should I feel obliged to go along with things that I do not agree to or that bother my moral conscience or ethical or religious convictions? There are some groups of people who feel alienated from certain aspects of their culture, and so they make an attempt to separate themselves from the mainstream and set up their own small society, ignoring the larger one around them as much as they can. This might seem like a good solution, but such groups often pay a high price for their separation and for cutting themselves off from the mainstream. They are forced to live a marginalized and alienated existence in their own society.

We have seen in Hegel's analysis of the role of Socrates in ancient Greece that traditional customary ethics is what governs society, but the key point is that the individual has the right to evaluate this with his or her own rationality and to assent to it or not. This is the right of conscience. Kierkegaard agreed with Hegel on this, and both of them viewed Socrates as a great revolutionary in his attempts to assert the rights of the individual. These are, however, not just issues of historical importance. Today we talk about things like civil courage, where individuals try to stand up for their beliefs in the face of a corrupt government or system. Journalists, political activists, and people of conscience today risk their lives, their reputations, and their livelihoods by speaking out publicly about the injustices that they see around them.

What should the rights of the individual be in such cases? Although Kierkegaard is generally known as a religious writer, his works also contain insightful considerations about issues of this sort concerning things such as politics and social theory. In this chapter we want to see how Kierkegaard, inspired by Socrates, explores some of these issues in the context of his first works after he completed his degree and set off on his career as an author.

6.1. Kierkegaard's Stay in Berlin

Kierkegaard stayed in Berlin from October 25, 1841 to March 6, 1842. While he was there he attended lectures at the university and began working on his next book. He rented a room at Jägerstrasse 57 just opposite Gendarmenmarkt.

The big event at the University of Berlin (see Fig. 6.1) was the recent appointment of the old philosopher Friedrich Wilhelm Joseph Schelling, who was the lone remaining survivor of the golden days of German idealism, with Fichte having died in 1814 and Hegel in 1831. Throughout the 1830s and at the beginning of the 1840s Hegel's students had a profound influence on intellectual life. The left Hegelians, which included figures such as Bruno Bauer, Friedrich Engels, Ludwig Feuerbach, Karl Marx, and David Friedrich Strauss, represented an alarming trend that was thought to undermine both religion and ethics, and so the King of Prussia was determined to do something about it. He decided to appoint Schelling in order to combat it. Although Schelling and Hegel had been close friends in their youth, their paths subsequently diverged to the point that there arose a polemic between them.

Schelling had been away from the public eye for many years, and so his appointment sparked considerable interest. Students and professors alike were keen to see what he would say about the Hegelians and

Fig. 6.1. The University of Berlin

what they would say in response. His lectures were overflowing with auditors and soon became the talk of the city; they were even reported on in the local newspapers. Kierkegaard attended these lectures, and he records his notes to them in his *Notebook 11*.[1] He was initially enthusiastic about Schelling, but in time grew tired of him and stopped taking notes altogether. In a letter to his brother from February of 1842 he writes, "Schelling talks the most insufferable nonsense," and adds, "I am too old to attend lectures, just as Schelling is too old to give them."[2] During the same time Kierkegaard also attended lectures by the Hegelian theologian Philipp Marheineke. He took quite detailed notes of Marheineke's lectures on Christian dogmatics in his *Notebook 9* and *Notebook 10*.[3] He also attended a course

---

[1] *Kierkegaard's Journals and Notebooks*, ed. by Niels Jørgen Cappelørn et al., vols 1–11, Princeton: Princeton University Press 2007ff., vol. 3, pp. 303–66, Not11:1–40.
[2] *Kierkegaard: Letters and Documents*, trans. by Henrik Rosenmeier, Princeton: Princeton University Press 1978, Letter 70, p. 141.
[3] *Kierkegaard's Journals and Notebooks*, vol. 3, pp. 243–73, Not9:1; pp. 285–98, Not10:8–9.

offered by the Hegelian logician Karl Werder, and took notes in the same notebooks.[4]

In addition to these academic pursuits, while he was in Berlin Kierkegaard attended the theater and contemplated what he wanted to do with his life. He had just completed his thesis on Socrates and irony, and this provided him with a model. He decided to develop a series of writings that would incorporate a number of Socratic elements, not least of all irony. He wanted to employ the same strategy as Socrates in order to undermine what he took to be the mistaken views of his own day.

In his work *The Point of View for My Work as an Author*, Kierkegaard gives an overview of all of his writings and explains his general authorial strategy. He says that his authorship began with *Either/Or*, that is, the work that he wrote after *The Concept of Irony*. In other words, he oddly does not count his master's thesis, *The Concept of Irony*, as a part of his authorship. In Kierkegaard studies this has often been interpreted to mean that Kierkegaard regarded his master's thesis as an immature early work, a piece of *juvenilia*, that does not need to be taken seriously. For this reason, Kierkegaard scholars have long focused on what have been regarded as his mature works, such as *Fear and Trembling* or the *Concluding Unscientific Postscript*, and have neglected *The Concept of Irony*. This is unfortunate, since this work is highly insightful for understanding what Kierkegaard regards as his official authorship.

Kierkegaard's decision to exclude *The Concept of Irony* from his authorship was made not because he believed it was an inferior work, but rather because it appeared *before* he hit upon his general idea for his authorship and thus was not a component of what he conceived of as his authorial strategy. It nonetheless is crucial for understanding his work since it in many ways serves as the basis for that strategy. So instead of being a part of the authorship proper, *The Concept of Irony* was a preparation for the authorship. But this means that its importance is increased rather than diminished since it provides an invaluable interpretive key to the rest of his writings.

[4] Ibid., vol. 3, p. 239, Not8:50; pp. 239f., Not8:52; pp. 274–8, Not9:2–9; p. 413, Not13:50.

6.2. The Debate about Mediation and the Conception of *Either/Or*

While he was in Berlin Kierkegaard began work on a new book, which was to become *Either/Or*. He conceived of this work in the midst of the critical discussions about Hegel's philosophy that were taking place in Berlin. In the second chapter we discussed the concept of *aporia* in Plato's dialogues, and in this context we noted that Hegel thought that it was a mistake for Socrates to stop with a negative result. Instead, the goal of philosophy was to see how the negative was necessarily related to the positive. Hegel believed that Socrates' negative method was important, but Socrates failed to take the important next step of constructing a positive philosophy. Hegel's Danish follower Hans Lassen Martensen thus encouraged his students to "go further than Socrates."

Hegel believed that philosophy was all about seeing the necessary organic relations between opposites. As we saw in the second chapter, being and nothingness are not two separate concepts, but rather each implies and presupposes the other. When a philosophy clings to just one side of such a dichotomy, it fails to grasp the wider truth. Hegel refers to such a one-sided approach as "dogmatism." In his book *The Encyclopedia of the Philosophical Sciences* he explains, "dogmatism consists in adhering to one-sided determinations of the understanding whilst excluding their opposites. This is just the strict 'either–or,' according to which (for instance) the world is *either* finite *or* infinite, but *not both*."[5] Here Hegel refers to the law of excluded middle, which states that either something is X or it is not. In other words, either the house is red or it is not, but it must be one of the two. Hegel makes a shorthand version of this by simply calling it the "either–or."

In Denmark in 1839 there was a debate about this point. The Bishop of Zealand, Jakob Peter Mynster, criticized Hegel, arguing that the law of excluded middle had been one of the cornerstones of logic (and common sense) ever since Aristotle, and it was absurd to deny it. In response, the Hegelian Martensen stated that key Christian dogmas such as the Incarnation or the Trinity could not be made sense of in terms of Aristotle's logic. According to this view, Jesus

[5] G. W. F. Hegel, *The Encyclopedia Logic. Part One of the Encyclopedia of the Philosophical Sciences*, trans. by T. F. Gerats, W. A. Suchting, and H. S. Harris, Indianapolis: Hackett 1991, § 32, Addition.

would have to be either God or human but not both. Martensen thus argued that some form of mediation must be presupposed if one wishes to maintain the Christian doctrine of the dual nature of Christ as both divine and human. He claims that Hegel's logic can account for this while Aristotle would have to reject it. Martensen writes, "The central point of Christianity—the doctrine of the incarnation, the doctrine of the God-man—shows precisely that Christian metaphysics cannot remain in an either/or, but that it must find the truth in a third which [the law of excluded middle] rules out."[6]

Kierkegaard followed this debate closely and seized upon the formulation "either/or" for the title of his new book. The work is divided into two parts by two authors. Part One is written by the anonymous A, the aesthete, and Part Two by B or Judge William. In the Preface of the work, the reader is told that the two texts were found by accident by Victor Eremita, who decided to publish them as editor. Kierkegaard attempts to depict two opposing world-views. He tries to develop a kind of dialogue between the aesthete, who makes a case for his carefree existence, and the judge, who argues for the virtues of a stable, predictable bourgeois life. But this dialogue reaches no positive conclusion. Kierkegaard does not come in at the end to say who won the debate. He simply presents the two positions to the readers as two important views of the age and then leaves it to them to decide for themselves which one they find more attractive. So with the work he presents an either/or and refuses to take the next step that Hegel demands by getting past the negation and constructing something positive. Kierkegaard's choice of the phrase "either/or" as a title is an invitation to embrace negation, opposition, and contradiction and resist the urge to resolve them. In this sense he is following in the path of Socrates. *Either/Or* can be seen as a kind of Socratic dialogue that ends in *aporia*.

Kierkegaard has the aesthete refer to this discussion about Hegel's logic at the beginning of the work in a short section entitled "Either/Or: An Ecstatic Discourse." The aesthete makes use of the law of excluded middle—a given thing must be either X or not X—and

[6] Hans Lassen Martensen, "Rationalism, Supernaturalism and the *principium exclusi medii*," in *Mynster's "Rationalism, Supernaturalism" and the Debate about Mediation*, ed. and trans. by Jon Stewart, Copenhagen: Museum Tusculanum Press 2009 (*Texts from Golden Age Denmark*, vol. 5), p. 130.

derives a number of different formulations, some of them seemingly absurd: "Marry, and you will regret it. Do not marry, and you will also regret it. Marry or do not marry, you will regret it either way."[7] Here the dichotomy is introduced: either marry or do not marry. According to Hegel's logic, these oppositions must be resolved or mediated. But Kierkegaard's aesthete insists on holding firmly to the opposition. With regard to Hegelian mediation, he writes, "But this is a misunderstanding, for the true eternity does not lie behind either/or but before it."[8] In other words, the truth appears not when the dichotomy or opposition is mediated and resolved (with the either/or behind it), but rather when one is confronted with the opposition. The resolution of such conceptual conundrums is possible in the realm of thought but cannot be achieved in life.

6.3. The Aesthete A as a Romantic Ironist: Diapsalmata

After he returned to Copenhagen Kierkegaard published *Either/Or* on February 20, 1843, two years after *The Concept of Irony*. Building on his previous analysis of German Romanticism, Kierkegaard now tries to create a literary character like that of the Romantic ironist in the figure of the aesthete. So one can say that in *The Concept of Irony* he gave a third-person description of the modern ironist, but then in *Either/Or* he moved to a first-person description from the perspective of the ironist himself. Moreover, *The Concept of Irony* was presented as an academic work and thus quotes extensively in German and Greek, whereas *Either/Or* was intended as a literary work, which allowed Kierkegaard a greater degree of compositional freedom.

The first volume of *Either/Or*, ostensibly written by the aesthete A, consists of a series of different texts, in which we can discern many traces of Kierkegaard's earlier analysis of Romantic irony from his previous work. For example, the final text in this first part is entitled "The Seducer's Diary," which tells the story of a certain Johannes who seduces the naïve young woman Cordelia. Johannes is presented as

---

[7] Kierkegaard, *Either/Or 1*, trans. by Howard V. Hong and Edna H. Hong, Princeton: Princeton University Press 1987, p. 38.

[8] Ibid., p. 39.

calculating and unfeeling. He seems to disregard all conventional ethics in order to satisfy his desires.

Many of the issues broached in *The Concept of Irony* in connection with the discussion of Schlegel's *Lucinde* are also incorporated into *Either/Or*. The discussion of love and marriage is taken up in Part Two of the work, authored by Judge William, the married civil servant. The judge attempts to make a case for marriage in opposition to the doctrine of Romantic love advocated by the aesthete.

But one of the clearest texts that illustrates the aesthete as a Romantic ironist is the first chapter of the book entitled the "Diapsalmata." This is a series of scattered aphorisms written and collected by the aesthete. The aphorisms initially seem unrelated to one another. They ramble from one topic to another with no clear organization or meaning. The aesthete appears to jot down whatever happens to pop into his mind after he has an experience or reads a text. When one reads these aphorisms, at first one has the impression that they are rather flippant and perhaps a bit confusing, but as one continues to read, the world-view and personality of the aesthete gradually begin to emerge. Let's take a few examples.

The aesthete writes, "I prefer to talk with children, for one may still dare to hope that they may become rational beings; but those who have already become that—good Lord!"[9] What does this tell us about the aesthete? Children may not yet be rational, but their naïve spontaneity is still preferable to the inauthenticity of adult culture. We have been taught to repress our feelings and to obey the rules. Adults develop different ways to hide their true feelings; they engage in strategies and intrigues in order to get what they want. But this undermines honest and open human relations and corrupts individuals. Children are mercifully free of this since it takes time to learn such things. Thus, the aesthete prefers to talk with children, who are still in touch with their own basic human feelings and emotions. They are true to themselves and do not try to dissemble who they are. To be sure, they have not yet developed their rational capacity and thus might be subject to temper tantrums occasionally, but even in this there is a certain authenticity and one knows exactly what a child wants and does not want. By contrast, with adults one is never certain since they often strategically hide who they really are and what their

---

[9] Ibid., p. 19.

true intentions might be. Although adults have developed their rationality, it is used in a negative way to plot and deceive others. By saying that he prefers to talk with children, the aesthete is thus offering an indictment against bourgeois culture, which corrupts people and destroys the true human spirit found in childhood.

In another aphorism, the aesthete exclaims, "I do not feel like doing anything,"[10] and he goes on to enumerate a string of different activities that he does not feel like doing, some of which are even the opposite of one another. What does this tell us about this person? The Romantic ironist is a nihilist, who does not believe that there is anything that has any intrinsic truth or value, and the absence of any external values that could be used to orient his life leaves him at the mercy of his personal and often arbitrary whims of the moment. We remember how the ironist exploited this in order to invent himself, so to speak. But the negative side of this disposition is that if nothing is true or valuable, then there is no reason to do anything. For the person who truly believes this, it would be very difficult to be motivated to do anything at all. This is the view of the aesthete, and it leaves him in a state of lethargy with no inclination to do anything at all.

In another aphorism, the aesthete claims, "The most ludicrous of all ludicrous things, it seems to me, is to be busy in the world, to be a man who is brisk at his meals and brisk at his work."[11] Here the aesthete criticizes the sense of importance that people invest in bourgeois life. They take themselves very seriously, and their work and activities become monumental labors of world-historical importance. From the perspective of the nihilist, nothing in bourgeois life has any deeper or lasting meaning. Seduced by the routine of daily life, people become unreflective and fail to see the wider perspective. Instead, they deceive themselves and try to conceive of their lives as profoundly important and meaningful. They do not see that they will die, and all of it will come to nothing. They could be struck by a falling roof tile and die on the spot. This example that the aesthete uses sounds absurd at first, but it underscores the fragility of life and human existence. It reminds us that however busy we are with our lives and daily activities, we should not lose sight of the ultimate questions. We become absurd and comic when we pretend that we

[10] Ibid., p. 20.   [11] Ibid., p. 25.

will live forever and when we invest our trivial pursuits and endeavors with great importance.

The voice of the nihilist comes out perhaps most clearly in the aphorism that begins, "How empty and meaningless life is."[12] The aesthete contemplates the death of a man. When we experience the death of another person, it is always an occasion to recall our own mortality, and we comfort ourselves that we still have some time left to live. But the aesthete suggests that this is little consolation in the big picture. Even a long human life is short on a larger cosmic scale. What is really won by living a few years longer? Moreover, the length of life does not invest it with any meaning. From this perspective even things that might seem important are in fact matters of indifference. Two aphorisms further down, he beckons, "Come, sleep and death; you promise nothing, you hold everything."[13]

In another aphorism, the contrast between childhood and adulthood is again thematized. The aesthete recalls that when he was young he did not laugh at things, presumably since he was only learning how the world worked. But then when he learned about life and society, he could only laugh at it. He gives a long list of things taken to be important by bourgeois society and claims that he now deems them worthy of laughter. He writes,

> I saw that the meaning of life was to make a living, its goal to become a councilor, that the rich delight of love was to acquire a well-to-do girl, that the blessedness of friendship was to help each other in financial difficulties, that wisdom was whatever the majority assumed it to be, that enthusiasm was to give a speech, that courage was to risk being fined ten dollars, that cordiality was to say "May it do you good" after a meal, that piety was to go to communion once a year. This I saw, and I laughed.[14]

In each case he enjoins his reader to posit a higher ideal. Love must be something more than just marrying a rich girl. Friendship must be something more than just loaning money to someone in need. Religious piety must be something more than just going to communion once a year. He does not elaborate on these things, but it is clear that he thinks that bourgeois culture makes a mockery of them. By means of these rich aphorisms Kierkegaard introduces his reader to

---

[12] Ibid., p. 29.   [13] Ibid., p. 30.   [14] Ibid., p. 34.

the character of the aesthete, who represents a large constellation of modern problems such as relativism, nihilism, and alienation.

In his *Journal JJ*, also from 1843, Kierkegaard looks back on *Either/ Or* and reflects on different aspects of it. In one entry entitled "My Judgment on *Either/Or*," which was apparently written before the work appeared, he refers to Socrates in an odd way: "There was a young man, happily gifted as an Alcibiades. He lost his way in the world. In his need he looked about for a Socrates but among his contemporaries found none. He then begged the gods to transform him himself into one."[15] It is difficult to avoid seeing in this remark an autobiographical reflection of some sort. Kierkegaard had from an early age been aware that he was a "gifted" young man, and this impression was no doubt strengthened after the successful completion of *The Concept of Irony*. But he was also regarded as something of an aesthete,[16] and the description of a young man who "lost his way in the world" might well have been an accurate portrayal of him, not least of all after his break-up with Regine and his trip to Berlin. In this sense he seems to identify with Alcibiades, the young man in Plato's *Symposium* who had intellectual talents but led a dissolute life. According to the journal entry, the young man sought someone who could guide him, just as Alcibiades sought a mentor in Socrates. But upon finding no one, Kierkegaard wished that he could himself become Socrates. Kierkegaard thus seems to have recognized in himself characteristics of both of these famous Greek figures, and he wished to overcome the side of his character that was like Alcibiades by becoming more like Socrates. This is important since it seems to confirm that it was around the time of the composition of *Either/Or* that Kierkegaard hit upon the idea of modeling his authorship and thought on Socrates.

6.4. The Immediate Reception of *Either/Or*

Today we know *Either/Or* as Kierkegaard's breakthrough work, but at the time, its reception was very mixed. It caused a stir in the

---

[15] *Kierkegaard's Journals and Notebooks*, vol. 2, p. 146, JJ:54.
[16] Kierkegaard's old teacher Ernst Bojesen states that many people regarded him as an "ingenious *Taugenichts*" or a good-for-nothing. See *Søren Kierkegaards Skrifter*, vols 1–28, K1–K28, ed. by Niels Jørgen Cappelørn et al., Copenhagen: Gad Publishers 1997–2013, vol. K28, p. 355.

intellectual circles of the Danish Golden Age. People were intrigued by the odd pseudonym Victor Eremita, and they saw in the book something very original. But the work was also offensive to some people. Part One, that is, the part written by the aesthete, seemed to many to display a tone of arrogant superiority that some people also saw in Kierkegaard's own personality. The aesthete seems to take himself to be more intelligent than his fellow citizens and to place himself beyond the sphere of bourgeois ethics. Especially "The Diary of the Seducer" from the first part of the work offended the sensibilities of the contemporary reader. Johannes the seducer's cynical, manipulative behavior made for uncomfortable reading, and one asked what kind of a mind could have produced such a figure.

The leading literary critic of the day, Johan Ludvig Heiberg, gave a short review of the work in his journal *Intelligensblade* on March 1, 1843. Heiberg seems to have been rather annoyed after reading Kierkegaard's book, which he regarded as poorly organized and rambling. His review is thus largely dismissive of Kierkegaard's effort. He begins by making fun of the length of the work, by writing,

> It is therefore almost with respect to its volume that the book must be called a monster, for it is impressive in its size even before one yet knows what spirit lives in it, and I do not doubt that if the author wanted to let it be exhibited for money, he would take in just as much as by letting it be read for money.[17]

While he grants that the book contains some occasional interesting reflections or formulations, he concludes that it is confusing and difficult to follow. Moreover, he claims, the text is somewhat long-winded, and the reader wants to move ahead more quickly than the author. Heiberg imagines a reader who, after having finished Part One, loses patience and closes the book with the words, "Enough! I have enough of *Either*, and I'll have no *Or*."[18]

Kierkegaard was deeply offended by the review and never forgave Heiberg. Still under the pseudonym Victor Eremita, he responded with an article in the newspaper *The Fatherland* dated March 5, 1843, entitled, "A Word of Thanks to Professor Heiberg." He takes the same approach as Socrates does with his interlocutors. He begins

---

[17] Johan Ludvig Heiberg, "Litterær Vintersæd," *Intelligensblade*, vol. 2, no. 24, March 1, 1843, p. 288.
[18] Ibid., p. 291.

by acknowledging Heiberg's expertise in literary affairs, just as Socrates ironically acknowledges the expertise of his interlocutors. Kierkegaard then goes on to mock satirically different passages from Heiberg's review. Heiberg casts his review in terms of the experience of an imaginary reader, whom he refers to with the impersonal pronoun "one." Kierkegaard humorously seizes on this and constantly refers to "one's" views of the work. At the end Kierkegaard exuberantly thanks Heiberg for his insightful review, doing so with such enthusiasm that there can be no doubt about the sarcasm. He has Victor Eremita write, "For all this I thank you, Professor! I rejoice that learning is so swiftly imitated. I thank you for wanting to communicate it so quickly. If I were to choose the person in literature whom I would thank first of all, I would choose you, Professor!"[19] This ironic expression of gratitude can be seen to mirror Socrates' more reserved sarcasm when he claims, for example, to want to learn from Euthyphro and to want to become his student.

The natural reaction of most writers who suffer a negative book review is to respond by trying to point out the things that the book does well and thus to try to refute the criticisms that have been raised against it. But Kierkegaard does not try to defend the merits of his work in any positive way. Instead, his approach is negative just like that of Socrates. He seems on the face of it to grant the truth of Heiberg's claims and then indirectly and ironically to undermine them.

6.5. The Next Works in Kierkegaard's Authorship

With *Either/Or* Kierkegaard began a remarkably productive period of writing. Only eight months after the publication of the work, three new books appeared on the same day, October 16, 1843. These works were *Three Upbuilding Discourses*, which appeared in Kierkegaard's own name, *Repetition*, written by the pseudonymous author Constantin Constantius, and *Fear and Trembling* by Johannes de silentio.

---

[19] Kierkegaard, "A Word of Thanks to Professor Heiberg," in *The Corsair Affair and Articles Related to the Writings*, trans. by Howard V. Hong and Edna H. Hong, Princeton: Princeton University Press 1982, p. 20.

Three Upbuilding Discourses was the first of a series of collections of edifying works that Kierkegaard published between 1843 and 1844. In each of these years, he produced individual collections of two, three, and four upbuilding discourses, respectively. These were then later collected by the publisher P. G. Philipsen and published under the title of *Eighteen Upbuilding Discourses* in 1845. After this was sold out, a similar collection was published as *Sixteen Upbuilding Discourses* in 1852. These texts are generally regarded as some of the key works of Kierkegaard as a Christian author. They were published under Kierkegaard's name and not attributed to pseudonymous authors. They are, moreover, intended to be more popular works than the pseudonymous writings. They address the common religious believer without any sophisticated or complex argumentation; there is no direct reference to Greek or German philosophers by name, but Socrates is nonetheless present and referred to as "the wise man of old."

Kierkegaard returned to Berlin for a short stay in May 1843, and this provided him with the inspiration for the short book *Repetition*. This novella is the story of a young man who asks the question of whether or not repetition is possible. Like Kierkegaard, the protagonist had been in Berlin before, and he hits upon the idea of making a return trip to see if he can repeat his experience. He returns to the Prussian capital and tries to visit the old places that he went to during his first visit. But he finds that many things have changed in the interim, and it is impossible to recreate his original experience. Not only has the city itself changed, but also he has changed, and so the way in which he experiences the city is also different. His conclusion from this experiment is that no true repetition is really possible since things are always changing.

The concept of repetition is an important idea for Kierkegaard. He speaks of repetition in the sense of appropriation. There are, for example, a number of abstract ethical principles that the individual must appropriate in terms of his or her particular situation. When one appropriates these rules in concrete action one is in a sense repeating the original rule. If there were no element of repetition here, then one could not be said to be following the rule. In this sense Kierkegaard explores the concept in the context of ethics.

The third work that appeared on the same day, *Fear and Trembling*, is one of Kierkegaard's best-known books. Its central motif is the Old Testament story of God's command to Abraham that he sacrifice his son Isaac. The work is divided into three chapters called "Problemata" or "Problems," which refer to the problems raised by Abraham's reaction to the command of God. In this work Kierkegaard, through his pseudonymous author, focuses on the difficult demands of faith, using Abraham as his example. Although Abraham's situation is quite special, since it is not every day that people are asked by God to sacrifice their sons, scholars have often taken his analysis here to be presenting an example of the difficulties involved in Christian faith.

6.6. The Universal and the Single Individual

The first of the three Problemata in *Fear and Trembling* raises the question: "Is there a teleological suspension of the ethical?" The chapter begins with a contrast between the universal and the single individual. Kierkegaard refers explicitly to a section of Hegel's book *The Philosophy of Right*, which is a work on ethics and political philosophy that was published in 1821. We saw earlier that Hegel was interested in exploring what he called the ethical life of a people, for example, the ancient Greeks. This was the large sphere of interconnected elements of the public social order: ethics, law, traditional customs, religious practices, and so forth. This conception of ethics is what Kierkegaard associates with the universal. It is universal since it is something that everyone knows and participates in intuitively. Ethical duties are defined as cultural norms. According to this view, we know what our ethical duties are simply by looking at what the traditions of our society tell us. In this sense ethics is by definition what established custom dictates.

For someone who defends this view, the great sin is to act in contradiction to the universally accepted ethics. When one acts for one's own selfish interests and disregards the universal duties that bind one, then one acts unethically. The individual's needs and desires are always subordinate to the demands of his or her culture. If I steal, it is because I value my own desires more than the requirements of my culture, and so the result is both immoral and illegal. To put it in philosophical language, if I commit such a crime, I put the individual (my personal desire) above the universal (society, law, custom). This seems entirely uncontroversial.

But Kierkegaard introduces an example that makes this picture more complex. He tries to understand the meaning and implications of the story of Abraham and Isaac in Genesis, chapter 22. Isaac is Abraham's only son, who is apparently destined to be the next great patriarch to lead the people. But God commands Abraham to sacrifice him on Mount Moriah. Needless to say, this was presumably extremely vexing to Abraham since this meant not only killing his beloved son, but also ending his family line. But Abraham, intending to obey God, takes Isaac with him to Mount Moriah, where he prepares everything for the sacrifice. At the crucial moment when it is time for him to actually kill Isaac, an angel appears and stops him, and provides a ram for him to sacrifice instead.

Kierkegaard points out that this story raises questions for the conception of ethics that we just discussed. According to the universal ethics, it is wrong and illegal to murder someone, not to mention for fathers to kill their own sons. So Abraham is acting in a way that is ethically wrong, when seen from this perspective. It is as if he, as an individual, is willfully ignoring the universal ethics of the community. But Abraham has received a revelation from God that requires him to put aside in this one instance the usual rules, practices, and traditions that govern the ethics of his people. This is what Kierkegaard means by the phrase "the suspension of the ethical." In order to fulfill God's command, Abraham must *suspend* ethics and act, as it were, on the basis of something higher. This is called a "teleological" suspension, since ethics are suspended for a higher *telos* or end.[20] Our intuitions seem in a sense to be split here since, on the one hand, we want to say along with Hegel that it is wrong to kill innocents and there is nothing higher than this universal, but then, on the other hand, we also want to say that one should obey the command of God. But what if these two are in contradiction with one another as they are here?

Kierkegaard points out that on Hegel's point of view we would have to regard Abraham as a murderer, but there seems something not quite right about this since we want to see Abraham as a faithful and pious man merely obeying the will of God. But according to the view of universal ethics, there is nothing higher than the universal, and thus the idea of a divine revelation being a reason to suspend the ethical cannot be recognized. This tension is the key interpretative

---

[20] Kierkegaard, *Fear and Trembling*, trans. by Howard V. Hong and Edna H. Hong, Princeton: Princeton University Press 1983, p. 59.

point in the text. It seems that Kierkegaard, via his pseudonymous author, wants to defend the view that there can be a suspension of the ethical in cases like this. It appears that he wants to criticize the universal view of ethics as being too narrow, since it fails to take into account exceptions to the rules. But what is interesting about the text is that he does not make this argument directly.

He does not try to enumerate reasons for why Abraham is justified in doing what he is doing. On the contrary, he says flatly that this cannot be done. The third Problema is dedicated to an analysis of Abraham's silence, and Kierkegaard concludes that Abraham has no choice but to keep silent about the motivations for his action. It would be wrong if he were to try to convince people that he was acting justly since he was merely fulfilling God's command. He cannot attempt to make arguments of this kind since it all boils down to a matter of faith, and faith is something private. Faith concerns the single individual, but language consists of universals. So if Abraham were to try to articulate his faith verbally, he would inevitably end up describing it with universals.[21] His description would thus be a distortion of what he wants to express. Abraham cannot convey to anyone else his own private faith. This is something that is non-discursive and ineffable. Thus, Abraham must simply carry out the action and keep silent about it. He knows full well that he must accept the consequences if he were to be caught and prosecuted, but his individual and incommunicable faith is more important than the consequences that can result from his defiance of universal laws and duties.

6.7. The Paradox of Faith

The conclusion that Kierkegaard seems to want to draw from his analysis in *Fear and Trembling* is less about ethics or political philosophy and more about religious faith. Indeed, throughout the work he talks about a knight of faith, modeled on Abraham. Although the story of Abraham and Isaac is of course one that belongs to Judaism and the Old Testament, scholars have generally taken Abraham's

---

[21] Ibid., p. 60.

obedience to God also to be a model for Christian faith that Kierkegaard wants to recommend.

So what does Kierkegaard say about faith in this context? In a famous line, he writes, "Faith is namely this paradox that the single individual is higher than the universal."[22] This is a sentence that scholars have argued about extensively. His point seems to be that there are instances, like that of Abraham, where the individual takes precedence over the universal, that is, accepted customs and universal ethics. Or, put differently, not all actions based on one's own individuality and at the expense of the universal ethics should be summarily dismissed as evil.

The key thing to note is the way in which Kierkegaard puts this point. As we know, Christian apologetics is the branch of theology that attempts to defend the doctrines of Christianity. It tries to offer arguments and good reasons for believing in things such as the incarnation, the ascension, the virgin birth, and so forth. The goal of Christian apologetics is to convince skeptics or nonbelievers of the truth of the Christian faith. But note that Kierkegaard's approach is entirely different from this: he says not that faith is reasonable or comprehensible, but instead that it is a paradox that cannot be grasped discursively. He says that Abraham acts "by virtue of the absurd."[23] This is not a recommendation for faith or an argument to convince skeptics. If a skeptic were to demand a solid reason for thinking that Abraham received a revelation from God, and our response was that Abraham believed by virtue of the absurd, this would not go very far to convince anyone. To say that something is absurd is usually to discount it and cannot be construed as a positive argument for a position.

Understanding faith as a paradox is what has been called a "negative concept," that is, a concept that does not have concrete, positive content, but rather leaves things open. By proposing the concept of faith as a paradox, Kierkegaard does not resolve the problem about faith, but rather he problematizes the issue and in effect invites us, his readers, to continue to explore it on our own. Here we can see the spirit of Socrates once again in Kierkegaard's text. Socrates claims to be ignorant, and therefore he does not present any positive doctrine. Instead, he merely criticizes the views of others and reduces them to

---

[22] Ibid., p. 55.   [23] Ibid., p. 56.

contradiction and absurdity. In a sense Kierkegaard is doing the same thing here. He claims that faith is not something positive or concrete, but rather it is a paradox, a contradiction. Like Socrates' approach, this is negative. Nothing is really resolved, but rather the issue is left open as a problem.

6.8. The Modern Conflict of Law and Conscience

Readers of Kierkegaard today are often perplexed and even amused by his theory of faith as a contradiction or a paradox. How is this somewhat odd theory of faith relevant for us in the modern world today? At bottom, the issue in *Fear and Trembling* is the relation of religious faith to the secular world with its laws, customs, and traditions. Abraham is a great model of piety and religious faith, but his actions potentially lead him into conflict with the laws of his people. One might think that this is just an old story that now has no relevance, since no one would think of making human sacrifices today. But when one considers the matter further, one quickly realizes that in fact this is a central and unresolved issue of our own time.

Most countries in Europe and the West legally guarantee the religious freedom of their citizens. This is a part of the Western heritage from the Enlightenment. There are laws intended to ensure that each individual has the right to pursue their religious practice without harassment or impediment, regardless of how unpopular those practices might be. But things are not always so simple since there are always limits to this. These limits to religious freedom appear at the moment that religious practices come into contradiction with civil law. If my religion dictated that I murder people, for example, as human sacrifices, then the state obviously could not allow this. There are less dramatic examples of this conflict in cases, for example, where a religion requires its followers to take certain hallucinogenic drugs in connection with their religious rites, but these substances may be illegal. Or some religions sanction polygamy, which is not allowed by the state. Examples of this kind demonstrate that while religious freedom is a basic right, it is not unlimited. Rather, it must be exercised in a way that is consistent with civil law.

Kierkegaard's view, or that of his pseudonymous author Johannes de silentio, raises difficult problems for this picture. His troubling claim is that there can be cases where the individual is higher than the universal, where there can be a suspension of the generally accepted ethical and legal norms of the state and the society. Most scholars have understood Kierkegaard as suggesting that Abraham's action to sacrifice his son is not only acceptable but even praiseworthy from a religious perspective, despite being unacceptable from a civil perspective. According to this view, Kierkegaard's message is that when one has a firm religious conviction or when one receives a revelation from God to do something, this is an absolute command that trumps ethics and civil law. One must simply follow this obediently.

But this view might seem to lead to dangerous consequences. One often hears of criminals who in their defense claim that God told them to do what they did. Many terrorists also believe they are fulfilling the will of God with their actions. In such cases most of us are disinclined to accept this as a reason for the murder of innocent people. Does Kierkegaard's analysis of Abraham open the door for this kind of thing? If he were alive today, would Kierkegaard defend the actions of terrorists as great acts of piety? If we look more closely, we can see that there are important elements in Kierkegaard's analysis that separate him from the modern murderer or terrorist. Perhaps most importantly, Kierkegaard emphasizes the paradoxical nature of faith: it is something that is contradictory and absurd. Moreover, faith is something entirely inward and cannot be communicated directly to another person. For this reason Abraham remains silent. By contrast, the modern murderer or terrorist tries to use the religious motivation for his actions as an argument in defense of it. In other words, the murderer says that God told him to kill someone, and the point of this is to explain the action and to defend it. But from Kierkegaard's perspective this would be a misunderstanding. One can never use the idea that one received a revelation from God or is acting on God's will as a defense of one's actions. It is true that one might believe this in the quiet of one's mind or, as Kierkegaard says, in one's inward-ness, but the moment one tries to communicate it, one shows that one does not understand the nature of faith. He claims that faith is not objective, discursive, or communicable in this way. This is a fundamental difference between Kierkegaard's view and that of the murderer or terrorist, who seeks to explain, justify, and defend his actions based on reasons, arguments, and discursive communication.

Kierkegaard's account of Abraham is also different from the arguments of terrorists in another important respect. Terrorists tend to have a political agenda of some sort, claiming that the existing political order is corrupt or unjust, and this argument is used to justify their actions. They claim that they are in fact working toward a better world or a more just society, but that certain sacrifices must be made in order to realize this. But this is very different from the picture of Abraham that Kierkegaard portrays. Abraham's goal must be independent of all human interests and advantages. He is not sacrificing Isaac for the sake of improving society. Kierkegaard makes this point explicitly by contrasting Abraham with other famous cases, where people have been called on to sacrifice their children for some higher good of the state, such as Agamemnon's sacrifice of his daughter Iphigenia for the sake of launching the Greek expedition against Troy. There are no utilitarian considerations in the action of Kierkegaard's Abraham, and on this point as well, this case differs from that of the modern terrorist. By sacrificing his son, Abraham is certainly not hoping to achieve some concrete goal such as starting a military expedition or improving society. His action does not serve any higher end, but is performed simply to obey God's command. So while it might look at face value as if Kierkegaard is offering a theory that might justify illegal and immoral acts and atrocities, a closer look shows that this is not the case. No justification or defense can be sought from the side of religious faith.

All of this raises topical questions about the limits of religious freedom. Where exactly is the line where religious freedom stops and civil law begins? Can or should civil law make exceptions to accommodate certain religious practices or should it lay down a consistent position that everyone in a society is obliged to follow? Is religious faith compromised or convoluted if it is obliged to bend to the rules of mainstream society? Does civil law discriminate against certain minority religions in society? These are all very important issues in our own day. It is thus a great mistake to believe that the question of religious freedom was resolved once and for all with the Enlightenment. Instead, with the granting of religious freedom a new set of issues and problems was ushered in.

7

Kierkegaard's Socratic Task and the Development of the Pseudonymous Works: 1844–6

The years 1844 to 1846 were perhaps the most productive in Kierkegaard's entire life. In this chapter we want to explore the series of famous works that he penned during this time, among others, the *Philosophical Fragments*, *The Concept of Anxiety*, *Prefaces*, *Stages on Life's Way*, and the *Concluding Unscientific Postscript*. These books present a complex series of works ostensibly authored by different pseudonyms, each with his own agenda and intentions. At first glance, this might all look very confusing, but in this chapter we will try to make sense of Kierkegaard's plan with these works and their complex relations to one another.

While Socrates is never again made the central object of investigation as he was in Kierkegaard's master's thesis, he nonetheless haunts these later works in ways that are often not easy to see. This is particularly interesting when we consider that these works treat important Christian concepts such as the incarnation, the revelation, faith, sin, and forgiveness. Many people might think that it is outrageous to believe that a pagan philosopher can help to understand these Christian concepts. Here we can catch a glimpse of the radicality of Kierkegaard's thought. He believes that Socrates has some important insights for Christians today. In one text, Kierkegaard acknowledges the objection, saying, "True, [Socrates] was no Christian, that I know." But then he goes on to make the highly provocative and indeed enigmatic statement, but "I also definitely remain convinced that he has become one."[1] So

---

[1] Kierkegaard, *The Point of View*, trans. by Howard V. Hong and Edna H. Hong, Princeton: Princeton University Press 1998, p. 54.

although Socrates was born and died centuries before Christ and the birth of Christianity, nonetheless Kierkegaard believes that Socrates became a Christian. What could he possibly mean by this?

7.1. Kierkegaard's *Philosophical Fragments*

Kierkegaard continued with his remarkable productivity and published *Philosophical Fragments or a Fragment of Philosophy* on June 13, 1844. It was published under the pseudonym Johannes Climacus, although his own name appears on the title page as the editor. The title of the work as "fragments" is often taken as a protest again systematic philosophy.

Socrates plays an important role, especially at the beginning of this work, where Kierkegaard has his pseudonymous author explore Socrates' role as a teacher. This might strike us at first sight as inconsistent with what he said earlier about Socrates' insistence on his own ignorance and his denial that he ever taught anything. But there is no inconsistency here, and Johannes Climacus emphasizes that in contrast to the philosophy and theology of the nineteenth century, which was focused on constructing things and on positive content, "Socrates lacked the positive."[2] What, then, does Climacus mean here by designating Socrates as a teacher, since usually teachers are thought to convey certain material, or, in Kierkegaard's language, something positive? Here Climacus makes reference to Socrates' art of maieutics or midwifery. Socrates does not produce the ideas or thoughts in the student, but rather helps the student to find them within himself. So in this sense Socrates is a teacher since he is the occasion for the student to arrive at the truth, but Socrates does not teach him the truth.

Philosophical Fragments is about the doctrine of the incarnation and revelation of Jesus Christ, but Kierkegaard is careful not to mention Jesus by name or to cast the analysis explicitly in terms of Christianity. He talks about merely "the god" in a way that could pertain to any revealed religion. Kierkegaard contrasts Socrates' role as midwife with the role of Christ as a savior, who is also the occasion

---

[2] Kierkegaard, *Philosophical Fragments*, trans. by Howard V. Hong and Edna H. Hong, Princeton: Princeton University Press 1985, p. 23.

for his followers to learn the truth. While Socrates is obviously not Christian, his idea of midwifery can be used to help us understand the Christian truth.

Kierkegaard also uses Socrates to introduce the notion of the absolute paradox. He begins Chapter 3 of the work by recounting a passage from Plato's dialogue the *Phaedrus*, where Socrates says that he was not interested in exploring the nature of mythological creatures such as "Pegasus and the Gorgons" because he was primarily concerned with discovering what he himself was as a human being. He claims to be ignorant of his own nature and wonders whether he might not be a monster like Typhon.[3] Kierkegaard has Johannes Climacus note that it is paradoxical "to want to discover something that thought itself cannot think."[4] For Socrates, this means apparently understanding what he is ultimately as a human being, which he can never quite grasp.

Human understanding learns new things by recognizing those aspects of them which are already familiar. It is thus unable to grasp something that lacks such familiar aspects and is absolutely different. Climacus suggests that we call the unknown "the god."[5] The analysis then subtly shifts over into a Christian context, although again this is not stated explicitly. The unspoken issue is the Christian doctrine of incarnation, according to which God became incarnated as a human being, Jesus Christ, in order to reveal himself. According to Johannes Climacus, this too involves a paradox. God is infinite and eternal, but became finite and temporal with the incarnation. Climacus calls this the absolute paradox. This contradiction is not something that the human mind can grasp or think, but it is something it must accept.

Kierkegaard's view here is a response to the idea of mediation that was found in the works of Hegelians such as Martensen. According to the Hegelian view, there are no absolute dichotomies or contradictions, and everything can be mediated. So, as we have seen, according to Martensen, there is no absolute difference between human and divine or between finite and infinite, temporal and eternal. Each is

---

[3] Ibid., p. 37. See also *Kierkegaard's Journals and Notebooks*, ed. by Niels Jørgen Cappelørn et al., vols 1–11, Princeton: Princeton University Press 2007ff., vol. 3, p. 393, Not13:28: "Socrates is supposed to have said that he doesn't know if he is a human being or an even more variable animal than Typhon (cf. Plato's *Phaedrus*)." Kierkegaard refers to Plato's *Phaedrus*, 230a.

[4] Kierkegaard, *Philosophical Fragments*, p. 37.   [5] Ibid., p. 39.

necessarily related to the other and thus mediated by it. Jointly they form a higher conceptual structure since they must be regarded as belonging together organically. When one understands the terms in this way, it is possible to give a philosophical explanation of the incarnation and the revelation of Christ. According to Hegel's speculative logic, there is no contradiction in thinking that God, as the infinite, became finite. It was this explanation that Kierkegaard objected to. With the doctrine of the absolute paradox, he clearly wants to insist that the revelation is an irreducible contradiction, an either/or that cannot be mediated. He uses Socrates as an example of someone who realizes there are some things that he cannot know or understand and accepts that there are some things that must be regarded as paradoxes.

7.2. Kierkegaard's *The Concept of Anxiety*

On June 17, 1844 Kierkegaard published *The Concept of Anxiety* under the pseudonym Vigilius Haufniensis or the "Watchman of Copenhagen." This work appeared only four days after *Philosophical Fragments* and on the same day as another book entitled *Prefaces*. *The Concept of Anxiety* is one of Kierkegaard's most scholarly works. It treats the complex set of issues concerning the freedom of the individual and hereditary sin. It is in this context that his influential analysis of anxiety appears. It seems odd, then, that in a work about the Christian dogma of sin the pagan philosopher Socrates would play a role. But once again it is clear that Kierkegaard is constantly looking to Socrates as a model and source of inspiration.

Socrates is mentioned at the very beginning of the work in the opening motto that follows the title page. He is compared positively to modern philosophy. The motto begins, "The age of making distinctions is past. It has been vanquished by the system."[6] This refers to the Hegelian doctrine of mediation that, as we have seen, brings together opposites or, as is implied here, eliminates distinctions. For Kierkegaard, by contrast, the key is to keep the oppositions and the contradictions in focus and not to mediate them. We saw that his

---

[6] Kierkegaard, *The Concept of Anxiety*, trans. by Reidar Thomte in collaboration with Albert B. Anderson, Princeton: Princeton University Press 1980, p. 3.

slogan "either/or" emphasizes that one is obliged to take one side or another, and no mediation is possible. Now here in the motto to *The Concept of Anxiety*, Socrates is invoked as someone who, like Kierkegaard, insisted on distinctions. The motto further acknowledges that this might seem somewhat eccentric in modern times, now that people are used to Hegel's philosophy. Kierkegaard quotes the German philosopher Johann Georg Hamann, who was also a great admirer of Socrates. Hamann writes, "For Socrates was great in 'that he distinguished between what he understood and what he did not understand.'"[7] By using this as the motto of the work, Kierkegaard indicates that he intends to follow the lead of Socrates and insist on unshakeable distinctions that resist mediation.

Kierkegaard dedicated *The Concept of Anxiety* to his old teacher Poul Martin Møller, who had died in 1838. As noted earlier, the dedication refers to Møller as "the confidant of Socrates."[8] This seems to confirm the idea that we discussed earlier, namely, that Møller's interest in Socrates and Socratic irony played an important role in Kierkegaard's intellectual development and might well have served as a part of the inspiration for his book, *The Concept of Irony*.

In the Introduction to *The Concept of Anxiety* Kierkegaard mentions Socrates when he presents the topic of the work: the concept of sin. He begins by claiming, "Sin does not properly belong in any academic field, but it is the subject of the sermon, in which the single individual speaks as the single individual to the single individual."[9] This assertion may strike theologians as odd, since traditionally the dogma of sin has been addressed by the scholarly field of theology and specifically dogmatics. Here at the outset Kierkegaard has his pseudonymous author indicate that his approach and understanding of sin will be something very different, indeed, something at odds with a scholarly account.

Usually we think of a sermon as something like a lecture, where the priest or pastor explains a certain biblical passage or idea to the congregation. But also here Kierkegaard wants to signal a different

---

[7] Ibid., p. 3. Kierkegaard quotes from Hamann's *Socratic Memorabilia*. For an English translation see *Hamann's Socratic Memorabilia: A Translation and Commentary*, by James C. O'Flaherty, Baltimore: The Johns Hopkins Press 1967, p. 143: "Socrates was, gentlemen, no mean critic. He distinguished in the writings of Heraclitus what he did not understand from what he understood, and drew a very proper and modest inference from the comprehensible to the incomprehensible."

[8] Kierkegaard, *The Concept of Anxiety*, p. 5.   [9] Ibid., p. 16.

understanding. While he admits that some pastors in his own day have been corrupted by scholarship and recent philosophical trends and thus give sermons that sound like lectures, this is not the true nature of the sermon. Then comes the truly surprising passage. Kierkegaard writes, "But to preach is really the most difficult of all arts and is essentially the art that Socrates praised, the art of being able to converse."[10] This seems very odd since Socrates of course never attended a Christian Church service and never heard a sermon in his entire life. But Kierkegaard has Vigilius Haufniensis compare Socrates' form of conversing and discussing with a Christian sermon. The key term in both cases is what Kierkegaard refers to as "appropriation," by which he means going beyond passive listening and making use of what one hears in a personal and meaningful way. The idea for Socrates is that through his questioning and conversation, the individual is led to find the truth within himself. This means taking something and giving it one's own interpretation or appropriation in one's own special context. So also with a sermon, the pastor, instead of simply preaching about some external fact or bit of knowledge, encourages the individual members of the congregation to find the truth of Christianity in themselves, each in their own way. The pagan Socrates is thus presented as a Christian role model since his maieutic approach leads to appropriation in a way that lecturing does not. Every follower of Christ must appropriate the Christian message for him- or herself. So, for Kierkegaard, the key here is that the truth both for Socrates and for Christianity is something inward that must be appropriated by people as individuals. So even though Socrates is not a Christian thinker, he can give us insight into Christianity.

In Chapter IV of *The Concept of Anxiety*, Kierkegaard has his pseudonymous author contrast Socrates with modern philosophy and specifically Hegel. This appears in the context of a discussion of the notion of negation and what Kierkegaard refers to as "inclosed reserve." The Danish term "*Indesluttethed*" means literally closing oneself off from the world or from other people. It is natural to understand negativity in this context, since when one is closed off into oneself, one negates the outside world. We have seen how important negation is in Kierkegaard's understanding of irony. Kierkegaard writes, "Thus irony has been explained as the negative.

---

[10] Ibid.

Hegel was the first to discover this explanation, but, strangely enough, he did not know much about irony."[11] Hegel's lack of understanding is then contrasted to Socrates' full appreciation of the importance of irony:

> That it was Socrates who first introduced irony into the world and gave a name to the child, that this irony was precisely inclosing reserve, which he began by closing himself off from men, by closing himself in with himself in order to be expanded in the divine . . . —this is something that no one is concerned with.[12]

Here Kierkegaard again emphasizes the element of subjectivity that Socrates introduced. There is something infinitely important and valuable in each and every individual, but to get to this one must occasionally get away from the crowd and from other people. This distancing oneself from others involves negation and irony. One must instead focus on one's own inwardness and religiosity. Kierkegaard takes Socrates to be the first one to have realized this. Here again we see an intriguing juxtaposition of an issue concerning Christian faith and the practice of a pagan philosopher, which Kierkegaard uses as a model. Inclosed reserve can thus be seen as another important Kierkegaardian concept that makes use of the idea of negation and irony from Socrates.

7.3. Kierkegaard's *Prefaces* and the Polemic with Johan Ludvig Heiberg

We saw in Chapter 6 how Heiberg wrote a critical review of *Either/Or* that earned him Kierkegaard's animosity. While Kierkegaard responded with the article "A Word of Thanks to Professor Heiberg," this was by no means the end of the conflict. At the beginning of 1844 Heiberg founded a new journal entitled *Urania*, which had an entirely new profile. He had become interested in astronomy, and it was intended to encourage new research in this field. On the second floor of his house Heiberg built his own private observatory. In this first issue of his new journal Heiberg wrote an article entitled "The Astronomical Year," which discussed cyclical natural occurrences

---

[11] Ibid., p. 134.   [12] Ibid.

such as the movements of the planets and the changing of the seasons. In this context he mentions Kierkegaard's *Repetition*, writing, "In a recently published work, which even has the word 'repetition' as its title, something very beautiful and fitting is said about this concept, but the author has not distinguished between the essentially different meanings which repetition has in the sphere of nature and in the sphere of spirit."[13] As in his earlier review of *Either/Or*, Heiberg acknowledges something positive in Kierkegaard's work, but then criticizes it for misunderstanding something quite fundamental. Kierkegaard was angered by Heiberg's remarks here just as he had been angered by the previous review of *Either/Or*. He drafted a couple of different articles in response to Heiberg, but in the end he never finished them, and they remained unpublished.[14]

He saved his response to Heiberg for his next book, entitled *Prefaces*. This book appeared on June 17, 1844 with the author listed as Nicolaus Notabene. This is a somewhat odd book in that it consists of a series of different prefaces to other texts that were never written. It appears that Kierkegaard had penned a handful of unpublished texts that he had just lying around, but they could not really be used for anything. Some of these texts included materials relevant for his criticism of Heiberg. So Kierkegaard hit upon the idea of publishing them in a single work with the title *Prefaces*. He had to give some kind of reason for why these texts were presented in this odd way, and so he concocted the following story. The author Nicolaus Notabene is a married man, and his wife is angry with him because he spends so much time writing books and not enough time with her. So she forbids him from writing books, but he cannot desist and circumvents the letter of her prohibition by writing only prefaces rather than books *per se*. This explains why the book consists of a series of eight prefaces that stand alone and are not prefaces to any particular book.

The work mentions Heiberg several times, and the perceptive reader can recognize Kierkegaard's response to both the review of

---

[13] Johan Ludvig Heiberg, "Det astronomiske Aar," *Urania*, 1844, pp. 77–160; p. 97. See also Kierkegaard, *Repetition*, trans. by Howard V. Hong and Edna H. Hong, Princeton: Princeton University Press 1983, Notes, pp. 379–83.

[14] For example, "Open Letter to Professor Heiberg, Knight of Dannebrog from Constantin Constantius," in *Repetition*, Supplement, pp. 283–98. "A Little Contribution by Constantin Constantius, Author of Repetition," ibid., Supplement, pp. 299–319.

Either/Or and the criticism of *Repetition*. Indeed, Notabene criticizes the entire culture of literary critics and the industry of book reviews in the second Preface. As we saw in Chapter 6, in his article "A Word of Thanks to Professor Heiberg" Kierkegaard satirized Heiberg's constant use of the impersonal pronoun "one" in his review of *Either/Or*. In the fourth of the Prefaces, he similarly writes,

> What, I wonder, will "one" say about this book now? My dear reader, if you are not able to find out in any other way, then our literary telegraph manager, Prof. Heiberg will probably be kind enough to be a tax collector again and tally the votes, just as he once did in connection with *Either/Or*.[15]

The last of Kierkegaard's Prefaces, namely, "Preface VIII," is also a criticism of Heiberg, but it is particularly interesting for our purposes since in it Kierkegaard again employs some of the strategies that he has learned from Socrates. Preface VIII is ostensibly a Preface to a new philosophical journal that Notabene wants to found. He begins by referring to Heiberg's journal *Perseus*, which began in 1837. The subtitle of *Perseus* is "A Journal for the Speculative Idea," which indicates Heiberg's intention to spread information about Hegel's speculative philosophy in Denmark. In the end Heiberg's journal saw only two issues and was then discontinued. Notabene contemplates his own prospects of succeeding with a new philosophical journal given Heiberg's failure.

He recalls that Heiberg, in his treatise *On the Significance of Philosophy for the Present Age*, claimed that philosophy was what was needed to help the age overcome the relativism and subjectivism that were so dominant.[16] Given this diagnosis, Heiberg's attempt to found a new philosophical journal made perfect sense, since he believed there was a need for philosophy. Notabene says that he too wants to serve philosophy, but his journal will take a different approach. Instead of using it to explain philosophy to his readers as Heiberg does, Notabene admits that he does not understand philosophy and that his journal will invite contributors to explain it to him. He says that his goal is to promote philosophy by asking people to

---

[15] Kierkegaard, *Prefaces*, trans. by Todd W. Nichol, Princeton: Princeton University Press 1998, pp. 23–4.

[16] Kierkegaard, "Preface VIII," in *Heiberg's Perseus and Other Texts*, ed. and trans. by Jon Stewart, Copenhagen: Museum Tusculanum Press 2011 (*Texts from Golden Age Denmark*, vol. 6), p. 163.

teach him about it: "Isn't this purpose good, and isn't it different from that of those who heretofore have tried to publish a philosophical journal? Even if it shares their wish to serve philosophy, the services are different: one serves it with his wisdom, another with his stupidity."[17]

Just as Socrates claimed to know nothing, Notabene claims to be ignorant. He refers to himself in an entirely humble and self-effacing manner, while recognizing Heiberg as one of the leading cultural figures in Danish letters.[18] Just as Socrates invites others to teach him and to explain to him what they know, so also Notabene invites contributors to his journal, who can teach him and explain the new philosophy. Like Socrates, Notabene refrains from making any positive claims himself, but instead simply listens to the claims of others and critically evaluates them. Heiberg was, of course, known for his promotion of Hegel's philosophy in Denmark, and so Notabene grants that Hegel's philosophy has explained everything.[19] This is the same as Socrates' point of departure: he always grants immediately the claims of his interlocutors to know something. Notabene merely states that he does not understand the account that Hegel's philosophy gives, and so he politely asks for an explanation of it. So also Socrates, after having heard the explanations or definitions given by his interlocutors, claims not to understand their explanation fully, and so he begins to ask questions, which reveal that the explanation is contradictory and thus unsatisfying. Notabene then, like Socrates, ironically states his expectation to be enlightened: "Since we now have many philosophers here in Denmark, who with industry and good fortune have comprehended this philosophy, I happily expect the instruction for which I have wished."[20] Socrates often begins by flattering his interlocutors for the knowledge they possess, thereby making it more difficult for them to refuse to answer his questions after they have accepted his recognition. So also Notabene seems to oblige the Danish followers of Hegel to respond since they are known to have an understanding of Hegel's philosophy, which Notabene is the first to recognize. But given their public reputation as experts in this philosophy, these people, like Heiberg, have no excuse for not responding to Notabene's call for papers. Heiberg appears in the role of one of Socrates' interlocutors, perhaps even one of the Sophists,

---

[17] Ibid., p. 164.   [18] Ibid., p. 161.
[19] Ibid., p. 169.   [20] Ibid.

someone who claims to know things and to teach things, but who in fact is ignorant and even ignorant of his own ignorance. Here we can see how Kierkegaard takes his initial inspiration from Socrates and then translates it into his own modern Danish cultural milieu.

7.4. Kierkegaard's *Stages on Life's Way*

Kierkegaard's next important work was *Stages on Life's Way*, which appeared on April 30, 1845 under the pseudonym Hilarius Bookbinder. It is in some ways a sequel to *Either/Or*. Like Victor Eremita, Bookbinder claims to have found by accident the texts that constitute the work. The book consists of three long chapters with what amount to four different texts by four different authors. First, there is "In vino veritas," which is attributed to William Afham. Then there is "Some Reflections on Marriage in Answer to Objections" attributed to a "Married Man," that is, Judge William, the author of the second part of *Either/Or*. The third large chapter consists of two works. First, there is a text entitled "'Guilty?'/'Not Guilty?'" by Quidam, the Latin name for "someone." With respect to form, this text recalls "The Seducer's Diary" from *Either/Or*. It is the story of a young man, who, like Kierkegaard, breaks off an engagement to his beloved fiancée, and, as the title indicates, it is a meditation on his degree of culpability in the matter. This inspires another long text called "Letter to the Reader," by Frater Taciturnus, who claims to have found the manuscript of "'Guilty?'/'Not Guilty?'" at the bottom of a lake.

Stages on Life's Way thus represents a complex embedding of stories within stories, a device that Kierkegaard borrows from Plato. While readers have been quick to try to identify Kierkegaard with, for example, Quidam, the text is set up in a way such that Kierkegaard himself hides behind the different authors. Not only is the work pseudonymous, but it also contains a handful of different authors with convoluted relations to one another. There are thus many levels of distancing of Kierkegaard as the author from the texts that comprise the work.

Kierkegaard's use of Socrates or a Socratic strategy plays an unmistakable role here. Indeed, Socrates is mentioned in all four texts. Perhaps most notable is the section "In vino veritas," where one can see clear signs of this influence. The title "In vino veritas" is Latin and means simply "in wine, the truth," that is, when people drink they lose their inhibitions and speak the truth. It presents a series of speeches given at a dinner party on the subject of love. The participants at the dinner party are well-known Kierkegaardian figures: Johannes the seducer, Victor Eremita, Constantin Constantius, and the Young Man from *Repetition*. This text is clearly modeled after Plato's *Symposium*, which likewise presents a banquet scene and a series of speeches on the topic of love in which Socrates participates.

Toward the end of *Stages on Life's Way* in the "Letter to the Reader," Frater Taciturnus discusses the issue of sin and forgiveness. He understands the original state of human beings as that of immediacy, that is, living in immediate harmony with nature and the world. Sin breaks this immediacy and ushers in the stage of reflection. The religious question is how to return to immediacy and undo the damage done by sin. Frater Taciturnus proposes a third stage as the forgiveness of sin, which he refers to as a "second immediacy." The harmony between humans and the world is restored, but it is no longer the same harmony as at the beginning. Clearly what is at issue here is the Christian doctrine of the forgiveness of sins by means of Jesus Christ.

Socrates is invoked in this context. Frater Taciturnus emphasizes the difficulty of this Christian doctrine and warns against those people who claim to understand it; here he is presumably referring to the academic theologians or well-educated clergy of the day. He anticipates that in the eyes of such people he will be regarded as a "stupid" person who asks "foolish questions,"[21] but claims it will not bother him since many people responded to Socrates the same way. Frater Taciturnus imagines what Socrates would say about the issue of sin and forgiveness and the responses of people in the nineteenth century. He has Socrates say, "Surely, what you are asking about is a difficult matter, and it has always amazed me that so many could believe that they understood a teaching such as that; but it has amazed me even more that some people have even understood much more."[22] Here we can see Kierkegaard, through his pseudonym, again taking up a Socratic posture vis-à-vis his contemporaries. He recognizes the difficulty and complexity of the issue, which the others fail to see. What does it mean to say that our sins are forgiven in Christ? He is

---

[21] Kierkegaard, *Stages on Life's Way*, trans. by Howard V. Hong and Edna H. Hong, Princeton: Princeton University Press 1988, p. 482.

[22] Ibid.

content to remain in a situation of ignorance and uncertainty, even if this means being ridiculed by those who in his eyes fail to appreciate the contradictory, paradoxical, and absurd nature of Christian belief. Kierkegaard thus employs Taciturnus' hypothetical Socrates to criticize what he takes to be the unwarranted presumption of his contemporaries.

7.5. The Conflict with *The Corsair*

One of the signal episodes of Kierkegaard's biography is his conflict with the satirical journal *The Corsair* (see Fig. 7.1). In Kierkegaard's time this was a popular publication that featured humorous articles that made fun of well-known figures. The articles were often accompanied by cartoons and comic illustrations that delighted the readers. It was published by a talented writer, Meir Goldschmidt, who continually found himself in legal trouble due to the journal's frequent conflict with the Danish censors. He was eventually compelled to engage a series of proxy editors, whose name appeared on the masthead, while he ran things behind the scenes. Thus, when the authorities tried to prosecute *The Corsair* with legal action, they had no other recourse but to punish the proxy editor who was legally responsible. One of his colleagues at the journal was another talented young writer and critic by the name of Peder Ludvig Møller, who played a key role in the conflict with Kierkegaard.[23]

Kierkegaard is known for his great animosity toward Goldschmidt and *The Corsair*, but this was not always the case. Prior to the actual conflict, the two had known each other for about ten years and were in fact on good terms.[24] In 1841 *The Corsair* published a book review of Kierkegaard's *The Concept of Irony*, and there was no problem or conflict in that context, even though the review satirized the language of the work.[25] Similarly, in 1843 *The Corsair* published a positive

---

[23] See K. Brian Soderquist, "Peder Ludvig Møller: 'If he had been a somewhat more significant person...,'" in *Kierkegaard and his Danish Contemporaries*, Tome III, *Literature, Drama and Aesthetics*, ed. by Jon Stewart, Aldershot: Ashgate 2009 (*Kierkegaard Research: Sources, Reception, and Resources*, vol. 7), pp. 247–55.

[24] *Encounters with Kierkegaard: A Life as Seen by His Contemporaries*, trans. and ed. by Bruce H. Kirmmse, Princeton: Princeton University Press 1996, pp. 65ff.

[25] See *The Corsair Affair and Articles Related to the Writings*, trans. by Howard V. Hong and Edna H. Hong, Princeton: Princeton University Press 1982, Supplement, pp. 92–3.

Fig. 7.1. Title page of *The Corsair*

review of *Either/Or* that recognized Kierkegaard's gift as a writer.[26] The controversy began at the end of 1845 with a review of *Stages on Life's Way* by Peder Ludvig Møller, published not in that journal but

---

[26] Ibid., Supplement, pp. 93–5.

in his own publication entitled *Gæa*. It was not uncommon for scholars and literary writers of the time to publish their own journals in this way, and we need only recall Kierkegaard's own publication, *The Moment*, some years later. Møller's *Gæa* was, unlike *The Corsair*, a serious organ for literature.

The article in question was a critical treatment of *Stages on Life's Way* entitled "A Visit to Sorø." Sorø is a small town in Denmark that was the home of the famous Sorø Academy, which employed a number of famous scholars and writers. One of these was the poet and novelist Carsten Hauch. In his article Møller creates a fictional dialogue that is said to take place at Hauch's home in Sorø, where *Stages on Life's Way* is the central object of discussion. Kierkegaard's work is criticized for its awkward style and the way in which the author puts his own ethical development on show. The article has a jocular and ribbing tone about it and cannot really be taken as a piece of serious literary criticism.

Kierkegaard responded to this article with a piece of his own entitled "The Activity of a Traveling Esthetician and How He Still Happened to Pay for the Dinner," which was published in the newspaper *The Fatherland* on December 27, 1845 and appeared under the name of his pseudonym Frater Taciturus.[27] Rather than respond to Møller's criticisms, Kierkegaard implies that Møller is trying to win public acclaim by associating himself with the literary elite of the day by, among other things, placing the discussion at the home of Carsten Hauch. So at the end of his article Kierkegaard associates Møller with *The Corsair*, by inviting him to show his true colors and issue his criticism in that journal. Kierkegaard's point was in effect to show that, while Møller was pretending to associate with the sophisticated literary elite of the country, in fact he was writing for a journal of ill repute.

Kierkegaard's action was a serious breach of academic ethics at the time.[28] His affirmation that Møller participated in *The Corsair* was unwelcome since Møller had wanted to keep his collaboration with Goldschmidt a secret. Hoping for an appointment to the University of Copenhagen, Møller was keen to present himself as a serious literary scholar and not someone who was writing for a disreputable

---

[27] Ibid., pp. 38–46.   [28] *Encounters with Kierkegaard*, p. 73.

journal. In private conversations Goldschmidt had assured Kierkegaard that he alone was responsible for *The Corsair*; he warned Kierkegaard not to implicate Møller in this, but his pleas were to no avail.[29] The disclosure had serious consequences for Møller's career and probably ruined his chances for academic employment. But an alternative interpretation might say that Møller's chances at a professorship were undermined not so much by his association with *The Corsair*, but rather by the general perception that Kierkegaard had gotten the better of him in the debate.[30]

Møller attempted to respond to Kierkegaard's article two days later in *The Fatherland*, where Kierkegaard's piece appeared.[31] Møller tries to deflect Kierkegaard's *ad hominem* criticism by saying that the dialogue he presented in his article was fictional and thus not an attempt to associate himself with leading literary figures such as Hauch. Kierkegaard quickly responded in an article entitled "The Dialectical Result of a Literary Police Action,"[32] in which he has Frater Taciturnus compare *The Corsair* with a prostitute and emphasize its goal to make money at the expense of others. This was a serious attack on *The Corsair* that deeply vexed Møller,[33] who saw his reputation damaged forever. This was Kierkegaard's last article in the conflict, but the damage was done.

Over the next few years Kierkegaard was frequently mentioned in a satirical way in *The Corsair*. Even worse, he was depicted in master-fully executed cartoon sketches that made fun of both his person and his writings (see Figs. 7.2 and 7.3). Kierkegaard felt humiliated when he found himself the object of public ridicule. He had always taken great care to cultivate a certain public image of himself and to maintain a certain relation to his readers, but now he saw that these things were not entirely in his control. He believed *The Corsair* was intent on ruining his reputation and came to regard himself as a martyr of unfair public opinion. While he enjoyed writing in ironic and sarcastic ways about others, he could not bear being the object of this same kind of criticism. He developed an uncompromising hatred toward primarily Goldschmidt for his role in this. His journals are full of venomous outbursts against Møller, Goldschmidt, and *The*

---

[29] Ibid., p. 71.   [30] Ibid., p. 72.
[31] *The Corsair Affair*, pp. 104–5.   [32] Ibid., pp. 47–50.
[33] *Encounters with Kierkegaard*, p. 75.

Corsair.[34] Even when this material was published after Kierkegaard's death, Goldschmidt showed great magnanimity in the matter and refused to criticize Kierkegaard as a person,[35] despite the abuse that Kierkegaard unreservedly hurled at him. In any case, this was without a doubt one of the great controversies in Danish literary history that left its mark on all three of the main figures who were involved in it.

Figs. 7.2 and 7.3. Satirical images of Kierkegaard from *The Corsair*

[34] See Johnny Kondrup, "Meïr Goldschmidt: The Cross-Eyed Hunchback," in *Kierkegaard and His Danish Contemporaries*, Tome III, *Literature, Drama and Aesthetics*, ed. by Jon Stewart, pp. 105–49.

[35] *Encounters with Kierkegaard*, pp. 79ff.

Figs. 7.2 and 7.3. Continued

7.6. Introduction to Kierkegaard's *Concluding Unscientific Postscript*

The *Concluding Unscientific Postscript*, which many regard as Kierkegaard's *magnum opus*, was published on February 28, 1846. Kierkegaard himself indicates that it played a very special role for him in the development of his work. The full title of the work is the *Concluding Unscientific Postscript to Philosophical Fragments: A Mimical–Pathetical–Dialectical Compilation: An Existential Contribution*. As the sequel to the *Philosophical Fragments*, it is ascribed to the same pseudonymous author of that work, Johannes Climacus.

Kierkegaard liked to take walks to Frederiksberg Garden, which is a park located in a suburb of Copenhagen, about a 30-minute walk from the old city. In the *Postscript*, his pseudonymous author Johannes Climacus recounts that four years previously he went there one Sunday afternoon and sat outside the café, smoking a cigar.[36] He claims that at this time he was considering the idea of becoming an author. One is tempted to read this story of Johannes Climacus biographically as referring to Kierkegaard himself. We know that four years prior to the *Postscript*, that is, in 1842, Kierkegaard was just returning from Berlin and was in fact contemplating what he wanted to do with his life. It was presumably during this time that he hit upon the idea of becoming an author and constructing his authorship with a series of pseudonymous and signed works.

In any case, the point of Johannes Climacus telling this story about the beginning of his writing career and his initial inspirations is to contrast this account in a humorous way with the account told by Johan Ludvig Heiberg of his conversion to Hegel's philosophy. As we discussed in Chapter 4, Heiberg attended Hegel's lectures in Berlin, and he gives a very excited and romanticized account of his first great insight into Hegel's philosophy, which served as the inspiration for many of his later works. He describes this as a kind of epiphany that he experienced on his return from Berlin to Kiel:

> While resting on the way home in Hamburg, where I stayed six weeks before returning to Kiel, and during that time was constantly pondering what was still obscure to me, it happened one day that, sitting in my room in the inn, the König von England with Hegel on my table and in my thoughts, and listening at the same time to the beautiful hymns which sounded almost unceasingly from the chimes of St. Peter's Church, suddenly, in a way which I have experienced neither before nor since, I was gripped by a momentary inner vision, as if a flash of lightning had illuminated the whole region for me and awakened in me

---

[36] Kierkegaard, *Concluding Unscientific Postscript*, vols 1–2, trans. by Howard V. Hong and Edna H. Hong, Princeton: Princeton University Press 1992, vol. 1, p. 185. See also ibid., p. 161.

the theretofore hidden central thought. From this moment the system in its broad outline was clear to me, and I was completely convinced that I had grasped it in its innermost core, regardless of however much there might be in the details which I still had not made my own and perhaps never will.[37]

Kierkegaard has Johannes Climacus satirize this account by referring to Heiberg as Dr. Hjortspring. He makes fun of Heiberg's conversion to Hegel's philosophy as a miracle that took place at Hotel Streit in Hamburg.[38] By contrast, Johannes Climacus gives a humble account of his own beginnings and his limited contributions to Danish literature. There is nothing romanticized about his portrayal of his decision to become an author in Frederiksberg Garden.

Climacus explains that as he sat in the café with his cigar he reflected on how he was getting older and had still not yet taken on any vocation. He saw other men using their talents in different fields in order to make life easier.[39] He recalls the technological advances of the day such as steamships and railroads. Similarly, Heiberg, by popularizing Hegel's philosophy, makes it easier for people to understand the German philosopher's difficult philosophical system. When Climacus considered what these other people were doing with their lives and how they were benefiting the age, the inevitable question arose about what he was doing with his life. He then hit upon the idea of what his vocation should be, and he decided he could best contribute by making things more difficult rather than making them easier. He points out that there is a danger in an age when things become too easy, and so it is important to have someone who can guard against this danger and point out the difficulties.

While there is an ironical or satirical tone in these passages, there is also something very serious about this. He refers to the *Philosophical Fragments*, the first work by Johannes Climacus. One of the goals of that book was in a sense to make the belief in Christianity more difficult by the analysis of the absolute paradox. So when Climacus says here that his planned life vocation was to make things difficult,

---

[37] Johan Ludvig Heiberg, "Autobiographical Fragments," in *Heiberg's On the Significance of Philosophy for the Present Age and Other Texts*, ed. and trans. by Jon Stewart, Copenhagen: C. A. Reitzel 2005 (*Texts from Golden Age Denmark*, vol. 1), p. 65.

[38] Kierkegaard, *Concluding Unscientific Postscript*, vol. 1, p. 184.

[39] Ibid., p. 186.

he means more specifically the idea of revising the conception of Christianity of the day and making it more difficult. This seems to be Kierkegaard's understanding of his own task, and he seems clearly to regard Socrates as a model for it. Like Socrates, Kierkegaard believes he could best contribute to improving his culture by playing the role of a gadfly.

7.7. Kierkegaard's "The Issue in the Fragments"

Climacus goes on to explain the goals and strategy of his previous work, the *Philosophical Fragments*. At the end of this discussion there is an interesting comparison with Socrates. Climacus states his intention was not to elaborate on Christian doctrine or dogma, but rather to address the question of how one becomes a Christian. In this context he says something quite counterintuitive. The missionary tradition in Christianity has set a well-known pattern for how Christians explain to nonChristians what Christianity is. The goal of the missionary is to convert the nonbeliever. The means to conversion is usually argument and different forms of persuasion. The missionary tries to demonstrate the confusion and contradictions involved in the nonbeliever's world-view and the consistency and plausibility of Christianity. The whole point of this is to show that it is attractive to be a Christian and unattractive to be a nonbeliever. Now against this background, it is very odd when Johannes Climacus says that his goal is not to make becoming and being a Christian easier, but rather more difficult. He writes, "I venture according to my poor ability to take on the responsibility of making it difficult, as difficult as possible."[40]

This seems a very odd thing to say. Is the meaning of this that Johannes Climacus is a kind of anti-missionary, whose goal is not to persuade people to become Christians, but rather just the opposite, to repel them from Christianity? The key here is to understand what he means by Christianity. Since Christianity promises salvation and eternal happiness, it is a matter of the utmost importance to be sure about. It would be disastrous if one believed that one was a Christian,

---

[40] Ibid., p. 381.

but instead had a mistaken conception of what Christianity was. Kierkegaard believed that the understanding and practice of Christianity in his own day was largely misconceived and deviated radically from the original Christianity taught by Jesus. When Climacus says that his goal is to make it more difficult to be a Christian, he does not mean that he wants to undermine Christianity *per se*, but rather that what he wishes to challenge is a mistaken version of Christianity that makes things too easy. This needs to be undermined, so that one can come to grasp the true version of Christianity which is much more difficult.

According to Climacus, Christianity concerns the inwardness of each individual and not discursive arguments or demonstrations. He rejects the idea that Christianity is a doctrine.[41] This is also a radical and counterintuitive claim. Throughout the history of Christianity there have constantly been attempts to formalize the teachings of Christ as a fixed doctrine. This began with the very first Church councils and continued through history, with countless theologians and scholars developing their own system of Christian dogmatics, that is, the field of theology that tries to understand the different dogmas. Moreover, the religious controversies that led to schisms in the history of the Church concerned disputes about the interpretation of specific dogmas or doctrines. In religious wars people fought and died for what they believed to be the truth of specific doctrines. Likewise, people were persecuted, tortured, and executed for not believing in certain doctrines. Given all this, it is strikingly odd when Johannes Climacus implies that it is a mistake to understand Christianity as a doctrine. He writes, "The introducing that I take upon myself consists, by repelling, in making it difficult to become a Christian and understands Christianity not as a doctrine but as an existence-contradiction and existence-communication."[42] *Philosophical Fragments* had argued that Christianity is based on paradoxes

---

[41] Ibid., p. 382.

[42] Ibid., p. 383. See also *Kierkegaard's Journals and Notebooks*, vol. 7, p. 188, NB17:33: "This Socratic thesis is of utmost importance in Christianity: Virtue cannot be taught; that is, it is not a doctrine, it is a being-able, an exercising, an existing, an existential transformation, and therefore it is so slow to learn, not at all as simple and easy as the rote-learning of one more language or one more system. No, in respect to virtue there is always particular emphasis on *the internal*, the inward, 'the single individual.' Here I come again to my thesis—Christianity is not a doctrine but an existence-communication."

such as God becoming man, the finite becoming infinite, and the eternal becoming temporal. Because these ideas are inherently contradictory, they preclude rather than lead to a positive doctrine. Kierkegaard believed Christianity could never be comprehended by the human mind or explained to another person. Rather, it must simply be accepted on faith in the inwardness of one's own heart. This seems to be what Climacus means by "existence-communication," which is just the opposite of an objective, direct, or straightforward communication of a fact about the world. Instead, an existence-communication concerns something that is paradoxical, contradictory, and absurd—a communication based on lived experience rather than speaking and listening.

Toward the end of this discussion Kierkegaard has Climacus discuss Plato's dialogue, the *Greater Hippias*, which addresses the concept of beauty. Just as Climacus wants to introduce people to Christianity, so also the goal of Plato's dialogue is to introduce people to the concept of beauty. This is one of Plato's so-called aporetic dialogues, and so after many failed attempts to define beauty, the discussion ends with no conclusion. At the end Socrates states simply that he "has benefited from the conversation" since he found the issue of defining beauty to be difficult.[43] Climacus sees this as analogous to his approach to Christianity. He does not attempt to teach a positive doctrine about Christianity, just as Socrates does not attempt to teach a straightforward definition of beauty. Instead, the idea of Christianity and the concept of beauty are themselves problematized. Climacus takes this to be important and indeed beneficial in his own age, which in his opinion is dominated by confused and mistaken conceptions of Christianity. So if his readers come away from his text questioning and doubting their views of Christianity, they will benefit even if he has not taught them a positive doctrine. So here again we see Socrates providing a model for Kierkegaard's project. Like the Socrates of the *Greater Hippias*, who makes things more difficult with regard to the concept of beauty, so also Kierkegaard sees himself as making things more difficult with regard to Christianity.

---

[43] Kierkegaard, *Concluding Unscientific Postscript*, vol. 1, p. 384. It should be noted that Kierkegaard uses a quotation from the *Greater Hippias* as the motto for the *Concluding Unscientific Postscript*: "But I must ask you, Socrates, what do you suppose is the upshot of all this? As I have said a little while ago, it is the scrapings and shavings of argument, cut up into little bits." Ibid., p. 3. The quotation is from the *Greater Hippias*, 304a.

7.8. Kierkegaard's "A First and Last Explanation"

Why did Kierkegaard regard the *Concluding Unscientific Postscript* as such an important work? The key lies in the word "concluding" in the title. The obvious interpretation of this term is that the work is intended as the sequel to the *Philosophical Fragments* and is thus intended to conclude or complete that work. But there is also a deeper, biographical explanation. As previously noted, all of Kierkegaard's siblings, with the exception of his elder brother, died a premature death. Needless to say, this had a profound effect on him. He developed the idea that he too would die before he reached the age of 34. In his recollections of Kierkegaard, Hans Brøchner records this, when he writes, "Kierkegaard once told me . . . that as a young man he had for many years had the firm conviction that he would die when he reached the age of thirty-three. (Was it Jesus' age which also was to be the norm for Jesus' imitator?)."[44] When he reached the age of 34 still alive and well, Kierkegaard could not bring himself to believe it and even checked the official registry to confirm the actual date of his birth.[45] In any case, this meant that as he was writing his famous works, he always had in the back of his mind that he only had a few years to live. He thus strategically planned his books in such a way that they would culminate in one final work, which would be the *Concluding*

---

[44] *Encounters with Kierkegaard*, p. 240. In a letter to his brother from 1847, Kierkegaard writes, "The birthday on which you congratulate me and about which you say that it 'often and uncustomarily has been in your thoughts these days,' that birthday has also frequently and for a long time preceding it been in my own thoughts. For I became 34 years old. In a certain sense it was utterly unexpected. I was already very surprised when—yes, now I may say it without fear of upsetting you—you became 34 years old. Both father and I had the idea that nobody in our family would live past his 34th year. . . . The 34th year was, then, to be the limit, and father was to outlive us all. That is not the way it has turned out—I am now in my 35th year." *Kierkegaard: Letters and Documents*, trans. by Henrik Rosenmeier, Princeton: Princeton University Press 1978, Letter 149, p. 211.

[45] In his account Brøchner adds, "This belief was so ingrained in him that when he did reach this age, he even checked in the parish records to see if it really were true; that was how difficult it was for him to believe it" (*Encounters with Kierkegaard*, p. 240). See also *Kierkegaard's Journals and Notebooks*, vol. 4, p. 123, NB:210: "How strange, that I have turned 34. It is utterly inconceivable to me. I was so sure that I would die before or on this birthday that I could actually be tempted to suppose that my birthday was erroneously recorded and that I will still die on my 34th."

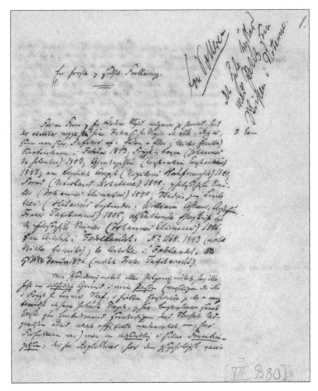

Fig. 7.4. Draft of "A First and Last Explanation"

Unscientific Postscript. This would be the book that brought together the different strands of his authorship.

Since Kierkegaard believed that he would die after the publication of the *Concluding Unscientific Postscript* in 1846, he decided to make a statement about his works as a whole at the end of the book, presumably thinking that this would be his last chance to do so. Once he had completed the book, he then added at the very end a final section entitled "A First and Last Explanation" (see Fig. 7.4). This appears on unnumbered pages, separate from the body of the work.

Throughout the years prior to this Kierkegaard had been meticulous about keeping up the facade of the pseudonymous authors that he had created. He went to great lengths to distance himself from his works and to see to it that they were attributed to the fictional authors. He never personally negotiated the contracts for his pseudonymous works with the printer and the publishing house, but instead sent his friend Jens Finsteen Giødwad to do so. In this way he could remain hidden behind the pseudonymous author. As we have seen, when Heiberg criticized *Either/Or*, Kierkegaard responded by publishing "Public Confession," not in his own name but in the name of the pseudonymous editor of the work, Victor Eremita.

Kierkegaard was assisted in this attempt to present the pseudonyms as real authors by the literary customs of the day. In Golden Age Denmark there was nothing new or original about writing in pseudonyms, and many of the great figures of the day also made use of them, including figures such as Heiberg and Mynster. Scholarly etiquette of the time dictated that a reader or critic respect the pseudonym and not betray the identity of the true author. Thus, in Heiberg's criticisms of *Either/Or* and *Repetition* he is careful never to mention Kierkegaard by name.

In "A First and Last Explanation" Kierkegaard takes the extraordinary step of revealing that he is the author of the pseudonymous works leading up to and including the *Postscript* itself. It seems on the face of it that his main goal was just to make it known that he was the author of *Either/Or*, *Fear and Trembling*, etc., if he should die and people did not know. In this sense it seems in many ways natural that he would want to take credit for his work of many years. But the matter is not quite so straightforward, since once he states this, he goes on to make a request of his readers, namely, that when they refer to a work, they attribute it not to him but to the pseudonymous author. So while Kierkegaard claims legal responsibility for the pseudonymous works, he seems to want to maintain a distanced relation to them, which was clearly a part of the original plan with the pseudonyms in the first place. By requesting his readers to refer to these works as authored by the pseudonyms, he suggests the views expressed by the pseudonyms were not necessarily his own. In recent years this has also been the source of debate among Kierkegaard scholars. Some argue that the pseudonyms are simply a literary tool that Kierkegaard uses for different reasons, but in the end they have no bearing on the content of his works and can be safely ignored. Others argue that they are of absolute importance, and one should take Kierkegaard at his word and be wary of associating the views of the pseudonymous authors with those of Kierkegaard himself.

7.9. The Parallel Authorship

In 1848, two years after the publication of the *Postscript*, Kierkegaard wrote a retrospective overview of his works entitled *The Point of View for My Work as an Author*. He only decided to publish a short version of this in 1850 under the title *On My Work as an Author*. But when *The Point of View* was discovered among his manuscripts after his death, his brother Peter Christian Kierkegaard published the complete version in 1859. In these works Kierkegaard reflects on his many books and their relations to one another.

In a journal entry from 1849 Kierkegaard indicates that his literary production is to be understood as "a unified project." He refers to what he calls a "comprehensive plan in the production as a whole."[46] This is surprising to some readers, since we know that Kierkegaard was an outspoken critic of any form of systematic thinking. What could it then possibly mean when he seems to regard his collective literary work as a kind of unified system? This is what is explained in *The Point of View*.

Kierkegaard published works both under different pseudonyms and under his own name. The pseudonymous works treat themes such as aesthetics, philosophy, and psychology, while the signed works were primarily religious discourses, akin to sermons. Kierkegaard refers to the pseudonymous works as "the aesthetic authorship" and the signed works as "the religious authorship," although it is clear that the pseudonymous works, such as *Fear and Trembling*, *Philosophical Fragments*, and *The Concept of Anxiety*, also treat religious subjects. A case might be made that the pseudonymous works were aimed at a more sophisticated audience, since they at times refer to academic debates and quote in foreign languages. By contrast, the edifying works seem to be directed toward the common believer, who does not necessarily have any scholarly training. Kierkegaard's strategy, therefore, seems to have been to try to reach different kinds of people through his writings in a way that was most suitable for them.

In his description of these two different parts of his authorship, Kierkegaard portrays himself as following Socrates' maieutic art.[47]

---

[46] *Kierkegaard's Journals and Notebooks*, vol. 5, p. 286, NB10:38.

[47] Kierkegaard, *The Point of View*, trans. by Howard V. Hong and Edna H. Hong, Princeton: Princeton University Press 1998, p. 7: "It began *maieutically* with aesthetic production, and all the pseudonymous writings are *maieutic* in nature. Therefore this writing was also pseudonymous, whereas the directly religious—which from the beginning was present in the gleam of an indication—carried my name."

He explains that he intended for his aesthetic works to practice a maieutic strategy of leading his readers unknowingly to Christianity. Then they would be in a position to appreciate the edifying works and the religious messages that they convey. At first glance, it might seem unclear how Kierkegaard can claim that he is doing the same thing that Socrates was, given that his works look so different from Socrates' questioning. But the point seems to be that Kierkegaard's pseudonymous writings are maieutic in the Socratic sense in that they problematize a number of issues that the readers thought they had understood. By rendering their views problematic, Kierkegaard's works then require the readers to look within for new answers. He is careful not to allow his pseudonymous authors to present solutions to the issues raised, and this then leaves it to the readers to find the truth in themselves. This also meant that his pseudonymous writings were not aimed at a large audience or "the crowd," but instead addressed each individual and his or her religious inwardness in the same way that Socrates' questioning was directed at a specific person.[48] So judging from Kierkegaard's own account here, one can say that Socrates' conception of maieutics provided the model for the entire pseudonymous part of the authorship.

In *The Point of View for My Work as an Author* Kierkegaard explains that he intended for the two sets of works to run parallel with and complement each other. So the idea was that for each pseudonymous work that he would publish, there would also appear a signed work parallel to it. In this way two different authorships would arise together (see Fig. 7.5). When one looks at the publication dates of Kierkegaard's works, this conception of his authorship does for the most part seem to hold true.[49] *Either/Or* was published on February 20, 1843 and its corresponding text, *Two Upbuilding Discourses*, was published only three months later on May 16, 1843. Similarly, the pseudonymous works *Fear and Trembling* and *Repetition* were published on October 16, 1843, and on exactly the same day the signed collection *Three Upbuilding Discourses* appeared. One can continue to follow these parallels up to the publication of the *Concluding Unscientific Postscript* in 1846.

---

[48] Ibid., p. 9.

[49] See Niels Jørgen Cappelørn, "The Retrospective Understanding of Søren Kierkegaard's Total Production," in *Kierkegaard: Resources and Results*, ed. by Alastair McKinnon, Montreal: Wilfrid Laurier University Press 1982, pp. 18–38.

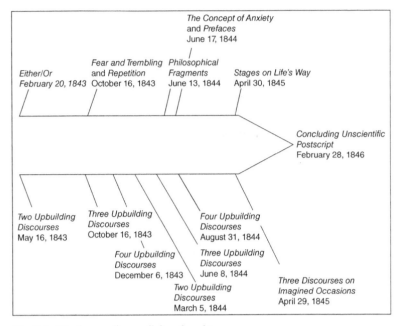

Fig. 7.5. Kierkegaard's parallel authorship

This scheme also shows the importance of the *Concluding Unscientific Postscript* in bringing together the two different strands. In *The Point of View*, Kierkegaard writes, "The first division of books is aesthetic writing; the last division of books is exclusively religious writing—between these lies the *Concluding Unscientific Postscript* as the turning point."[50] What does Kierkegaard mean by calling the *Postscript* "the turning point" in his literary work?[51] He did not die as he expected in 1846, and he found that he could not stop writing after the *Postscript*. Since the *Postscript* had completed his original agenda, the publications that followed it are different. Scholars generally divide Kierkegaard's life and work into two periods—the first leading up to and culminating in the *Postscript*, and the second beginning after the *Postscript* and culminating in his attack on the Church and his death in 1855. It is said that while the first half of the

[50] Kierkegaard, *The Point of View*, p. 31.
[51] See ibid., p. 31, p. 55. See also *Kierkegaard's Journals and Notebooks*, vol. 5, p. 289, NB10:40.

authorship gave primacy to the pseudonymous aesthetic works, the second half inverted this, putting the primary focus on the religious writings.

7.10. The Journals and Notebooks

A parallel shift can also be discerned in Kierkegaard's journals.[52] He was an avid journal writer and meticulously kept running journals throughout his lifetime. People often think of his journals as a personal diary, but this is rather misleading since Kierkegaard used his journals for many other functions beyond simply recording the events of his daily life. Indeed, they were used to jot down a clever turn of phrase or thought, to note something interesting that he read, or to record something that he could come back to and use in his writings.

The journals also fall into two large categories that correspond temporally with the two periods of the authorship. The journals in the first set are given double numbers: AA, BB, CC, etc. until KK. Kierkegaard began *Journal AA* in 1835, when he was still a student at the University of Copenhagen, and he continued to write in his *Journal JJ* into the year 1846. At roughly the same time as these early journals Kierkegaard also wrote a series of notebooks which later editors have simply numbered sequentially, that is, *Notebook 1*, *Notebook 2*, etc., until *Notebook 15*. It is here that we find, for example, his lecture notes to Schelling's lectures and notes to his readings. These early journals and notebooks correspond to the first part of the authorship.

The second set of journals, the so-called NB journals, corresponds to the second half of the authorship. When Kierkegaard saw that he did not die as he had anticipated, he continued to write journals. After he thought he had given his definitive statement of his authorship in "A First and Last Explanation," as time went on he still felt the need to

---

[52] The best introduction to Kierkegaard's journals and notebooks to date is Niels Jørgen Cappelørn et al., *Written Images: Søren Kierkegaard's Journals, Notebooks, Booklets, Sheets, Scraps, and Slips of Paper*, trans. by Bruce H. Kirmmse, Princeton and Oxford: Princeton University Press 2007. A highly interesting study of this material can be found in Henning Fenger, *Kierkegaard, The Myths and Their Origins: Studies in the Kierkegaardian Papers and Letters*, trans. by George C. Schoolfield, New Haven and London: Yale University Press 1980.

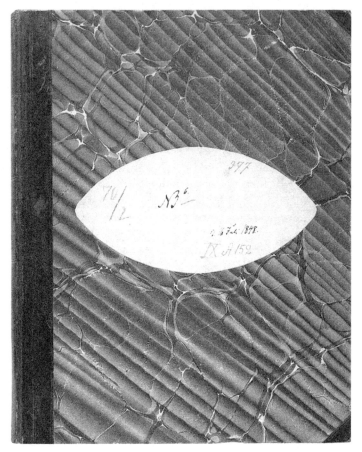

Fig. 7.6. The cover of Kierkegaard's *Journal NB6*

say more, and so he named his next journal, which he began immediately after the publication of the *Concluding Unscientific Postscript*,
the *NB* journal (see Fig. 7.6). The initials "NB" stand for the Latin
words "*nota bene*" or "note well." The idea seems to be that these are
supplemental remarks or reflections about his authorship. Even into
1847 he remained unsure about whether or not he was going to die.
The *NB* journal grew to be very large. At some point he realized that
he was in fact going to live, and so he decided to continue with a new
journal, which he called *NB2*. He worked on the sequence of the NB
journals until his death, with his final journal being *NB36*.

The NB journals run parallel to the second half of the authorship and are somewhat different in character from the early journals. While the early journals contain very diverse kinds of material and skip from topic to topic very quickly, the NB journals display a greater degree of continuity. They contain endless reflections on Kierkegaard's self-understanding and his complicated and often inimical relations to others. In any case, the journals constitute a rich source of information about both Kierkegaard's life and works, and provide interesting perspectives that are not always afforded by his published writings.

7.11. Socrates and Christianity as Subjective Truth

At the beginning of this chapter we noted that Kierkegaard made the odd claim that he believed that Socrates became a Christian. Now, after looking at some of Kierkegaard's works from the years 1844–6, we can perhaps begin to gain some insight into what he meant by this. Usually we associate Christianity with a set of dogmas and doctrines that did not appear until several hundred years after Socrates' death. If this is what Christianity is, then surely it cannot make any sense to say that Socrates was a Christian or could have become one, since he was never familiar with these teachings and had no way of subscribing to them. But, as we have seen, Kierkegaard concluded it is a mistake to reduce Christianity to dogmas and doctrines. This is the conception of Christianity that theologians, philosophers, and other kinds of scholars tend to have, but Kierkegaard argues that their conception of Christianity is misguided or even corrupt.

What, then, is Kierkegaard's conception of Christianity and what does it have to do with Socrates? This is not so easy to identify or to describe clearly, since Kierkegaard seems very intent on avoiding giving his readers any direct information in this regard. But we can gain a glimpse of this if we recall the different analyses that we examined in this chapter. Kierkegaard's different authors claim consistently that Christianity is concerned with passion and inward personal decisions regarding ideas that are paradoxical and contradictory. This is just the opposite of the conception of Christianity of the scholars of the day, who try to understand and explain the paradox and the absurdity of the key dogmas. Kierkegaard believes that Socrates can play an important negative role here. With Socrates' critical disposition, he can help people to undermine the different positive doctrines about Christianity. He can help people to return to the paradox, the absurdity, and the contradiction intrinsic to Christianity.

Needless to say, this is a provocative and controversial position. On the one hand, Kierkegaard's view of Christianity as fundamentally tied to the individual subject is attractive to many people today. There seems to be something intuitively correct about focusing on the inwardness and subjectivity of the individual when talking about Christianity or indeed religion in general. There is also something attractive about the view that one can believe in the conviction of one's heart without needing to convince anyone else of it. For Kierkegaard, any such attempt to try to convince other people of the truth of Christianity would distort its inward nature. Each individual must come to Christian faith on their own.

On the other hand, there is something a bit unsettling about the radicality of Kierkegaard's emphasis on the subjectivity of the individual. Some scholars have expressed concerns that Kierkegaard opens the door for arbitrariness and relativism. If the truth of Christianity is just about my inwardness, my subjective passion, and my incommunicable decisions, then is there any real connection to any objective truth? Usually Christianity is defined on the basis of certain doctrines, for example, that God became a human being, and that Jesus performed miracles and returned to life after being crucified. The usual assumption has always been that if these things are not true, then this would undermine the truth of Christianity, and it does not matter what I might think about this personally in my inwardness or passion. For this reason critics of Christianity have always attacked these kinds of things to show that they are not credible, while proponents of Christianity have done their best to defend them. On both sides there is agreement that much is at stake in these kinds of things being true or false. Some people have argued that, by locating faith in the inwardness of the individual, Kierkegaard neglects this other objective dimension of Christianity. Does not being a Christian mean having a relation to these outward, objective things? Can one really be a Christian merely by focusing on one's inwardness and ignoring all these things that have traditionally been associated with Christianity?

The point here is not to praise or criticize Kierkegaard's views, but rather to understand them and appreciate their uniqueness and radicality. He raises issues that remain relevant for all of us, even if one is not a Christian or even religious. He raises the fundamental question that goes back to Socrates: What is the truth? Is it something out there in the world, a fact of the matter? When I look out and say that here and now the sun is shining, is this not true independent of my subjective disposition? Are there not things like this that are objectively true and that I can give arguments and reasons to support as true: the earth is the third planet from the sun, a molecule of water contains one oxygen atom and two hydrogen atoms, 2 plus 3 is equal to 5? Is the truth not something that is objective and greater than the personal opinions or dispositions of individuals, who might well be confused, mistaken, or deceived?

Or is the truth something subjective in me? When I read a poem, view a painting, or hear a song, I get a feeling that I cannot necessarily describe or articulate in words but that I am somehow certain about even if other people disagree with me. I am convinced that the poem, the painting, or the song captures something true and beautiful even if no one else seems to think so. In ethics I might have a deep-seated conviction that I owe my friend something even if other people or even my friend himself might not think so. I alone feel convinced of this. When I am listening to a sermon or reading a sacred text, I might have the feeling of having a personal and special relation to God or of a deep conviction of the truth of religion, even if other people might regard me as silly, old fashioned, or superstitious. I cannot point to anything in the world to demonstrate the truth of these things, but I just seem to know them to be true in my own heart. My certainty that I am correct is not diminished by my inability to demonstrate it to anyone else. Are there thus not some truths that are as personal or subjective as Kierkegaard claims?

Many people today have intuitions that are caught somewhere between these two views. Is the truth something objective or something subjective? Is the truth something about me as an individual or is it something about the world that has nothing to do with me?

8

Kierkegaard's Socratic Task
and the Second Half of
the Authorship: 1846–55

The last decade of Kierkegaard's life was in many ways the most dramatic. This was the time of the Revolutions of 1848 and of Kierkegaard's public attack on the Danish State Church in his final years. As we saw in the last chapter, this period represents what Kierkegaard scholars refer to as the second half of the authorship, namely, the period from 1846 after the *Concluding Unscientific Postscript* to Kierkegaard's death in 1855. In this chapter we want to explore some of his main works from these years, such as *A Literary Review of Two Ages*, *Upbuilding Discourses in Various Spirits*, *The Sickness unto Death*, *Practice in Christianity*, and *The Moment*. We will see how some of the themes and motifs that we have examined so far reappear in these works. In our exploration of these texts it will become evident that as Kierkegaard grew older, he continued to return to the figure of Socrates and never abandoned the great hero of his youth.

8.1. Kierkegaard's Views of Society and
His Relation to King Christian VIII

Only a month after the *Postscript*, on March 30, 1846, Kierkegaard published a work called *A Literary Review of Two Ages*. This short book is a review of a novel entitled *Two Ages* by Thomasine Gyllembourg, the mother of Johan Ludvig Heiberg. Gyllembourg's work contrasts the period of Romanticism and Napoleon with that of the

Restoration. This contrast is portrayed through the story of a couple of different generations of a family living in Copenhagen. Kierkegaard seizes on the novel to develop some of his own ideas about society. Scholars often point to this work as Kierkegaard's most important statement of social–political thought.

It cannot really be said that Kierkegaard was a major figure in the field of social–political philosophy in the way that one can talk about thinkers such as John Locke, Karl Marx, or John Stuart Mill. Kierkegaard never wrote any extensive treatise on political philosophy, and his *A Literary Review of Two Ages* can hardly be compared with the classics of political philosophy, such as Locke's *Second Treatise of Government* or Rousseau's *The Social Contract*. In some ways Kierkegaard does not appear to have been much interested in politics due to his strong emphasis on the inward religious nature of the individual. This emphasis seems in many ways to undermine a social or political theory. But with that said, there can be no doubt that Kierkegaard does have some insights that can be used in the context of social–political philosophy, and in recent years Kierkegaard scholars have been increasingly attentive to this dimension of his thought.

One of these insights is the concept of leveling. This is an important idea that Kierkegaard explores in *A Literary Review*. Kierkegaard was at heart a royalist and wary of the changes that were beginning to take place and would culminate in the Revolutions of 1848. He was also mistrustful of the trend toward democracy with a broad spectrum of voters. The fundamental idea of democracy is that everyone has the same rights to vote and to have their say in how the government should be run. Kierkegaard was worried about this development since he feared that it would create a public opinion that would be grounded in the masses. Thus, public opinion would undermine the individuality of everyone since it would be a projection of a larger group.

The concept of leveling appears in this context. Kierkegaard was concerned that the rush toward democracy would work against anyone who dared to differ from the majority. Feeling more comfortable with the old system of aristocratic patronage, he feared democracy would discourage individual genius and achievement. Public opinion encourages people to be conformist. No one wants to appear different from anyone else. Public opinion can easily turn against a person who stands out in some way and expose him or her to ridicule. This was the way that Kierkegaard understood what happened to him in connection with his polemical exchange with the journal *The Corsair*. He believed himself to have been unfairly persecuted by *The Corsair*, which managed to turn the general public opinion against him. Kierkegaard believes that this kind of phenomenon is a pernicious aspect of modern life. Anyone who dares to be different or who possesses great gifts that make the mediocre masses envious will be subject to criticism and mockery. Such a person who towers above others will be brought down to the common level of the masses. This is what Kierkegaard understands by leveling. Instead of encouraging people to cultivate and develop their individual genius, modern democratic culture actively undermines and works against this. In this regard he believes that the old order of things was better, where recognition was given to, for example, nobility, and public opinion did not carry so much weight. In that world it was easier for people to stand out without being subject to the persecution of mass public opinion.

Although Kierkegaard was a royalist, he had a reserved relation to the king. At the time, the King of Denmark was Christian VIII, who had ruled since 1839. The king and his wife were interested in Kierkegaard, and he was summoned to a series of three audiences. The first took place at Amalienborg Palace on March 13, 1847. Kierkegaard records these encounters in his *Journal NB9*.[1] It seems that the king was interested in using Kierkegaard as a kind of advisor in affairs concerning intellectual life in the kingdom. The king knew that Kierkegaard had been in Berlin and attended Schelling's lectures. As we discussed in Chapter 6, Schelling had been appointed by the King of Prussia for the purpose of combatting the forces of left Hegelianism. Many of Hegel's students became active politically and came to play important roles in the Revolutions of 1848. Christian VIII was presumably interested to hear what Schelling had done and to what extent his appointment had been successful in this regard. He was interested in appointing Kierkegaard to an academic position at the Sorø Academy, presumably with a similar strategic idea in mind.

---

[1] *Kierkegaard's Journals and Notebooks*, ed. by Niels Jørgen Cappelørn et al., vols 1–11, Princeton: Princeton University Press 2007ff., vol. 5, pp. 229–36, NB9:41–3. See also *Encounters with Kierkegaard: A Life as Seen by His Contemporaries*, trans. and ed. by Bruce H. Kirmmse, Princeton: Princeton University Press 1996, p. 211.

But Kierkegaard refused to be drawn into politics in this way. Indeed, he was reluctant even to meet the king and fearful of any closer contacts with him.[2] For example, when the king made it known that he wanted to see him, Kierkegaard initially used as an excuse that he did not have suitable attire and could not come. But the king insisted, and he was obliged to visit the Palace. During their discussion the king, without asking Kierkegaard, simply informed his servants that Kierkegaard would be staying for dinner. This was obviously intended as an honor, but Kierkegaard rather brazenly refused, insisting that this was impossible for him.[3] When the king continued to make overtures, Kierkegaard simply stated that he was a private person, thus implying that such contact was not desirable to him.

So while we can say that politically speaking Kierkegaard was a royalist, this statement should be qualified. He was not uncritical of royalty and enjoyed making fun of people who held high positions or enjoyed noble titles. While he was worried about the democratic developments that led to the Revolutions of 1848, he did not want to be drawn into any direct political role. He wanted to keep his primary focus on the inward life of the individual.

8.2. Socrates in *Upbuilding Discourses in Various Spirits* and *Works of Love*

In the years following the publication of the *Concluding Unscientific Postscript* and *A Literary Review*, Kierkegaard continued to publish prolifically. In 1847 *Upbuilding Discourses in Various Spirits* and *Works of Love* appeared under his own name. These works refer to Socrates not by name, but rather as the "simple wise man of antiquity" or "the simple wise man of old."[4] In *Upbuilding Discourses in Various Spirits* Socrates is held up as a positive contrast to what

---

[2] *Encounters with Kierkegaard*, p. 211.   [3] Ibid., pp. 211f.
[4] Kierkegaard, *Works of Love*, trans. by Howard V. Hong and Edna H. Hong, Princeton: Princeton University Press 1995, pp. 371–3; *Christian Discourses. The Crisis and a Crisis in the Life of an Actress*, trans. by Howard V. Hong and Edna H. Hong, Princeton: Princeton University Press 1997, p. 133.

Kierkegaard calls "the crowd,"[5] that is, the mass public about which he had expressed concerns in *A Literary Review of Two Ages*. As we have just seen, Kierkegaard has a negative view of the idea of people as a collective unit, such as a political party, a lobby, an interest group, or public opinion. He believes that this distorts or even destroys the voice of the individual. One dares not oppose the voice of the majority for fear of being the subject of its criticism. For this reason Kierkegaard hails Socrates, who stubbornly insisted on the individual. The truth is to be found in each particular person, not in the collective group.

In *Works of Love* Kierkegaard explores the meaning of the biblical command to love one's neighbor. The subtitle of the work is "Some Christian Deliberations in the Form of Discourses," and in a draft Kierkegaard explains the nature and goal of a deliberation in contrast to other genres such as edifying discourses. He explains, "A deliberation does not presuppose the definitions as given and understood; therefore, it must not so much move, mollify, reassure, persuade, as *awaken* and provoke people and sharpen thought."[6] Here one can already see the shadow of Socrates as someone who claims to know nothing and thus starts without any presuppositions, but then goes on to examine people and make their own thinking more rigorous. This of course can involve a kind of provocation, since people are under many illusions about what they think they know. The goal is to shake people up with respect to their assumed conceptions of love. Kierkegaard then refers to the deliberation with another image from Socrates: "A deliberation ought to be a 'gadfly.'"[7] Moreover, just as Socrates used irony in the service of trying to attain the truth, so also in a deliberation, "[i]rony is necessary."[8] So Kierkegaard seems to be saying that *Works of Love* is a form of writing that follows closely Socrates' form of philosophizing.

In one passage he compares Socrates' practice with Christian love,[9] arguing that true love entails helping the other person to stand on their own and thus to be free as Socrates does with his questioning. The goal of the Socratic method is to show the interlocutor that in fact

---

[5] Kierkegaard, *Upbuilding Discourses in Various Spirits*, trans. by Howard V. Hong and Edna H. Hong, Princeton: Princeton University Press 1993, pp. 95–6.

[6] Kierkegaard, *Works of Love*, Supplement, p. 469.

[7] Ibid.   [8] Ibid.

[9] Kierkegaard, *Works of Love*, pp. 276–8.

he does not know the things he thought he knew. Thus, the views of the other person are reduced to absurdities and contradictions. Socrates attempts to show this not by telling the other person what the truth is, but rather by extracting it from the other person by means of questioning. As we learned, this is what Socrates refers to as his art of midwifery or maieutics. In this way Socrates can claim that he was not the author of any new knowledge or information, but rather merely assisted in its coming to the world, just like a midwife assists in delivering babies.

Kierkegaard emphasizes that while Socrates is helping the other person in this way, he must remain as unselfish and anonymous as possible.[10] His actions can be conceived as an act of self-sacrifice since his attempts to help others often lead them to be angry with him. No one likes discovering that the things they hold to be true are in fact confused and mistaken, and the sense of humiliation that this causes was the source of great hostility against Socrates in ancient Athens. For this reason Socrates cannot make a great show of helping other people, but instead he must play down his own role and play up the fact that the other person is reaching the truth on their own. Kierkegaard refers to this in a somewhat odd way as "deceiving the other into the truth."[11] Socrates' interlocutor is unaware that Socrates is helping him by eliminating his false beliefs and illusions and leading him to stand on his own feet afterwards. In the end, he has Socrates to thank for being free, but he will probably never realize it.

This seems clearly to be the model for Kierkegaard for what he is doing with his writings. On the negative side he is combatting what he takes to be mistaken conceptions of Christianity that come from the Church, academic theologians and philosophers, or mainstream culture. Then on the positive side he, just like Socrates the midwife, is enjoining each individual to find his or her own individual way to the

---

[10] In a journal entry from 1851 Kierkegaard objects to criticisms of Socrates on this point: "It is sheer genial drivel to charge that Socrates was motivated by self-love in acting indirectly, maieutically, in ironic isolation. No, according to Socrates' way of thinking, this is precisely what it is to love. If it is true that every man has to help himself, if it is the ideal to stand alone, then it is entirely valid to prevent the one who is being helped from becoming dependent upon the helper—for in that case he is not helped. This was Socrates' idea..." (*Søren Kierkegaard's Journals and Papers*, vols. 1–6, ed. and trans. by Howard V. Hong and Edna H. Hong, Bloomington and London: Indiana University Press 1967–78, vol. 1, pp. 45f., no. 109).

[11] Kierkegaard, *Works of Love*, p. 277.

Christian truth. In this manner he believes that he is helping other people to stand on their own and be free.

In a journal entry from 1847, the same year as *Works of Love*, Kierkegaard states directly that he is following Socrates by employing the maieutic art in the context of what he takes to be the mistaken conceptions of Christianity:

> Now people can do whatever they want to me—insult me, stop reading me, take a poke at my head, kill me—they can never, in all eternity, deny what was my idea and my life, one of the most original thoughts in many years, and the most original thought in the Danish language: that Christianity needed a maieutic practitioner and that I understood how to be one—although no one knew how to appreciate this.[12]

Kierkegaard thus identifies with Socrates as someone who is misunderstood by his age and who evokes the anger of his contemporaries. Most importantly, he describes as "my idea and my life" the Socratic practice of maieutics in a Christian context. He goes on to explain more precisely what this means. He states that the practice of maieutics "assumes that people possess what is highest but wants to help them become aware of what they possess."[13] The problem is that in Christendom the conceptions of Christianity that people have been taught are confused and antithetical to the true nature of the religion. But despite being constantly exposed to these mistaken views, people still have the possibility of attaining the correct form of faith in their inwardness and subjectivity. So the task of what Kierkegaard calls the "maieutic practitioner" is to disabuse people of the erroneous views that they are used to hearing and get them in touch with their own inwardness and passion.

8.3. Kierkegaard's *The Point of View*

In the last chapter we mentioned Kierkegaard's posthumously published book *The Point of View for My Work as an Author*. Of particular importance in our context is the fact that he refers to Socrates several times and makes it clear that he is following the

---

[12] *Kierkegaard's Journals and Notebooks*, vol. 4, pp. 102–3, NB:154.
[13] *Kierkegaard's Journals and Notebooks*, vol. 4, p. 103, NB:154.

Greek philosopher in certain aspects. For example, in the Introduction to the work, Kierkegaard explains that *The Point of View* is not a defense of his work, and he compares this with Socrates' behavior at his trial. He writes, "If in nothing else, on this point, I truly believe that I have something in common with Socrates."[14] He recalls that Socrates mentions that his daimon never tried to prevent him from speaking or acting the way he did at his trial, and so Socrates took this to mean that he was in no danger since if he were doing something wrong, his daimon would have warned him as it always did.[15] Kierkegaard interprets this to mean that Socrates never really tried to defend himself at his trial or rather that his divine daimon had prevented him from doing so. Kierkegaard believes that such a defense would have been a contradiction, presumably since Socrates' work was always negative and to defend himself would have amounted to stating positive claims.

One can discuss the validity of Kierkegaard's interpretation here since it does seem that Socrates tries to explain and thus defend his actions to the jurors, but then in Kierkegaard's favor is the fact that when Socrates had the opportunity to propose an alternative sentence, he did not really make any serious attempt to get a lighter punishment, but rather proposed that he receive free meals at the Prytaneum. In any case, Kierkegaard sees himself as following Socrates in not defending his work since, he says, "there is in me and in the dialectical nature of my relationship something that makes it impossible for me and impossible in itself to conduct a 'defense' of my authorship."[16] So on this score, it seems that Kierkegaard clearly identified with the fate of Socrates and regarded himself to be persecuted unjustly by what he called "the crowd."

Elsewhere Kierkegaard returns to his concerns about the rising demands for democracy, which he believes in some ways destroys the individual. In democracy what is important is not the individual as individual, but rather the collection of people in larger groups, that is, in political parties. One's voice as an individual is only heard when that voice is shared by a number of other voices. Thus, Kierkegaard

---

[14] Kierkegaard, *The Point of View*, trans. by Howard V. Hong and Edna H. Hong, Princeton: Princeton University Press 1998, p. 24.

[15] Kierkegaard had already mentioned this in *The Concept of Irony* to illustrate the negative nature of the daimon. See *The Concept of Irony*, trans. by Howard V. Hong and Edna H. Hong, Princeton: Princeton University Press 1989, pp. 159f.

[16] Kierkegaard, *The Point of View*, p. 24.

develops a number of concepts, such as "the crowd," "the masses," and "public opinion," which he uses to characterize what he takes to be pernicious new developments in his own age. His own emphasis, by contrast, was to insist on the irreducible value of the individual. He believes that even if one has an opinion that is not shared by others and thus is obliged to stand alone as an individual, this should be respected and regarded as having some validity. But in a democracy it can never really carry any real weight until it is shared by a larger group.

Also on this point Kierkegaard believes that he has something in common with Socrates. He explains how his emphasis on "the single individual" was regarded as eccentric and points out that Socrates was regarded as eccentric for the same reason.[17] Noting Hegel's characterization of Socrates as the inventor of ethics in the sense of the inventor of the idea of subjective freedom, Kierkegaard sees himself as reintroducing subjective freedom in his own day. In the age of modern democracy, it is the crowd that is malign, and so he takes a part of his task to be to struggle against this tendency by focusing on the individual.

In these reflections on his work Kierkegaard reserves a special place for Socrates, whom he acknowledges as his teacher.[18] This confirms that Kierkegaard's appreciation of Socrates was not just a fleeting youthful interest in his master's thesis, but rather an absolutely determining factor in his work as a whole.

8.4. The Revolutions of 1848 and *The Sickness unto Death*

In 1848 there were revolutions breaking out across Europe. People protested against the rule of absolute monarchy and demanded that the power of the kings be limited by a constitution. This was the most radical period of political change in Europe since the French Revolution of 1789. The Revolution began in France and quickly spread to include the German states, the Italian states, the Habsburg Empire, Poland, Belgium, Romania, and so on. It reached Denmark on March 21, 1848, when the National Liberals marched to the Royal Palace and

---

[17] Ibid., pp. 68f.   [18] Ibid., p. 55.

demanded that the new King Frederik VII create a democratic constitution. The king agreed, and negotiations went on for more than a year until the new constitution was agreed upon and signed into law on June 5, 1849.

Kierkegaard published *The Sickness unto Death* on July 30, 1849, shortly after the introduction of the new Danish Constitution and thus the completion of the bloodless revolution. Kierkegaard introduces a new pseudonymous author by the name of Anti-Climacus, who catalogues the different forms of despair that humans suffer from. He understands despair as a form of sin and in the end recommends embracing Christianity as a solution to despair. Although one might think that this work is irrelevant for Kierkegaard's concerns with Socrates, in fact Anti-Climacus also holds up Socrates as a model for what is needed in his own day.

In a short section Anti-Climacus compares Socrates' understanding of sin with the Christian understanding. The discussion must be seen against the background of the political turmoil that was taking place in Denmark at the time. In the course of the negotiations in the Constitutional Assembly, there were of course many conflicting voices. Each person seemed to have his own clear idea of what was needed at the time. In *The Sickness unto Death* Kierkegaard refers to this in a somewhat odd way. He does not evoke some particular political leader, group, or modern cause, but instead hearkens back to Socrates. He writes,

> Socrates, Socrates, Socrates! Yes, we may well call your name three times; it would not be too much to call it ten times, if it would be of any help. Popular opinion maintains that the world needs a republic, needs a new social order and a new religion—but no one considers that what the world, confused simply by too much knowledge, needs is a Socrates.[19]

Why would he think that of all people the ancient philosopher Socrates was of urgent importance in the wake of the 1848 Revolutions in Europe?

Kierkegaard suggests that what his age needs is an "ironic-ethical correction,"[20] which is what Socrates provided for his contemporaries.

---

[19] Kierkegaard, *The Sickness unto Death*, trans. by Howard V. Hong and Edna H. Hong, Princeton: Princeton University Press 1980, p. 92.
[20] Ibid.

Socrates corrected the folly of his fellow countrymen by his irony, by claiming to know nothing, and by pretending to believe that other people knew all the things they said that they did. In Kierkegaard's time, people were quite convinced that they knew what was needed for the state. They each had their own idea of the nature of the constitution and the structure of the government. Kierkegaard seems to suggest here that they are misguided and really do not know. What is needed is for someone to show that they do not know by means of a modern version of Socratic irony. He notes that people are anxious to go beyond Socrates and to construct some positive doctrine or present some solution to the political confusion of the day. But, he claims, instead of overcoming Socratic ignorance and going beyond Socrates, what is needed rather is a return to Socrates, that is, a return to Socratic ignorance.

As we have seen, his goal is to point out that Christianity cannot be explained or understood discursively since it is based on paradox, absurdity, or contradiction. So to attempt to comprehend it can only serve to distort its true nature. Kierkegaard thus writes,

> I consider it an outright ethical task, perhaps requiring not a little self-denial in these very speculative times, when all "the others" are busy comprehending [Christianity], to admit that one is neither able nor obliged to comprehend it. Precisely this is no doubt what our age, what Christendom needs: a little Socratic ignorance with respect to Christianity.[21]

Socrates is thus held up as a corrective to the errors of nineteenth-century philosophy and theology. Socratic ignorance is the means to correct the mistaken conceptions of Christianity.

Kierkegaard recalls that Socrates regarded his activities as divinely sanctioned based on the oracle's statement. Socrates believed that by the oracle saying that he was the wisest, he had been enjoined to examine the purported wisdom of others and undermine it when it proved to be unfounded. Kierkegaard regards his own mission as a parallel one with that of Socrates, but, instead of the issue being one of knowledge, it is one of the nature of Christianity. Kierkegaard goes around Copenhagen and explores the different conceptions of Christianity which he believes to be mistaken. In his works he tries to point out the contradictions and problems with these conceptions in order

---

[21] Ibid., p. 99.

to undermine them, just as Socrates did with the different claims to knowledge that he encountered. But Kierkegaard resists the urge to prop up a different positive conception of Christianity in contrast to the ones he is criticizing, just as Socrates refuses to present any positive doctrine of the truth himself. Instead, they are both content to remain in negativity. Kierkegaard thus uses Socratic ignorance to guard Christianity against the mistaken positive claims of philosophy and theology of the day.

8.5. Kierkegaard's *Practice in Christianity*

In 1850 Kierkegaard published *Practice in Christianity* under the name Anti-Climacus, the same pseudonym that he used for *The Sickness unto Death*. The work is divided into three sections or numbers. The first of these treats the passage from Matthew chapter 11, verse 28, where Jesus says to "Come here, all you who labor and are burdened, and I will give you rest." Kierkegaard had previously given a sermon on this passage in the Church of Our Lady (see Fig. 8.1) for the Friday Communion on June 18, 1847. He then published this in 1848 in Part Four of *Christian Discourses*. A part of Kierkegaard's inspiration for this analysis might well have come from the sculpture of Jesus by the famous Danish sculptor Bertel Thorvaldsen that stands at the altar of the Church of Our Lady and which is inspired by the same biblical verse.

In the second part of the work Kierkegaard discusses Matthew, chapter 11, verse 6, where Jesus says, "Blessed is he who is not offended at me." Through his pseudonymous author, Kierkegaard tries to bring us back to the time of Jesus and to capture the experience of the people who saw him and heard him preach. He points out that they did not see a God, but rather a humble man. There was nothing triumphant about Jesus as he was going around the countryside with his flock of disciples spreading his message. Most importantly, Kierkegaard emphasizes that many people were offended by the idea that Jesus was the Son of God and the savior. They could not reconcile this with his humble and meek appearance. So instead of believing, they were offended by the idea. The point here is that this is an important and essential part of Christian belief that we cannot forget if we hope to maintain a veridical picture of Christianity. Anti-Climacus insists that Christianity requires "the possibility of offense."

Fig. 8.1. The interior of the Church of Our Lady

When Jesus is portrayed as a powerful and triumphant figure, this is a distortion of the historical Jesus. This is not what his contemporary followers saw, but yet they chose to believe anyway. In other words, many more people would presumably have believed right away if they could immediately see that Christ was a powerful, superhuman figure. Such portrayals, however, eliminate the possibility of offense, since no one would be offended by the idea of a triumphant, powerful figure being regarded as a savior or the Son of God. But this constitutes a misunderstanding and distorts the nature of faith. According to Kierkegaard, we must be like the contemporaries of Jesus and believe in spite of his humble appearance, regardless of whether others are offended. But if there is no possibility of offense, then there is no belief.

In connection with this discussion Kierkegaard refers to Christ as "a sign of contradiction"[22] by virtue of his being both human and divine or the "God-man." In other words, our common sense tells us that something must be one thing or the other. We can well understand the idea of a God and the idea of a human being, but the idea of both together is a contradiction. The fundamental idea of Christianity is thus something that is contradictory to our understanding. Kierkegaard's claim is that this contradiction needs to be maintained since this is what is required for faith. Here he again departs from the long tradition of Christian apologetics, which tries to make the idea of the double nature of Christ more comprehensible and understandable. Their goal is to make it easier to understand this key Christian doctrine. But Kierkegaard stubbornly insists that this is a mistake. True Christian faith involves not explaining or dissolving this difficulty, but rather cultivating and emphasizing it.

Here we again see the influence of Socrates on Kierkegaard's project. Concepts such as "offense" and "the sign of contradiction" are intended to emphasize the difficulty of faith rather than make it easier. These are not positive doctrines that explain things; rather, they are negative and show us the limits of our explanations and understanding. So just as Socrates questioned people and made knowing more difficult by exposing the mistaken views of his interlocutors, so also Kierkegaard makes Christian faith more difficult by exposing the mistaken conceptions of his contemporaries about it. But Kierkegaard's Socrates says that he himself is ignorant and does not present a solution to the problem. So also Kierkegaard, through his pseudonyms, does not present a solution by giving his own theory of the incarnation or the nature of Jesus. Instead, he simply says that it is a contradiction that cannot be grasped by the understanding and leaves it at that.

---

[22] Kierkegaard, *Practice in Christianity*, trans. by Howard V. Hong and Edna H. Hong, Princeton: Princeton University Press 1991, p. 124.

8.6. The Attack on the Church

In the last years of his life, 1854–5, Kierkegaard mounted a relentless attack on the Danish State Church and its most distinguished representatives. He issued his criticism in a series of polemical articles in the newspaper *The Fatherland* and his own publication *The Moment*. He accused the pastors and bishops of corruption, hypocrisy, and distorting the Christian message. This attack was scandalous for Danish society and was a topic that was avoided in polite conversation for years after Kierkegaard's death.

The immediate occasion for the attack was a sermon that was given by his old rival Martensen, who had just been appointed as Bishop of Zealand and the head of the Danish State Church. In his sermon Martensen referred to his predecessor, the recently deceased Jakob Peter Mynster (see Fig. 8.2), as "a witness to the truth." Kierkegaard took issue with this characterization in an article entitled "Was Bishop Mynster a 'Truth-Witness?'" published on December 18, 1854 in the newspaper *The Fatherland*. This was the occasion for Kierkegaard to develop his conception of what he calls "New Testament Christianity" and to show how radically it differs from the lives of Mynster and Martensen.

By "New Testament Christianity" Kierkegaard seems to mean the form of Christianity that was practiced by its first followers as recorded in the New Testament. He points out that Christianity at that time required great demands on the believer. The early Christians lived in poverty and were often martyrs for their faith. They were ridiculed and detested by the mainstream Roman society. At that time, in the ancient Roman world, to identify oneself as a Christian was to risk one's life. Christians had to meet in secret to hold their church services. In the face of this, belief was a very difficult matter. Christianity was then a small, marginalized religion, and the beliefs of its followers also exposed them to social ostracism. Thus, for Kierkegaard, to be a witness to the truth of Christianity requires considerable sacrifice.

In this context Kierkegaard again sees a parallel with Socrates. The true Christian was one who had to be prepared for martyrdom: to be tortured and even killed for his beliefs. Socrates was in a sense a martyr for philosophy, relentlessly seeking the truth, even if it made him enemies. People came to resent him since he exposed them for their ignorance and arrogance. Even at the end he never recanted or

Fig. 8.2. Bishop Jakob Peter Mynster (1775–1854)

regretted his actions, but instead stuck steadfastly to his beliefs. This kind of resolve is needed for a return to New Testament Christianity. The person who, like Kierkegaard, exposes the hypocrisy and corruption of the clergy will be subject to ridicule and hatred just as Socrates was. From the conflict with *The Corsair*, Kierkegaard learned what it was like to experience this, and he regarded himself as a martyr.

He then compares his idea of New Testament Christianity with what he sees in the Danish State Church. He looks at the highest officials of the Danish Church and finds that they are far from making sacrifices for their faith. They are in no danger of being persecuted. There is no chance that they will have to risk their lives. On the contrary, they are among the most respected members of society, and they receive a regular salary from the state. Kierkegaard argues that this is wholly inconsonant with the true nature of Christianity, as one finds it in the New Testament. Instead of losing their livelihood by being Christians, the priests are earning their living from it. Instead of being detested outcasts of society, the priests are leading pillars of it. Kierkegaard believes that this is a fundamental distortion of the true nature of Christianity. He demands that the priests either reform themselves in order to come more in line with the hard demands of New Testament Christianity or give up calling themselves Christians.

Kierkegaard also criticizes lay people who call themselves Christians simply because they were born in a Christian country, where they automatically become members of the State Church. This again is, according to Kierkegaard, not in keeping with the true nature of the Christian doctrine, which demands a conscious act of belief on the part of the individual. If no conscious choice has taken place, then one cannot rightly call oneself a Christian.

With these views Kierkegaard issues a demanding challenge to his contemporaries and warns against religious complacency. Being a Christian is something that one needs to work at every day and every hour. It requires one to make all sorts of sacrifices with regard to normal bourgeois life. Kierkegaard's warning to the future was clearly for people to be attentive to this and always to keep in focus the difficult demands of New Testament Christianity and not to allow themselves to be seduced by a lukewarm version of it, which is, to his mind, a grotesque distortion.

8.7. The Last Issue of *The Moment*

While Kierkegaard was composing his articles for *The Fatherland* and *The Moment*, he lived in a building right across the street from the Church of Our Lady and the Bishop's Palace. He was thus living literally just a stone's throw away from Bishop Martensen's residence. While he was living here he published nine issues of *The Moment* and had just completed the tenth and final issue when he fell fatally ill.

The Moment, no. 10 is an interesting work since Kierkegaard reflects on his own strategy in his attack on the Church, and here once again we can see some interesting hints of the figure of Socrates emerge. In the section called simply "My Task," Kierkegaard reminds his readers that he has not called himself a Christian and that it is of the utmost importance that people bear this in mind. This might come as a surprise to some people, since every introductory text or encyclopedia article on Kierkegaard begins by saying that he is a

Christian writer. What, then, can he mean when he says that he never called himself a Christian?

Church history is full of different sects and factions that claimed to know the truth about Christianity and criticized others for not knowing it. They thus took a kind of moral high ground by viewing themselves as the true Christians, while others fell short of the mark. Kierkegaard is anxious to avoid this kind of relation, where he props himself up as the moral authority. If he were to assert that he were the true Christian, then he would open himself up to criticisms from his opponents, who could claim that he was a hypocrite. In order to avoid this, he simply says that he does not call himself a Christian. In *The Point of View for My Work as an Author*, he explains this point as follows: "If it is an illusion that all are Christians, and if something is to be done, it must be done indirectly, and not by someone who loudly declares himself to be an extraordinary Christian, but by someone who, better informed, even declares himself not to be a Christian."[23]

Instead, he takes a different strategy, painting a picture of New Testament Christianity that is so difficult to live up to that it ends up being a kind of unattainable ideal. He justifies his criticism not on the basis of his own authority, but rather on the basis of this ideal, which nineteenth-century Danish Christianity does not measure up to. This ideal allows him to criticize what he takes to be the corrupt and false Christianity of his contemporaries without him having to commit himself to saying that he personally embodies the ideal. In short, the ideal does the critical work for him, and he simply has to point it out.

This too is a Socratic strategy. Like Socrates, Kierkegaard ostensibly claims to know nothing. Socrates then goes around and asks others what they know, just as Kierkegaard explores the conception of Christianity of other people. Just as Socrates then discovers that, although other people claim to know certain things, they are in fact ignorant, so also Kierkegaard sees that, although his contemporaries claim to be pious Christians, they have a mistaken understanding of Christianity. Socrates keeps driving at the truth and continues to ask people what they know in the hope of one day finding it. It is as if he

---

[23] See *The Point of View*, p. 43. See also ibid., p. 54.

has a conception or ideal of it that he can never manage to attain, just as Kierkegaard has an ideal of Christianity and says that he does not call himself a Christian. Neither Socrates nor Kierkegaard claims that he has reached this ideal. Their task was to show that other people have not attained it, even though they may claim to have done so. Thus, Kierkegaard writes,

> The only analogy I have before me is Socrates; my task is a Socratic task, to audit the definition of what it is to be a Christian—I do not call myself a Christian (keeping the ideal free), but I can make it manifest that the others are that even less.[24]

This makes it clear that Kierkegaard used Socrates, a pagan philosopher, in his attempt to criticize what he took to be the mistaken conceptions about Christianity in his own time. When confronted with the words of the oracle that there was no one wiser than he, Socrates interpreted this to mean simply that while everyone else claimed to know something and yet was ignorant, he at least knew that he was ignorant, and on this sole point he was wiser than the others. Similarly, Kierkegaard can point out that the version of Christianity that the others are following is mistaken, although everyone else believes that they are pious Christians. The difference between Kierkegaard and them is simply that he realizes that he is not a Christian, while the others continue to believe themselves to be so. Thus, like Socrates, he avoids making the positive claim about his own status, but instead his project is the negative one of exposing the problems with the views of others.

Socrates struggled against the Sophists; they taught for money, and they had no problem in presenting something as true. Kierkegaard sees a parallel with the clergy and theologians of his day who were well paid by the state. They too teach for a fee; indeed, they are financially supported by the state. They claim to teach the truth of Christianity, but, according to Kierkegaard, the conception of Christianity that they present is deeply problematic. So, for Kierkegaard, these are the modern Sophists, while he is the modern Socrates.

---

[24] Kierkegaard, *The Moment and Late Writings*, p. 341. See also *Søren Kierkegaard's Journals and Papers*, vol. 1, p. 46, no. 109: "I began with the Socratic . . . ."

8.8. Kierkegaard's Illness and Death

The public conflict with the Danish Church doubtless took its toll on Kierkegaard, who never enjoyed robust health even in his best days. Due perhaps to stress and overwork, Kierkegaard became seriously ill and, after collapsing, was admitted to Frederik's Hospital on October 2, 1855. He was visited regularly by certain members of his extended family, for example, his nephews, but he refused to see his elder brother Peter Christian. He was angry with Peter Christian who, at the Roskilde Ecclesiastical Convention on July 5, 1855, had given a speech which took a critical stance toward Kierkegaard's attack on the Church.[25] The ailing Kierkegaard was, however, regularly visited by his friend Emil Boesen, who left behind an account of Kierkegaard's final days.[26]

As Kierkegaard's condition continued to deteriorate, hope began to slip away. Boesen asked if he would take Holy Communion, but Kierkegaard refused. He claimed that he would only take it from a layman, not a pastor.[27] But this was, of course, not legal since only ordained pastors were permitted to perform such ceremonies. So Kierkegaard declared that he would die without the communion. He explained to Boesen, "The pastors are civil servants of the Crown and have nothing to do with Christianity."[28]

Kierkegaard suffered from a paralysis that immobilized his legs and lower body. His condition gradually worsened to the point that he could hardly hold up his head or move at all. He became weaker and weaker with each day, and reached a point where he was not able to recognize anyone or even to speak. Finally, he died on the evening of November 11, 1855. By the time that he died, Kierkegaard had exhausted his finances. He had lived his entire life on the money that he had inherited from his father, and most all of this was spent by 1855. When he died, the only thing that he had left was his extensive book collection.

8.9. Kierkegaard's Funeral and Burial

Kierkegaard's funeral took place on Sunday, November 18, 1855 in the Church of Our Lady. The situation was awkward given his attack

---

[25] *Encounters with Kierkegaard*, pp. 259ff., p. 304.   [26] Ibid., pp. 121f.
[27] Ibid., pp. 125f.   [28] Ibid., p. 126.

Fig. 8.3. Eggert Christopher Tryde (1781–1860)

on the Church. For this reason few members of the clergy dared to show up for fear of being perceived to be sympathetic to Kierkegaard's cause. The only exceptions were Kierkegaard's brother, Peter Christian Kierkegaard, who was the only remaining relative in Kierkegaard's immediate family, and Archdeacon Eggert Christopher Tryde, who was the presiding pastor (see Fig. 8.3). It was a difficult proposition for Tryde since, on the one hand, he could hardly criticize Kierkegaard's attack on the Church for fear of seeming to speak ill of the dead, but then, on the other hand, he could hardly ignore it completely since it was a fresh controversy that had attracted a large amount of public attention.

Peter Christian gave the eulogy and recounted the life of his father and the loss of his siblings.[29] He could not avoid completely the issue of the controversy surrounding the attack on the Church, although he said that the funeral was not the appropriate place to discuss it. Nonetheless, he emphasized that he thought that his brother had gone too far in his criticism, and that much of what Søren had said

---

[29] Ibid., p. 132.

in the context of his articles in *The Fatherland* and *The Moment* could not be accepted.

A large number of people were in attendance; indeed, there was standing room only in the church. It was said that there were few distinguished members of society, but rather most of the people who came were from the lower social classes. This might be taken to imply that Kierkegaard's works were popular among ordinary people, who were not trained scholars or academics. Or it might be explained by the fact that Kierkegaard was a well-known public figure who was seen regularly on his daily walks through Copenhagen. There was also doubtless an element of sensationalism involved, since people were keen to see how the official Church establishment would deal with this awkward and sensitive situation.

After the funeral in the church, the procession made its way to Assistens Cemetery for the burial itself. Here Kierkegaard was to be interred in the family grave, where his mother, his father, and his siblings were buried. Tryde had just completed the simple burial ceremony when suddenly, Kierkegaard's nephew, a young man named Henrik Lund, began to speak. Lund was a medical student who was doing his residency at Frederik's Hospital at the time and had witnessed Kierkegaard's final days firsthand.

To the surprise of absolutely everybody, he addressed the crowd at the grave in a polemical and agitated tone. Tryde tried to object that since Lund was not ordained, he had no right to speak during the ceremony, but the sentiment of the crowd of people present supported Lund, loudly encouraging him, and so there was little that Tryde could do to prevent it. Lund began by speaking about his relation to Kierkegaard as the son of the deceased's sister, Nicoline Christine Kierkegaard, who had died in 1832. But, Lund explained, he was more than just Kierkegaard's relative; he was also his friend. Moreover, he agreed with Kierkegaard's views. Lund pointed out that at the funeral everyone seemed to be talking around the point and carefully avoided any mention of Kierkegaard's actual writings and opinions. So he felt obligated to say something about Kierkegaard's criticism of the Church in his recent articles in *The Fatherland* and *The Moment*.

Lund's main argument was that the official funeral and burial of Kierkegaard by the State Church were merely a vindication of the correctness of Kierkegaard's criticism. In his attack on what he derogatorily called "the official Church," Kierkegaard complained that being a Christian had become a simple matter of course, and thus the actual content of Christianity, which makes very difficult demands on its followers, is distorted and even destroyed. In the last years of his life Kierkegaard had done everything he could to criticize and distance himself from this view of the official Church, but yet despite all this, the Church still nonetheless seemed to regard him as a loyal member and was now giving him an official church burial. Lund argues that this would never happen in other religions such as Judaism or Islam. If someone had attacked the religious establishment of these religions in the same way that Kierkegaard attacked the Danish Church, then there would have been no question of giving him the usual funeral rites. But the Danish Church nonetheless still clearly regards Kierkegaard as a member and accords him the rites of burial as such. For Lund, this is a clear demonstration of the fact that the Danish Church has no meaningful conception of Christianity, just as Kierkegaard had argued.[30]

Toward the end of his outburst Lund issues a violent reproach of the Church. He asks if the official Danish Church does not represent the true Christian Church, what, then, does it represent? To Tryde's horror, his answer was that it was a corrupt institution utterly compromised by its relations to worldly powers. Lund enjoined the onlookers to leave the official Church and protested against the funeral proceedings as violating Kierkegaard's beliefs and wishes. Since he was dead and could not defend himself, Lund, as his friend, felt obliged to do so on his behalf. When he was done, some people applauded, and even shouted "Bravo," and "Down with the clergy!"[31]

This was a major scandal at the time, which was recounted again and again by witnesses at the graveside to those who were not present. Some people agreed with the sentiment that informed Lund's protest, but thought that he had gone too far to express himself in the way that he did. Others loyal to the Church were outraged by it. There were newspaper articles about the outburst, and Lund himself published his speech in full three days later on November 22, 1855 in *The Fatherland*. Needless to say, the Church establishment did not take this well. Bishop Martensen exercised his authority in the matter by bringing legal proceedings against Lund, who was eventually compelled to pay a rather large fine.

---

[30] Ibid., p. 134.   [31] Ibid., p. 133.

The Lund affair thus exacerbated the controversy already gener-ated by Kierkegaard's own articles. As a result, in the years following Kierkegaard's death, his name in Denmark was always associated with something scandalous and unpleasant. There can be little doubt that this had a negative effect on the initial reception of his thought, since it discouraged people from exploring his work in a scholarly fashion given that people were afraid of being associated with the scandal he had caused. It took some time for the scandal to die down and for a new generation to come of age that was no longer affected by it in the same way. Thus, the reception of Kierkegaard's thought was slow to start, but once it began, it continued to grow as the years passed.

8.10. Kierkegaard's Legacy

What can we say about Kierkegaard's legacy or the reception of his thought by later philosophers, theologians, and writers? When his-torians of ideas try to tell the story of the history of philosophy, they do not really have time to go into great detail with respect to any individual thinker. Instead, they tend to paint in large strokes and to see certain continuities that allow them to treat groups of thinkers together under broad headings. They thus tell the story of different schools of thought: rationalism, idealism, empiricism, materialism, realism, etc. In short, it is the story of -isms. But this approach invariably leads to certain distortions with respect to the nuances of the thought of the individual thinkers. There has been no shortage of attempts to see Kierkegaard as a member of a certain school of thought or -ism.

The existentialists were quick to hail him as an important fore-father of their school.[32] They saw in Kierkegaard's writings important analyses of freedom, alienation, authenticity, meaninglessness, despair, and anxiety. These were all points of great inspiration for authors such as Simone de Beauvoir, Albert Camus, Martin Heidegger, Karl Jaspers, Gabriel Marcel, Jean-Paul Sartre, and others associated with the existentialist tradition.

---

[32] See *Kierkegaard and Existentialism*, ed. by Jon Stewart, Aldershot: Ashgate 2011 (*Kierkegaard Research: Sources, Reception, and Resources*, vol. 9).

Philosophers and literary theorists associated with the movements of deconstruction and post-modernism have also seen Kierkegaard as an important precursor of some of their central ideas.[33] They have been particularly attracted to Kierkegaard's interest in irony. They have seen Kierkegaard's use of the pseudonyms as a support of their views about the death of the author. They celebrate Kierkegaard's use of different perspectives and authorial voices as a forerunner of what has been referred to as the indefinite deferral of meaning. Figures such as Jean Baudrillard, Gilles Deleuze, Jacques Derrida, Jacques Lacan, and Paul de Man have been important figures in this dimension of the reception of Kierkegaard's thought.

Theologians and religious writers have, of course, also been keen to make use of Kierkegaard's writings.[34] Kierkegaard's initial reception internationally came from Germany, where he was seen as an important influence on the movement known as "dialectical theology," which includes figures such as Karl Barth, Emil Brunner, Rudolf Bultmann, and Paul Tillich. Although a Lutheran himself, Kierkegaard has been a source of inspiration for thinkers of other faiths and denominations including Reformed Protestantism, Catholicism, and Judaism.

Also, literary writers, including novelists, playwrights, and literary critics, have found in Kierkegaard an important source of inspiration.[35] Writers from countries around the world have attempted to create Kierkegaardian characters or to explore, in a literary way, emotions such as anxiety and despair that Kierkegaard discussed in his works. Likewise, attempts have been made to imitate and further develop Kierkegaard's own, often pioneering, literary techniques. Well-known authors such as Ibsen, Joyce, Kafka, Thomas Mann, Rilke, and Strindberg all make active use of Kierkegaard and owe a debt to him.

When one traces the history of ideas it can perhaps be useful to see the way in which Kierkegaard's writings were appropriated by

---

[33] See *Kierkegaard and Post/Modernity*, ed. by Martin J. Matuštík and Merold Westphal, Bloomington, Indianapolis: Indiana University Press 1995.

[34] See *Kierkegaard's Influence on Theology*, Tomes I–III, ed. by Jon Stewart, Aldershot: Ashgate 2012 (*Kierkegaard Research: Sources, Reception, and Resources*, vol. 10).

[35] See *Kierkegaard's Influence on Literature and Criticism*, Tomes I–V, ed. by Jon Stewart, Aldershot: Ashgate 2013 (*Kierkegaard Research: Sources, Reception, and Resources*, vol. 12).

these later thinkers. But we need to be careful about automatically associating him with later schools of thought and intellectual trends. Kierkegaard was a unique figure, and his writings resist the usual designations. To see him as a member of a specific school can lead to distortions of his thought. Later thinkers tend to pick and choose certain aspects of his thinking that are relevant for their intellectual agenda. Regardless of how important these aspects are, this approach invariably leads to a selective interpretation, and so we should probably be a bit cautious about labeling Kierkegaard in any definitive way. But, to be sure, to call Kierkegaard an existentialist or a postmodernist and to associate him with later thinkers creates a new context of thought which can be fruitful and useful to explore. But this is, of course, different from Kierkegaard's own thought in its original context.

It is safe to say that Kierkegaard's work cannot be reduced to a single aspect or a single intellectual trend. To appreciate fully his writings requires that we look at them from different perspectives and with different interpretations. One might be tempted to say of the reception of Kierkegaard's thought what he said of the reception of Socrates' philosophy. Since Socrates was a negative thinker in the sense that the Greek philosopher always claimed ignorance and refrained from giving any positive view in his own name, this left a vacuum for later interpretation to fill. As a result, there were many different competing philosophical schools that later claimed their origin in Socrates. So also with Kierkegaard, his own Socratic mission made it such that he too was in many regards a negative thinker. This made it possible for him to be appropriated by many different schools of thought, some of which were even in conflict with one another. This negative or open-ended dimension of his thought perhaps explains why he continues to appeal to so many different readers with very different kinds of interests.

8.11. Christian Appropriation

We recall from Chapter 2 that as a young student Kierkegaard came to Gilleleje in the summer of 1835 to try to figure out what he wanted to do with his life. It was here that he expressed his deep desire to find a truth that had a profound meaning for him personally, as he put it, "a truth for which [he was] willing to live and die."[36] It seems certain that both Kierkegaard's experience in Gilleleje and his master's thesis on Socrates and irony had a profound influence on his later development.

Only about a month after Kierkegaard's death a little-known Danish theologian named Hans Frederik Helveg published an article entitled "Hegelianism in Denmark." This title is somewhat misleading since Helveg only briefly mentions at the beginning some of the main works and figures in the movement of Danish Hegelianism. In fact, the large part of the article is dedicated to a book review of Kierkegaard's *The Concept of Irony*. The connection here is not in itself surprising since, as we have seen, Kierkegaard drew much of his inspiration from Hegel and especially the German philosopher's interpretation of the Greek world and the figure of Socrates. So it makes sense that Helveg would treat *The Concept of Irony* as an important part of the Danish Hegel reception.

Although modern scholarship tends somewhat to ignore *The Concept of Irony* and downplay its significance, Helveg saw the importance of this work for Kierkegaard generally. He writes,

> The members of the Faculty of Philosophy who were supposed to judge the work hardly suspected that in this effort of a young author they had not so much a qualification for a master's degree but a program for life, that here it was a matter not of giving a solution to an academic problem but of a *task of life*.[37]

Helveg emphasizes that Kierkegaard was not concerned with abstract academic knowledge and instead emphasized knowledge that was true for him personally and relevant for his life. To back up his assertion Helveg cites a sentence at the end of *The Concept of Irony* where Kierkegaard claims, "If our generation has any task at all, it must be to translate the achievement of scientific scholarship into personal life, to appropriate it personally."[38]

On the face of it, Kierkegaard seems to be making a kind of protest against academic learning just for its own sake. The point of going to university and learning new things is not just to understand the

---

[36] *Kierkegaard's Journals and Notebooks*, vol. 1, p. 19, AA:12.

[37] Hans Frederik Helveg, "Hegelianismen i Danmark," *Dansk Kirketidende*, vol. 10, no. 51, December 16, 1855, p. 830.

[38] Kierkegaard, *The Concept of Irony*, trans. by Howard V. Hong and Edna H. Hong, Princeton: Princeton University Press 1989, p. 328.

way the world works; instead, this knowledge should be transformed or translated into something personal. Each person must, as Kierkegaard says, "appropriate" knowledge in the context of their own situation and life. So the idea of appropriation is absolutely central to Kierkegaard's understanding of the proper acquisition and application of knowledge.

Kierkegaard's use of Socrates lends further support to Helveg's thesis. But now, here at the end of our investigation we can see that there is much more in this single sentence than what Kierkegaard could have realized at the time. As we have seen, Kierkegaard had an early academic interest, namely, Socrates and his conflict with the Greek world. He made this academic interest the subject of his master's thesis. But after this was done, he took the further step that he claims here is so important: he *appropriated* that knowledge in accordance with his own modern situation. He was attracted to many aspects of Socrates' thought and decided to use him as a model. But the world of ancient Greece in which Socrates lived was of course very different from Kierkegaard's Golden Age Denmark. So Kierkegaard needed to *appropriate* the main elements from the thought of Socrates and transfer them to his own time. So the key terms from the thought of Socrates such as irony, ignorance, negation, *aporia*, maieutics, the gadfly, and so on, all came to take on a new meaning in the context of Kierkegaard's own life and time. Helveg was entirely right: Socrates was, for Kierkegaard, not just an object of scholarly investigation, but also a model to follow in his personal life.

Kierkegaard was familiar with the scholarly field of theology, which he learned about at the University of Copenhagen. Again, as we have seen in the Gilleleje entry in his journals, Kierkegaard is only interested to a certain degree in theology as an academic discipline. Instead, he believes that Christianity is not a doctrine or an objective truth that can be taught in books or in the classroom. Instead, Christianity is a belief that must be *appropriated* by each individual personally in inwardness and passion. Christianity is all about the subjectivity of each individual. There are no easy answers, since each person is obliged to *appropriate* the Christian message in one's own life and context. No one can tell another person how this should be done.

So Kierkegaard believes that Socrates can help us in the modern world. With his irony and negativity he can help us to undermine mistaken views and modern illusions that people today suffer from.

With his idea of maieutics or midwifery he can help us to understand that each and every one of us individually has the truth within himself and that each and every human being has an infinite value that should be respected. These are important messages for us today living in the twenty-first century, regardless of whether we regard ourselves as religious or not. We struggle to understand our role in the fast-moving, anonymous society around us. What is my importance? What is the meaning and value of my life? Do I really count for anything as a person or am I simply a number or a statistic? Kierkegaard is not just a figure locked into his own time, who with every passing day becomes less and less relevant, only to end up an object of interest for a cadre of specialists in the history of ideas. On the contrary, every day as society continues to develop and new technical innovations change our ways of living, interacting, and thinking about ourselves, Kierkegaard becomes more and more relevant. He might have died in 1855, but he is still very much with us today, for anyone who has the ability to read his works and appreciate his ideas.

Bibliography

I. Introductions to Kierkegaard

Allen, E. L., *Kierkegaard: His Life and Thought*, London: Nott 1935; New York: Harper 1936.

Arbaugh, George E. and George Bartholomew Arbaugh, *Kierkegaard's Authorship: A Guide to the Writings of Kierkegaard*, Rock Island, Illinois: Augustana College Library 1967; London: Allen & Unwin 1968.

Billeskov Jansen, F. J., *Søren Kierkegaard: Life and Work*, Copenhagen: Royal Danish Ministry of Foreign Affairs, Ministry of Culture and Ministry of Education 1994.

Brandt, Frithiof, *Søren Kierkegaard, 1813–1855: His Life, His Works*, trans. by Ann R. Born, Copenhagen: Det Danske Selskab in cooperation with The Press and Information Department of the Danish Foreign Office 1963.

Caputo, John D., *How to Read Kierkegaard*, London: Granta Books 2007; New York: W. W. Norton & Company 2008.

Carlisle, Clare, *Kierkegaard: A Guide to the Perplexed*, London: Continuum 2006.

Collins, James, *The Mind of Kierkegaard*, Chicago: Regnery 1953; 2nd revised edition, Princeton: Princeton University Press 1983.

Diem, Hermann, *Kierkegaard: An Introduction*, trans. by David Green, Richmond, Virginia: John Knox Press 1966.

Evans, C. Stephen, *Kierkegaard: An Introduction*, Cambridge: Cambridge University Press 2009.

Ferreira, M. Jamie, *Kierkegaard*, Malden, Massachusetts: Wiley-Blackwell 2009.

Gardiner, Patrick, *Kierkegaard*, Oxford: Oxford University Press 1988.

Hampson, Margaret Daphne, *Kierkegaard: Exposition and Critique*, Oxford: Oxford University Press 2013.

Hohlenberg, Johannes, *Søren Kierkegaard*, trans. by T. H. Croxall, New York: Pantheon 1954; London: Routledge 1954; New York: Farrar, Straus and Giroux 1978.

Jolivet, Régis, *Introduction to Kierkegaard*, trans. by W. H. Barber, London: Muller 1950.

Kirmmse, Bruce H., *Kierkegaard in Golden Age Denmark*, Bloomington and Indianapolis: Indiana University Press 1990.

Malantschuk, Gregor, *Kierkegaard's Way to the Truth: An Introduction to the Authorship of Søren Kierkegaard*, trans. by Mary Michelsen, Minneapolis: Augsburg Publishing House 1963.

Pattison, George, *Kierkegaard and the Crisis of Faith: An Introduction to His Thought*, London: SPCK 1997.

Purkarthofer, Richard, *Kierkegaard*, Leipzig: Reclam 2005.

Rocca, Ettore, *Kierkegaard*, Rome: Carocci editore 2012.

Rohde, H. P., *Søren Kierkegaard: An Introduction to His Life and Philosophy*, trans. by A. M. Williams, London: Allen & Unwin 1963.

Shell, Patrick, *Starting with Kierkegaard*, London: Continuum 2011.

Vardy, Peter, *Kierkegaard*, London: Harper Collins 1996.

II. Biographies of Kierkegaard

Brandt, Frithiof, *Den unge Søren Kierkegaard*, Copenhagen: Levin & Munksgaard 1929.

Cain, David, *An Evocation of Kierkegaard*, Copenhagen: C. A. Reitzel 1997.

Garff, Joakim, *Søren Kierkegaard: A Biography*, trans. by Bruce H. Kirmmse, Princeton: Princeton University Press 2005.

Grimsley, Ronald, *Søren Kierkegaard: A Biographical Introduction*, London: Studio Vista 1973.

Hannay, Alastair, *Kierkegaard: A Biography*, Cambridge: Cambridge University Press 2001.

Lowrie, Walter, *Kierkegaard*, London, New York, and Toronto: Oxford University Press 1938.

Lowrie, Walter, *A Short Life of Kierkegaard*, Princeton: Princeton University Press 1942.

Mendelssohn, Harald von, *Kierkegaard. Ein Genie in einer Kleinstadt*, Stuttgart: Klett-Cotta 1995.

III. Works on Kierkegaard's Relation to Plato and Socrates

Anz, Wilhelm, "Die platonische Idee des Guten und das sokratische Paradox bei Kierkegaard," in *Die antike Philosophie in ihrer Bedeutung für die Gegenwart. Kolloquium zu Ehren des 80. Geburtstages von Hans-Georg Gadamer*, ed. by Reiner Wiehl, Heidelberg: Winther 1981, pp. 23–36.

Arnarsson, Kristian, "Erindring og gentagelse. Kierkegaard og Grækerne," in *Filosofi og samfunn*, ed. by Finn Jor, Kristiansand: Høyskoleforlaget 1998, pp. 197–203.

Ashbaugh, A. Freire, "Platonism: An Essay on Repetition and Recollection," in *Kierkegaard and Great Traditions*, ed. by Niels Thulstrup and Marie Mikulová Thulstrup, Copenhagen: C. A. Reitzel 1981 (*Bibliotheca Kierkegaardiana*, vol. 6), pp. 9–26.

Bejerholm, Lars, "Sokratisk metod hos Søren Kierkegaard och hanns samtid," *Kierkegaardiana*, vol. 4, 1962, pp. 28–44.

Bergman, Shmuel Hugo, "The Concept of Irony in Kierkegaard's Thought," in his *Dialogical Philosophy from Kierkegaard to Buber*, Albany, New York: State University of New York Press 1991, pp. 25–45.

Borgvin, Rune, "En sammenligning av bestemmelsen av sokratisk og romantisk ironi i 'Om Begrebet Ironi,'" in *Kierkegaard 1993—digtning, filosofi, teologi*, ed. by Finn Hauberg Mortensen, Odense: Institut for Litteratur, Kultur og Medier, Odense Universitet 1993, pp. 153–60.

Carlsson, Ulrika, "Love among the Post-Socratics," *Kierkegaard Studies Yearbook*, 2013, pp. 243–66.

Come, Arnold, "Kierkegaard's Ontology of Love," in *Works of Love*, ed. by Robert L. Perkins, Macon, Georgia: Mercer University Press 1999 (*International Kierkegaard Commentary*, vol. 16), pp. 79–119.

Cooper, Robert M., "Plato and Kierkegaard in Dialogue," *Theology Today*, vol. 31, 1974–5, pp. 187–98.

Cooper, Robert M., "Plato on Authority, Irony, and True Riches," in *Kierkegaard's Classical Inspiration*, ed. by Niels Thulstrup and Marie Mikulová Thulstrup, Copenhagen: C. A. Reitzel 1985 (*Bibliotheca Kierkegaardiana*, vol. 14), pp. 25–62.

D'Agostino, Francesco, "La fenomenologia dell'uomo giusto: Un parallelo tra Kierkegaard e Platones," *Rivista Internazionale di Filosofia del Diritto*, vol. 49, 1972, pp. 153–72.

Daise, Benjamin, *Kierkegaard's Socratic Art*, Macon, Georgia: Mercer University Press 1999.

Deuser, Hermann, "Kierkegaards Sokrates—Modell und Umkehrung antiker Philosophie," in his *Kierkegaard. Die Philosophie des religiösen Schriftstellers*, Darmstadt: Wissenschaftliche Buchgesellschaft 1985 (*Erträge der Forschung*, vol. 232), pp. 31–57.

Ferreira, M. Jamie, "The 'Socratic Secret': The *Postscript to the Philosophical Crumbs*," in *Kierkegaard's Concluding Unscientific Postscript: A Critical Guide*, ed. by Rick Anthony Furtak, Cambridge: Cambridge University Press 2010, pp. 6–24.

Friis Johansen, Karsten, "Kierkegaard und die griechische Dialektik," in *Kierkegaard and Dialectics*, ed. by Hermann Deuser and Jørgen K. Bukdahl, Aarhus: University of Aarhus 1979, pp. 51–124.

Gallino, Guglielmo, "Kierkegaard e l'ironia socratica," *Filosofia*, vol. 45, 1994, pp. 143–61.

Greve, Wilfried, *Kierkegaards maieutische Ethik*, Frankfurt am Main: Suhrkamp 1990.

Grunnet, Sanne Elisa, *Ironi og subjektivitet. En studie over S. Kierkegaards disputats Om Begrebet Ironi*, Copenhagen: C. A. Reitzel 1987.

Heerden, Adriaan van, "Does Love Cure the Tragic? Kierkegaardian Variations on a Platonic Theme," in *Stages on Life's Way*, ed. by Robert L. Perkins, Macon, Georgia: Mercer University Press 2000 (*International Kierkegaard Commentary*, vol. 11), pp. 69–90.

Henningsen, Bernd, "Søren Kierkegaard: Sokrates i København," in his *Politik eller Kaos?*, Copenhagen: Berlingske Forlag 1980, pp. 134–233.

Himmelstrup, Jens, *Søren Kierkegaards Opfattelse af Sokrates. En Studie i dansk Filosofis Historie*, Copenhagen: Arnold Busck 1924.

Holm, Isak Winkel, "Myte: Platon," in his *Tanken i billedet. Søren Kierkegaards poetik*, Copenhagen: Gyldendal 1998, pp. 117–56.

Holm, Søren, *Græciteten*, Copenhagen: Munksgaard 1964 (*Søren Kierkegaard Selskabets Populære Skrifter*, vol. 11).

Howland, Jacob, *Kierkegaard and Socrates: A Study in Philosophy and Faith*, New York: Cambridge University Press 2006.

Howland, Jacob, "Lessing and Socrates in Kierkegaard's *Postscript*," in *Kierkegaard's Concluding Unscientific Postscript: A Critical Guide*, ed. by Rick Anthony Furtak, Cambridge: Cambridge University Press 2010, pp. 111–31.

Humbert, David, "Kierkegaard's Use of Plato in His Analysis of the Moment in Time," *Dionysius*, vol. 7, 1983, pp. 149–83.

Jensen, Povl Johannes, "Kierkegaard og Platon," in *Studier i antik og middelalderlig filosofi og idéhistorie*, ed. by Bo Alkjær, Ivan Boserup, Mogens Herman Hansen, and Peter Zeeberg, Copenhagen: Museum Tusculanum 1980, pp. 699–710.

Jensen, Povl Johannes, "Sokrates i Kierkegaards disputats," in his *Cum grano salis. Udvalgte foredrag og artikler 1945–1980*, Odense: Odense Universitetsforlag 1981, pp. 37–51.

Kangas, David, "Conception and Concept: The Two Logics of *The Concept of Irony* and the Place of Socrates," in *Kierkegaard and the Word(s): Essays on Hermeneutics and Communication*, ed. by Poul Houe and Gordon D. Marino, Copenhagen: C. A. Reitzel 2003, pp. 180–91.

Kirmmse, Bruce H., "Socrates in the Fast Lane: Kierkegaard's *The Concept of Irony* on the University's Velocifère (Documents, Context, Commentary, and Interpretation)," in *The Concept of Irony*, ed. by Robert L. Perkins, Macon, Georgia: Mercer University Press 2001 (*International Kierkegaard Commentary*, vol. 2), pp. 17–99.

Klint-Jensen, Henrik, "Platon—Kierkegaard. Tidsånden hos Platon og Søren Kierkegaard," *Fønix*, vol. 19, no. 4, 1995, pp. 24–38.

Klint-Jensen, Henrik, "Idé og dobbeltbevægelse—frigørelse hos Platon og Søren Kierkegaard," *Philosophia*, vol. 24, nos. 1–2, 1995, pp. 155–89.

Kloeden, Wolfdietrich von, "Sokrates," in *Kierkegaard's Classical Inspiration*, ed. by Niels Thulstrup and Marie Mikulová Thulstrup, Copenhagen: C. A. Reitzel 1985 (*Bibliotheca Kierkegaardiana*, vol. 14), pp. 104–81.

Kloeden, Wolfdietrich von, "Sokratische Ironie bei Plato und S. Kierkegaard," in *Irony and Humor in Søren Kierkegaard*, ed. by Niels Thulstrup and Marie Mikulová Thulstrup, Copenhagen: C. A. Reitzel 1988 (*Liber Academiae Kierkegaardiensis*, vol. 7), pp. 51–60.

Kloeden, Wolfdietrich von, *Kierkegaard und Sokrates. Sören Kierkegaards Sokratesrezeption*, Rheinland-Westfalen-Lippe: Evangelische Fachhochschule 1991 (*Schriftenreihe der Evangelischen Fachhochschule Rheinland-Westafalen-Lippe*, vol. 16).

Krentz, Arthur A., "The Socratic-Dialectical Anthropology of Søren Kierkegaard's 'Postscript,'" in *Anthropology and Authority: Essays on Søren Kierkegaard*, ed. by Poul Houe, Gordon D. Marino, and Sven Hakon Rossel, Amsterdam and Atlanta: Rodopi 2000, pp. 17–26.

Kuypers, Etienne, "Kierkegaards opmerkingen over de noodzaak van een Socratisch nihilisme," *Filosofie*, vol. 3, no. 4, 1993, pp. 22–8.

Kylliäinen, Janne, "*Phaedo* and *Parmenides*: Eternity, Time, and the Moment, or From the Abstract Philosophical to the Concrete Christian," in *Kierkegaard and the Greek World*, Tome I, *Socrates and Plato*, ed. by Jon Stewart and Katalin Nun, Aldershot: Ashgate 2010 (*Kierkegaard Research: Sources, Reception, and Resources*, vol. 2), pp. 45–71.

Leverkühn, André, "Engagement und Passion des dänischen Sokrates," in his *Das ethische und das Ästhetische als Kategorien des Handelns. Selbstwerdung bei Søren Kierkegaard*, Frankfurt am Main, Berlin, Bern, Brussels, New York, and Vienna: Peter Lang 2000, pp. 31–40.

Manheimer, Ronald J., "Educating Subjectivity: Kierkegaard's Three Socratic Postures," in his *Kierkegaard as Educator*, Berkeley and Los Angeles: University of California Press 1977, pp. 1–58.

Marini, Sergio, "Socrate 'quel Singolo.' A proposito di alcune annotazioni del 'Diario' kierkegaardiano," in *Nuovi Studi Kierkegaardiani*, Potenza: Ermes 1993 (*Bollettino del Centro Italiano di Studi Kierkegaardiani. Supplemento semestrale di "Velia. Rivista di Filosofia Teoretica,"* vol. 1), pp. 75–85.

Martinez, Roy, "Socrates and Judge Wilhelm: A Case of Kierkegaardian Ethics," *Philosophy Today*, vol. 34, 1990, pp. 39–47.

Martinez, Roy, *Kierkegaard and the Art of Irony*, New York: Prometheus Books 2001 (*Philosophy and Literary Theory*).

McDonald, William, "Indirection and *Parrhesia*: The Roles of Socrates' *Daimonion* and Kierkegaard's *Styrelse* in Communication," in *Kierkegaard and the Word(s): Essays on Hermeneutics and Communication*, ed. by Poul Houe and Gordon D. Marino, Copenhagen: C. A. Reitzel 2003, pp. 127–38.

McKinnon, Alastair, "Three Conceptions of Socrates in Kierkegaard's Writings," in *Kierkegaard oggi. Atti del covegno dell' 11 Novembre 1982*, ed. by Alessandro Cortese, Milan: Vita e Pensiero 1986, pp. 21–43.

Merrill, Reed, "'Infinite Absolute Negativity': Irony in Socrates, Kierkegaard and Kafka," *Comparative Literature Studies*, vol. 16, 1979, pp. 222–36.

Mjaaland, Marius G., "Death and Aporia," *Kierkegaard Studies Yearbook*, 2003, pp. 395–418.

Mjaaland, Marius G., "The Autopsy of One Still Living," in *Prefaces and Writing Sampler and Three Discourses on Imagined Occasions*, ed. by

Robert L. Perkins, Macon, Georgia: Mercer University Press 2006 (*International Kierkegaard Commentary*, vols. 9–10), pp. 359–86.

Mjaaland, Marius G., *"Theaetetus*: Giving Birth, or Kierkegaard's Socratic Maieutics," in *Kierkegaard and the Greek World*, Tome I, *Socrates and Plato*, ed. by Jon Stewart and Katalin Nun, Aldershot: Ashgate 2010 (*Kierkegaard Research: Sources, Reception, and Resources*, vol. 2), pp. 115–46.

Morris, T. F., "Kierkegaard's Understanding of Socrates," *International Journal for Philosophy of Religion*, vol. 19, 1986, pp. 105–11.

Muench, Paul, "The Socratic Method of Kierkegaard's Pseudonym Johannes Climacus: Indirect Communication and the Art of 'Taking Away,'" in *Kierkegaard and the Word(s): Essays on Hermeneutics and Communication*, ed. by Poul Houe and Gordon D. Marino, Copenhagen: C. A. Reitzel 2003, pp. 139–50.

Muench, Paul, "*Apology*: Kierkegaard's Socratic Point of View," in *Kierkegaard and the Greek World*, Tome I, *Socrates and Plato*, ed. by Jon Stewart and Katalin Nun, Aldershot: Ashgate 2010 (*Kierkegaard Research: Sources, Reception, and Resources*, vol. 2), pp. 3–25.

Muench, Paul, "Kierkegaard's Socratic Pseudonym: A Profile of Johannes Climacus," in *Kierkegaard's Concluding Unscientific Postscript: A Critical Guide*, ed. by Rick Anthony Furtak, Cambridge: Cambridge University Press 2010, pp. 25–44.

Müller, Paul, *Kristendom, etik og majeutik i Søren Kierkegaard's "Kjerlighedens Gjerninger,"* Copenhagen: C. A. Reitzel 1983.

Nagley, Winfield E., "Kierkegaard's Early and Later View of Socratic Irony," *Thought: A Review of Culture and Idea*, vol. 55, 1980, pp. 271–82.

Neumann, Harry, "Kierkegaard and Socrates on the Dignity of Man," *The Personalist*, vol. 48, 1967, pp. 453–60.

Olesen, Tonny Aagaard, "Kierkegaard's Socratic Hermeneutic," in *The Concept of Irony*, ed. by Robert L. Perkins, Macon, Georgia: Mercer University Press 2001 (*International Kierkegaard Commentary*, vol. 2), pp. 101–22.

Pattison, George, "A Simple Wise Man of Ancient Times: Kierkegaard on Socrates," in *Socrates in the Nineteenth and Twentieth Centuries*, ed. by Michael Trapp, Aldershot: Ashgate 2007, pp. 19–35.

Paula, Marcio Gimenes de, *Socratismo e cristianismo em Kierkegaard: o escândalo e a loucura*, São Paulo: Annablume editora 2001.

Pentzopoulou-Valalas, Thérèse, "Kierkegaard et Socrate ou Socrate vu par Kierkegaard," *Les Études Philosophiques*, vol. 2, 1979, pp. 151–62.

Pepper, Thomas, "Male Midwifery: Maieutics in *The Concept of Irony* and *Repetition*," in *Kierkegaard Revisited*, ed. by Niels Jørgen Cappelørn and Jon Stewart, Berlin and New York: Walter de Gruyter 1997 (*Kierkegaard Studies Monograph Series*, vol. 1), pp. 460–80.

Pivčević, Edo, "Sokrates, Climacus and Anticlimacus," in his *Ironie als Daseinform bei Søren Kierkegaard*, Gütersloh: Gütersloher Verlagshaus Gerd Mohn 1960, pp. 45–71.

Politis, Hélène, "Socrate, fondateur de la morale, ou Kierkegaard commentateur de Hegel et historien de la philosophie," in *Autour de Hegel. Hommage à Bernard Bourgeois*, ed. by François Dagognet and Pierre Osmo, Paris: Vrin 2000, pp. 365–78.

Pop, Mihaela, "L'influence platonicienne sur le concept kierkegaardien de moment," *Revue Roumaine de Philosophie*, vol. 45, nos. 1–2, 2001, pp. 165–75.

Porsing, Ole, "Græciteten, Sokrates og ironi," in his *Sprækker til det uendelige? Søren Kierkegaard i 1990'erne—en bog om bøgerne*, Århus: Slagmark 1996, pp. 17–22.

Possen, David D., "*Meno*: Kierkegaard and the Doctrine of Recollection," in *Kierkegaard and the Greek World*, Tome I, *Socrates and Plato*, ed. by Jon Stewart and Katalin Nun, Aldershot: Ashgate 2010 (*Kierkegaard Research: Sources, Reception, and Resources*, vol. 2), pp. 27–44.

Possen, David D., "*Phaedrus*: Kierkegaard on Socrates' Self-Knowledge—and Sin," in *Kierkegaard and the Greek World*, Tome I, *Socrates and Plato*, ed. by Jon Stewart and Katalin Nun, Aldershot: Ashgate 2010 (*Kierkegaard Research: Sources, Reception, and Resources*, vol. 2), pp. 73–86.

Possen, David D., "*Protagoras* and *Republic*: Kierkegaard on Socratic Irony," in *Kierkegaard and the Greek World*, Tome I, *Socrates and Plato*, ed. by Jon Stewart and Katalin Nun, Aldershot: Ashgate 2010 (*Kierkegaard Research: Sources, Reception, and Resources*, vol. 2), pp. 87–104.

Reece, Gregory L., *Irony and Religious Belief*, Tübingen: J. C. B. Mohr (Paul Siebeck) 2002 (*Religion in Philosophy and Theology*, vol. 5), pp. 5–29.

Richter, Liselotte, "Die Sünde: Auseinandersetzung mit Sokrates," in her *Der Begriff der Subjektivität bei Kierkegaard. Ein Beitrag zur christlichem Existenzdarstellung*, Würzburg: Verlag Konrad Triltsch 1934, pp. 13–28.

Rilliet, Jean, "Kierkegaard et Socrate," *Revue de Théologie et de Philosophie*, vol. 31, 1943, pp. 114–20.

Rubenstein, Mary-Jane, "Kierkegaard's Socrates: A Venture in Evolutionary Theory," *Modern Theology*, vol. 17, 2001, pp. 442–73.

Rubenstein, Mary-Jane, "Ecstatic Subjectivity: Kierkegaard's Critiques and Appropriations of the Socratic," *Literature and Theology*, vol. 16, 2002, pp. 349–62.

Rudd, Anthony, "The Moment and the Teacher: Problems in Kierkegaard's *Philosophical Fragments*," *Kierkegaardiana*, vol. 21, 2000, pp. 92–115.

Sarf, Harold, "Reflections on Kierkegaard's Socrates," *Journal of the History of Ideas*, vol. 44, no. 2, 1983, pp. 255–76.

Schär, Hans Rudolf, *Christliche Sokratik. Kierkegaard über den Gebrauch der Reflexion in der Christenheit*, Frankfurt am Main: Peter Lang Verlag 1977.

Scheier, Claus-Artur, "Klassische und existentielle Ironie: Platon und Kierkegaard," *Philosophisches Jahrbuch*, vol. 97, 1990, pp. 238–50.

Scholtens, W. R., "Kierkegaard en Sokrates, de plaats van de ironie in het geestelijk leven," *Tijdschrift voor geestelijk leven*, vol. 30, 1974, pp. 203–7.

Scopetea, Sophia, "A Flaw in the Movement," *Kierkegaardiana*, vol. 13, 1984, pp. 97–104.

Scopetea, Sophia, *Kierkegaard og græciteten. En kamp med ironi*, Copenhagen: C. A. Reitzel 1995.

Scopetea, Sophia, "Becoming the Flute: Socrates and the Reversal of Values in Kierkegaard's Later Works," *Kierkegaardiana*, vol. 18, 1996, pp. 28–43.

Sløk, Johannes, *Die Anthropologie Kierkegaards*, Copenhagen: Rosenkilde and Bagger 1954, pp. 52–77.

Sløk, Johannes, "Die griechische Philosophie als Bezugsrahmen für Constantin Constantinus und Johannes de silentio," *Classica et Mediaevalia. Francisco Blatt septuagenario dedicata*, ed. by Otto Steen Due, Holger Friis Johansen, and Bengt Dalsgaard Larsen, Copenhagen: Gyldendal 1973, pp. 636–58 (reprinted in *Materialien zur Philosophie Søren Kierkegaards*, ed. by Michael Theunissen and Wilfried Greve, Frankfurt am Main: Suhrkamp 1979, pp. 280–301).

Söderquist, K. Brian, "Kierkegaard's Nihilistic Socrates in *The Concept of Irony*," in *Tänkarnes mångfald. Nutida perspektiv på Søren Kierkegaard*, ed. by Lone Koldtoft, Jon Stewart, and Jan Holmgaard, Stockholm: Makadam Förlag 2005, pp. 213–43.

Söderquist, K. Brian, *The Isolated Self: Irony as Truth and Untruth in Søren Kierkegaard's On the Concept of Irony*, Copenhagen: C. A. Reitzel 2007 (*Danish Golden Age Studies*, vol. 1).

Stewart, Jon and Katalin Nun (eds), *Kierkegaard and the Greek World*, Tome I, *Socrates and Plato*, Aldershot: Ashgate 2010 (*Kierkegaard Research: Sources, Reception, and Resources*, vol. 2).

Stock, Timothy, "Love's Hidden Laugh: On Jest, Earnestness, and Socratic Indirection in Kierkegaard's 'Praising Love,'" *Kierkegaard Studies Yearbook*, 2013, pp. 307–29.

Strawser, Michael J., "How Did Socrates Become a Christian? Irony and a Postmodern Christian (Non)-Ethic," *Philosophy Today*, vol. 36, 1992, pp. 256–65.

Taylor, Mark C., "Socratic Midwifery: Method and Intention of the Authorship," in *Kierkegaard's Pseudonymous Authorship: A Study of Time and the Self*, Princeton: Princeton University Press 1975, pp. 51–62.

Thomas, J. Heywood, "Kierkegaard's View of Time," *Journal of the British Society for Phenomenology*, vol. 4, 1973, pp. 33–40.

Thomte, Reidar, "Socratic Midwifery: The Communication of the Truth," in his *Kierkegaard's Philosophy of Religion*, Princeton: Princeton University Press 1948, pp. 190–203.

Thulstrup, Marie Mikulová, *Kierkegaard, Platons skuen og kristendommen*, Copenhagen: Munksgaard 1970.

Thulstrup, Marie Mikulová, "Plato's Vision and its Interpretation," in *Kierkegaard's Classical Inspiration*, ed. by Niels Thulstrup and Marie Mikulová Thulstrup, Copenhagen: C. A. Reitzel 1985 (*Bibliotheca Kierkegaardiana*, vol. 14), pp. 63–103.

Thulstrup, Niels, "Kierkegaard's Socratic Role for Twentieth-Century Philosophy and Theology," *Kierkegaardiana*, vol. 11, 1980, pp. 197–211.

Torralba Roselló, Francesc, "Kierkegaard el heredero moderno de la mayéutica socrática," *Espiritu*, vol. 47, 1998, pp. 55–69.

Vergote, Henri-Bernard, *Sens et répétition. Essai sur l'ironie kierkegaardienne*, vols. 1–2, Paris: Cerf/Orante 1982.

Weiss, Raymond L., "Kierkegaard's 'Return' to Socrates," *The New Scholasticism*, vol. 45, 1971, pp. 573–83.

Widenmann, Robert J., "Plato and Kierkegaard's *Moment*," in *Faith, Knowledge, and Action: Essays Presented to Niels Thulstrup on His Sixtieth Birthday*, ed. by George L. Stengren, Copenhagen: C. A. Reitzel 1984, pp. 251–6.

Wild, John, "Kierkegaard and Classical Philosophy," *Philosophical Review*, vol. 49, no. 5, 1940, pp. 536–51.

Wisdo, David M., "Kierkegaard and Euthyphro," *Philosophy*, vol. 62, 1987, pp. 221–6.

Wood, Robert E., "Recollection and Two Banquets: Plato's and Kierkegaard's," in *Stages on Life's Way*, ed. by Robert L. Perkins, Macon, Georgia: Mercer University Press 2000 (*International Kierkegaard Commentary*, vol. 11), pp. 49–68.

Wyller, Egil A., "Platons øyeblikks-filosofi eller dialogen Parmenides' 3. hypothese," in *Tradisjon og fornyelse. Festskrift til A. H. Winsnes*, ed. by Asbjørn Aarnes, Oslo: Aschehoug 1959, pp. 7–26.

Wyller, Egil A., "Sokrates og Kristus hos Søren Kierkegaard. En henologisk interpretasjon av forfatterskapet," *Norsk filosofisk tidsskrift*, vol. 28, 1993, pp. 207–19.

Ziolkowski, Eric, "From *Clouds* to *Corsair*: Kierkegaard, Aristophanes, and the Problem of Socrates," in *The Concept of Irony*, ed. by Robert L. Perkins, Macon, Georgia: Mercer University Press 2001 (*International Kierkegaard Commentary*, vol. 2), pp. 193–234.

Index

Abraham 124–31
absurd, the 128, 154, 163, 164
actuality 77, 78, 83, 91, 93, 94
Adam and Eve 64
aesthetics v, 2, 75, 158, 159, 160, 161
Agamemnon 131
Alcibiades 121
alienation 4, 45, 51, 52, 64–6, 77, 111,
    121, 189
Anaxagoras 51
Andersen, Hans Christian (1805–75),
    Danish poet, novelist, and writer of
    fairy tales 8
Anti-Climacus 175, 177
Antigone 30, 31
anxiety 135, 189, 190
aporia 6, 14, 21, 35, 36, 50, 84, 115,
    116, 193
appropriation 104, 124, 137, 192, 193
Aristophanes 10, 11, 22, 28, 63, 82, 83
    The Clouds 11
Aristotle 65, 115, 116
Ast, Friedrich (1778–1841),
    German philosopher
    and philologist 79
attack on the church 180–2, 186
authenticity 109, 118, 189
autonomy 22–4, 49

Barth, Karl (1886–1968), Swiss
    Protestant theologian 190
Baudrillard, Jean (1929–2007), French
    sociologist 190
Bauer, Bruno (1809–82), German
    theologian 63, 112
Baur, Ferdinand Christian (1792–1860),
    German theologian 61
Beauvoir, Simone de (1908–86), French
    philosopher 189
Beck, Andreas Frederik (1816–61),
    Danish theologian 46, 61–4
being and nothingness 36, 37, 115
Bible 62, 170
    Genesis 64, 66, 126
    Ecclesiastes 73

Matthew 177
John 103
Boesen, Emil (1812–81), Danish
    pastor 20, 185
Bojesen, Ernst Frederik Christian
    (1803–64), Danish philologist and
    educator 105
Brøchner, Hans (1820–75), Danish
    philosopher 155
Brøndsted, Peter Oluf (1780–1842),
    Danish classical philologist 104
Brunner, Emil (1889–1966), Swiss
    Protestant theologian 190

Camus, Albert (1903–60), French
    author 189
Catholicism 91
Christ 60–2, 101, 103, 115, 116, 133–5,
    137, 143, 153, 177–9
Christendom 172, 176
Christian VIII of Denmark
    (1786–1848; King of Denmark,
    1839–48) 168, 169
Christianity 9, 16, 20, 23, 32, 33, 49, 61,
    63, 103, 104, 116, 128, 133, 137,
    151–4, 159, 163, 164, 171, 172,
    175–7, 179, 182–5, 188, 193
    New Testament 180–3
Church of Our Lady 177, 182, 185
conformity 86
conscience 45, 111
Constantin Constantinus 123, 143
Copenhagen's Flying Post 75
Corsair 144, 146–8, 168, 181
Creon 30, 31
crisis 75–8
crowd, the 159, 169, 173, 174

daimon 7, 18, 19, 21, 40–2, 46–8, 173
Danish Golden Age 8, 74, 99, 122, 157
Danish State Church 166, 180, 181,
    185, 193
De Man, Paul (1919–83), Belgian-born
    American literary critic 190
De omnibus dubitandum est 53, 59, 102

death of author 190
deconstruction 190
Deleuze, Gilles (1925–95), French
 philosopher 190
democracy 167, 173, 174
Derrida, Jacques (1930–2004), French
 philosopher 190
Descartes, René (1596–1650), French
 philosopher 53, 59, 89
despair 50, 57, 58, 175, 189, 190
dialectical theology 190
doubt 50, 53–5, 57, 58, 64, 102

Ehler's College 71
either/or 115–17, 135, 136
Engels, Friedrich (1820–95), German
 social scientist 112
Enlightenment 65, 70, 71, 76, 91,
 129, 131
ethics
 bourgeois 97, 98, 122
 Christian 21
 Sittlichkeit (customary ethics) 29, 30,
 38, 47, 51, 111
Euthyphro 12, 13, 14, 17, 33, 123
excluded middle, the law of 115, 116
existence-communication 153, 154
existentialism 2, 4, 189

faith 2, 125, 127–9, 132, 179
 knight of 127
family 88
Fatherland 62, 122, 146, 147, 180, 182,
 187, 188
Faust 48–50, 53, 65, 66
feeling/emotion 38, 70, 91, 118, 165
Feuerbach, Ludwig (1804–72), German
 philosopher 63
Fichte, Johann Gottlieb (1762–1814),
 German philosopher 71, 79, 89–94,
 96, 100, 112
finite and infinite 134, 154
forgiveness 132, 143
Frederik VII of Denmark (1808–63; King
 of Denmark, 1848–63) 175
Frederiksberg Garden 150, 151
freedom 98, 131, 189
 subjective 40, 45, 72, 78, 79, 84, 174
French Revolution (1789) 29

gadfly 7, 16–18, 21, 152, 170, 193
Gæa 146

German idealism 27, 112
Gilleleje 31, 33, 191, 192
Giødwad, Jens Finsteen (1811–91),
 Danish jurist and journalist 157
Goethe, Johann Wolfgang von
 (1749–1832), German poet, author,
 scientist, and diplomat 48, 71,
 77, 102
 Faust (1808, 1832) 48
going beyond 176
Goldschmidt, Meïr Aaron (1819–87),
 Danish author 144, 147
Good, the 37, 84
governance 19
Gyllembourg-Ehrensvärd, Thomasine
 Christine (1773–1856), Danish
 author 75, 166

Hamann, Johann Georg (1730–88),
 German philosopher 136
Hauch, Carsten (1790–1872), Danish
 author 146, 147
Hegel, Georg Wilhelm Friedrich
 (1770–1831), German
 philosopher 11, 22–5, 27–30,
 33–45, 46–8, 51, 52, 58, 60, 61, 69,
 72, 73, 75, 77–81, 83, 84, 89–96,
 100, 111, 112, 115–17, 125, 126,
 135–8, 140, 142, 150, 151,
 168, 174
 Phenomenology of Spirit (1807) 27
 Science of Logic (1812–16) 27
 *Encyclopedia of the Philosophical
 Sciences* (1817) 27, 115
 Philosophy of Right (1821) 27, 125
 Lectures on the Philosophy of Religion
 (1832) 28
 Lectures on the History of Philosophy
 (1833–36) 28, 35–40, 42, 43, 79,
 80, 90, 91
 Lectures on Aesthetics (1835–38) 28
 Lectures on the Philosophy of History
 (1837) 28
Hegelianism 100, 112, 134, 168
Heiberg, Johan Ludvig (1791–1860),
 Danish poet, playwright, and
 philosopher 74–8, 102, 122, 123,
 138–42, 150, 151, 157, 166
 *On the Significance of Philosophy for
 the Present Age* (1833) 75, 78, 140
 Perseus (1837) 140
 "The Astronomical Year" (1844) 138

Heiberg, Johanne Luise, born Pätges
(1812–90), Danish actress 75
Heiberg, Peter Andreas (1758–1841),
Danish author 74
Heidegger, Martin (1889–1976), German
philosopher 189
Helveg, Hans Frederik (1816–1901),
Danish pastor and
theologian 192, 193
Herodotus 9
Hilarius Bookbinder 142
history 63, 84, 95
Homer 9
humor 101

Ibsen, Henrik (1828–1906), Norwegian
playwright 190
identity, law of 90
immortality 101
incarnation 115, 116, 132–5
inclosed reserve 137, 138
Industrial Revolution 85
inwardness 38, 41, 63, 130, 138, 153,
154, 159, 164, 172, 193
Iphigenia 131
irony 2, 4, 6, 11, 24, 27, 28, 32, 35, 52, 53,
60, 68, 69, 71, 73, 77–9, 81–3, 85, 91,
95, 100–4, 137, 138, 170, 176, 190,
192, 193
controlled 12, 101–4
modern 72, 85
Romantic 12, 88, 96, 98, 100, 101,
108, 110, 117, 119
Socratic 12, 13, 21, 34, 47, 48, 59, 72,
79–81, 84, 94, 99, 101, 136, 193

Jaspers, Karl (1883–1969), German
philosopher 189
Jesus, *see* "Christ"
Johannes Climacus 56, 57, 65, 66, 133,
134, 150–4
Johannes the seducer 122, 143
Johannes de Silentio 123, 129
Joyce, James (1882–1941), Irish
author 190
Judaism 127
Judge William 99, 116, 118, 142

Kafka, Franz (1883–1924), Czech-
Austrian novelist 190
Kant, Immanuel (1724–1804), German
philosopher 24, 89, 92–4

Kierkegaard, Michael Pedersen
(1756–1838), Søren Kierkegaard's
father 8, 100
Kierkegaard, Peter Christian (1805–88),
Danish theologian (the brother of
Søren Kierkegaard) 9, 10, 158,
185, 186
Kierkegaard, Søren Aabye (1813–55)
*The Conflict between the Old and the
New Soap-Cellars* (*c.* 1837) 46,
53–5
From the Papers of One Still Living
(1838) 8
The Concept of Irony (1841) vi, vii, 2,
4, 5, 6, 10–12, 14, 22, 28, 41, 46, 50,
58–63, 68, 69, 71–3, 77, 78, 80, 81,
83, 84, 92–5, 97–105, 114, 117, 118,
121, 126, 136, 144, 192
Either/Or (1843) 5, 99, 114–16,
118–21, 123, 138, 139, 142, 145,
157, 159
"Public Confession" (1842) 63, 157
*Johannes Climacus, or De omnibus
dubitandum est* (*c.* 1842–43) 46, 56
"A Word of Thanks to Professor
Heiberg" (1843) 122, 138, 140
Two Upbuilding Discourses
(1843) 159
Three Upbuilding Discourses
(1843) 123, 124, 159
Repetition (1843) 123, 124, 139, 140,
157, 159
Fear and Trembling (1843) 5, 114,
123–5, 127–9, 157–9
Philosophical Fragments (1844) 21,
132, 133, 135, 138, 150–3, 155, 158
The Concept of Anxiety (1844) 99,
132, 135–7, 158
Prefaces (1844) 21, 132, 135, 138–42
Eighteen Upbuilding Discourses
(1845) 124
Stages on Life's Way (1845) 21, 107,
132, 142, 143, 145, 146
"The Activity of a Traveling
Esthetician and How He Still
Happened to Pay for the Dinner"
(1845) 146
Concluding Unscientific Postscript
(1846) 21, 33, 56, 100, 114, 132,
149–52, 155–60, 162, 166, 169
A Literary Review of Two Ages
(1846) 75, 166, 167, 169, 170

Kierkegaard, Søren Aabye (*cont.*)
  "The Dialectical Result of a Literary
    Police Action" (1846) 147
  *Upbuilding Discourses in Various
    Spirits* (1847) 166, 169
  Works of Love (1847) 21, 170, 172
  Christian Discourses (1848) 177
  "The Crisis and a Crisis in the Life of
    an Actress" (1848) 75
  *The Point of View for My Work as an
    Author* (c. 1848) 19, 114, 158–60,
    172, 173, 183
  The Sickness unto Death (1849) 21,
    166, 175–7
  Practice in Christianity (1850) 166,
    177, 179
  On My Work as an Author (1850) 158
  Sixteen Upbuilding Discourses
    (1852) 124
  The Moment (1855) 21, 146, 166, 180,
    182, 184, 187
  Journals, Notebooks, *Nachlass* 14, 27,
    31, 48, 50, 54, 100, 113,
    161–3, 168
Know thyself 42, 51

Lacan, Jacques (1901–81), French
  psychiatrist 190
Lenau, Nicolaus, *see* Strehlenau,
  Niembsch von
leveling 168
living poetically 95, 98, 102, 108, 109
Locke, John (1632–1704), English
  philosopher 167
logic 15, 90, 115–17, 135
love 170
  Christian 170
  Romantic 96–9
Lund, Ane Sørensdatter (1768–1834),
  Søren Kierkegaard's mother 8
Lund, Henrik (1825–89), nephew of
  Søren Kierkegaard 187–9

Macbeth 68
Madvig, Johan Nicolai (1804–86),
  Danish philologist 104, 105
maieutics 7, 19–21, 35, 133, 134, 158,
  159, 171, 172, 193, 194
Mann, Thomas (1875–1955), German
  author 190
Marcel, Gabriel (1889–1973), French
  philosopher 189

Marheineke, Philipp (1780–1846),
  German theologian 113
marriage 44, 70, 87, 98, 99, 106, 118
Martensen, Hans Lassen (1808–84),
  Danish theologian 23–7, 46, 49, 50,
  53–7, 59, 102, 104, 115, 116, 134,
  180, 188
  *On the Autonomy of Human Self-
    Consciousness* (1837) 23, 49
martyr 147
martyrdom 180
Marx, Karl (1818–83), German
  philosopher and
  economist 112, 167
masses, the 174
meaninglessness 2, 4, 67, 68, 120, 189
mediation 116, 117, 134, 135
melancholy 10, 107
Michelet, Karl Ludwig (1801–93),
  German philosopher 28
midwifery, *see* maieutics
Mill, John Stuart (1806–73), English
  philosopher 167
modernity 1, 4, 44, 86–8
Møller, Peter Ludvig (1814–65), Danish
  critic 144–7
Møller, Poul Martin (1794–1838),
  Danish poet and philosopher 99,
  100, 136
morality, reflective (*Moralität*) 38
Mynster, Jakob Peter (1775–1854),
  Danish theologian and bishop 115,
  157, 180, 181
mythology 63

Napoleon, I, i.e., Napoleon Bonaparte
  (1769–1821), French
  emperor 8, 166
Napoleonic Wars 29, 89
natural law 30
negation 37, 84, 138, 193
negativity 14, 59, 93, 98, 137, 177
  infinite 60
nihilism 4, 11, 68, 73, 76, 79, 81, 100,
  101, 119–21
Novalis, i.e., Baron Friedrich von
  Hardenberg (1772–1801), German
  lyric poet 71
Nytorv 7

offense 177, 179
Olsen, Regine (1822–1904) 99, 105–8

Oracle at Delphi 16, 17, 40–2, 47, 94, 176, 184
Ørsted, Hans Christian (1777–1851), Danish natural scientist 8, 104

paradox 128, 153, 163, 164, 176
  absolute 134, 135, 151
passion 163, 164, 172, 193
Perseus 49
Petersen, Frederik Christian (1786–1859), Danish philologist 104
Pharisees, the 6
pseudonyms/pseudonymity 56, 122, 124, 132, 150, 156–9, 190
Plato v, 6, 7, 9, 10, 12, 14, 16, 17, 21, 22, 28, 36, 41, 47, 63, 82, 83, 115, 121, 134, 142, 143, 154
  Apology 9, 12, 16–18, 41, 52
  Crito 9
  Euthyphro 6, 9, 12, 33, 35
  Greater Hippias 154
  Meno 19
  Phaedo 12
  Phaedrus 134
  Symposium 121, 143
Polyneices 30
post-modernism 4, 190
post-structuralism 4
preaching 137
Protagoras 38, 59
providence 19
public opinion 167, 174

Rahbek, Knud Lyne (1760–1830), Danish literary scholar 74
Regensen College 24
relativism 2, 11, 25, 38, 45, 58, 60, 76, 79, 84, 91, 121, 140, 164
repetition 124, 139
Restoration 166
revelation 126, 128, 130, 132, 133, 135
Revolutions (of 1848) 166–9, 174, 175
Rilke, Rainer Maria (1875–1926), German poet 190
Roman Empire 76
Romanticism 2, 11, 85, 86, 91, 94, 95, 102, 109, 166
  German 4, 69–71, 73, 79, 80, 90, 101, 117
Royal Theater in Copenhagen 75

Sartre, Jean-Paul (1905–80), French philosopher 189
Schelling, Friedrich Wilhelm Joseph von (1775–1854), German philosopher 112, 113, 161, 168
Schlegel, August Wilhelm von (1767–1845), German critic 71
Schlegel, Friedrich von (1772–1829), German Romantic writer 11, 69, 70, 79, 80, 93–8, 108, 110, 118
  Lucinde (1799) 70, 91, 96–8, 118
Schleiermacher, Friedrich (1768–1834), German theologian 24
School of Civic Virtue 9, 10, 105
self-deception 110
self-positing ego 91, 93, 94
sermon 137
Shakespeare, William (1564–1616), English dramatist 102
Sibbern, Frederik Christian (1785–1872), Danish philosopher 104
sign of contradiction 179
silence 127
sin 132, 143
  hereditary 135
single individual 174
Sittlichkeit, see ethics
skepticism 32, 50, 59
social-political thought 167
Socrates v, vi, vii, 4, 6, 7, 9–18, 20, 21, 22, 28–44, 46–66, 69, 79–84, 93, 94, 100, 101, 103, 105, 111, 112, 114–16, 121–4, 128, 132–4, 136–8, 140–4, 152, 154, 158, 159, 163–6, 169–77, 179–84, 191–3
  going beyond 37, 115, 176
  ignorance 12, 13, 21, 34, 51, 128, 133, 134, 141, 142, 176, 177, 179, 184, 191, 193
  irony *see* irony, Socratic
  method 33–5
Solger, Karl Wilhelm Ferdinand (1780–1819), German philosopher and aesthetic theorist 11, 69
Sophists, the 6, 15, 16, 21, 38, 46, 58–61, 81, 84, 141, 184
Sophocles 30
  Antigone 30
Sorø Academy 105, 146, 168
stages of existence v
Steffens, Henrik (1773–1845), Norwegian-Danish philosopher 71

Strauss, David Friedrich (1808–74), German theologian, historian and philosopher 61, 63 112
  The Life of Jesus Critically Examined (1835–36) 61–3
Strehlenau, Niembsch von, i.e., Nicolaus Lenau (1802–50), Austro-Hungarian poet 49
Strindberg, August (1849–1912), Swedish author 190
subjectivism 2, 4, 76, 140
subjectivity 25, 48, 52, 58, 69, 89, 91, 93, 138, 164, 172

teleological suspension of the ethical 125–7, 130
temporal and eternal 134, 154
Tennemann, Wilhelm Gottlieb (1761–1819), German historian of philosophy 42
thing in itself 92, 93
Thorvaldsen, Bertel (1770–1844), Danish sculptor 8, 177
Tieck, Johann Ludwig (1773–1853), German poet 11, 69, 71, 93, 94

Tillich, Paul (1886–1965), German-American Protestant theologian 190
Trinity 115
truth, subjective 31, 32
Tryde, Eggert Christopher (1781–1860), Danish theologian and pastor 186–8
Typhon 134

University of Copenhagen 10, 25

vaudeville 75
Victor Eremita 116, 122, 123, 142, 143, 157
Vigilius Haufniensis 135, 137

Warhol, Andy (1928–87), American artist 86
Werder, Karl Friedrich (1806–93), German philosopher and literary critic 114
witness to the truth 180

Xenophon 9, 10, 22, 28, 47, 63, 82, 83

Printed in Great Britain
by Amazon